World War II Veterans
in Hollywood

Also by Art Evans
and from McFarland

World War II Veterans in Motorsports (2019)

World War II Veterans in Hollywood

ART EVANS

Foreword by Perry King

McFarland & Company, Inc., Publishers
Jefferson, North Carolina

LIBRARY OF CONGRESS CATALOGUING-IN-PUBLICATION DATA

Names: Evans, Arthur G., author.
Title: World War II veterans in Hollywood / Art Evans.
Other titles: World War Two veterans in Hollywood
Description: Jefferson, North Carolina : McFarland & Company, Inc., Publishers, 2020 | Includes bibliographical references and index.
Identifiers: LCCN 2020014197 | ISBN 9781476677774 (paperback : acid free paper) ∞
ISBN 9781476639673 (ebook)
Subjects: LCSH: World War, 1939-1945—Veterans—Biography. | Motion picture actors and actresses—United States—Biography. | Celebrities—United States—Biography.
Classification: LCC D810.V42 E83 2020 | DDC 791.4302/8096970973—dc23
LC record available at https://lccn.loc.gov/2020014197

BRITISH LIBRARY CATALOGUING DATA ARE AVAILABLE

ISBN (print) 978-1-4766-7777-4
ISBN (ebook) 978-1-4766-3967-3

© 2020 Art Evans. All rights reserved

No part of this book may be reproduced or transmitted in any form or by any means, electronic or mechanical, including photocopying or recording, or by any information storage and retrieval system, without permission in writing from the publisher.

On the cover: Colonel James Stewart being awarded the *Croix de Guerre* with Palm in 1944 (United States Army Air Forces)

*McFarland & Company, Inc., Publishers
Box 611, Jefferson, North Carolina 28640
www.mcfarlandpub.com*

Acknowledgments

I want to acknowledge John and Ginny Dixon's contribution to this book. They are special friends and neighbors that spent untold hours researching, writing, proofing and indexing.

Actor Perry King has been most helpful in sending me remarks about those in the book that he knows or knew. I thank him also for writing the Foreword. Thanks to Gage Gill, who checked over the final drafts. And thanks to all the folks at McFarland who worked so hard on this book, particularly Steve Wilson, David Alff, Lisa Camp, Dylan Lightfoot and Kristal Hamby.

Table of Contents

Acknowledgments   v
Foreword by Perry King   1
Preface   3

1. Audie Murphy   5
2. Sterling Hayden   13
3. Eddie Albert   19
4. Jimmy Stewart   26
5. Joseph Wapner   33
6. Gene Autry   38
7. Neville Brand   44
8. Art Carney   49
9. Don Adams   55
10. Jackie Coogan   60
11. Douglas Fairbanks, Jr.   67
12. Charlton Heston   77
13. Jason Robards   85
14. James Arness   93
15. Peter (Aurness) Graves   99
16. Ernest Borgnine   101
17. Tony Bennett   110
18. Mickey Rooney   118
19. Tyrone Power   127
20. Charles Bronson   134

Table of Contents

21.	Tony Curtis	141
22.	Lee Marvin	149
23.	Rod Serling	157
24.	Kirk Douglas	163
25.	Charles Durning	172
26.	Henry Fonda	178
27.	Clark Gable	186
28.	Mel Brooks	196
29.	Rod Steiger	204
30.	Norman Lear	210
31.	Efrem Zimbalist, Jr.	218

Epilogue	224
Bibliography	227
Index	229

Foreword
by Perry King

When my friend Art Evans first sent me some of the stories for his new book about celebrities during World War II, I thought it was a wonderful premise for a fascinating read. If you love old movies, these short biographies will humanize the actors in those movies and make you care even more about them. Much of what Art found to write about is surprising and moving to learn. In my case I discovered that I knew some of his subjects and had the enormous pleasure of learning things about them that I had not known before.

For example, I think I have acted in two or more film projects with Charlie Durning, and during the shoot of *The Choirboys*, we spent a lot of time together. Charlie told me one night about some of his wartime experiences, in and out of combat, and I was chilled to learn what he went through. I had no idea how much combat he actually had taken part in, or how badly he had been wounded, until I read his biography in this book. He was one of the most enjoyable people to spend time with and work with I have ever known, and I suspect it was in part because of his war experiences: it made him value living greatly. He was an honorable, kind man, with a great sense of humor and enormous skill as a performer—and as a dancer!

Tony Curtis was also a hell of a lot of fun to be around and was very generous with helpful and precise advice. He, like Charlie, had a *joie de vivre* that carried you along with it, laughing and enjoying every moment. My experience with every one of those performers in Art's book whom I knew was similar. They all took great joy in work and in life and were universally kind and generous.

I never knew Clark Gable, but I remember with great fondness meeting Myrna Loy at a party in Hollywood in the mid 1970s. We talked for quite a while, and I told her that *Test Pilot* was one of my favorite films of all time. To my delight she said it was a personal favorite of hers, and she told me stories of what it was like to work with Gable and Spencer Tracy on the film. She said

Foreword by Perry King

that the three of them really developed a friendship much like that in the film, and they enjoyed the shoot as much as their characters enjoyed the fictional story of their relationship. When you watch that film you can see how comfortable and honest all three of them are together. It was that three-way bond that really made that picture, I feel. It is still a great movie after all these years.

So, I think that after you read Art's wonderful book, you'll never look at these famous faces the same way again. What you will see, after reading this fabulous collection of bios, is the real person behind the star persona. They were movie stars, true—but their lives were filled with sadness and joy, struggle, success, and occasional failure. I think every single one of these famous people would be deeply grateful to Art for telling us the true stories of his life.

Perry King

American actor Perry King is best known for his role in the TV series Riptide. *King received a Golden Globe nomination for his role in the TV film* The Hasty Heart, *which is a remake of the 1949 film of the same name.*

Preface

The Greatest Generation In Hollywood's Golden Age

The phrase "the Greatest Generation" was made popular by the renowned journalist Tom Brokaw in his 1998 book *The Greatest Generation*. It describes those who grew up in the United States during the deprivations of the Great Depression and went on to serve during World War II. The book is also, I think, great, and is recommended reading. Brokaw wrote: "It is, I believe, the Greatest Generation any society has ever produced." President Franklin Delano Roosevelt said, "This generation of Americans has a rendezvous with destiny."

Brokaw went on to write: "The young Americans of this time constituted a generation birth-marked for greatness, a generation of Americans that would take its place in American history. They were involved in a tumultuous journey through adversity and achievement, despair and triumph."

One of the best known of the Hollywood heroes was Audie Murphy, who was America's most decorated soldier. He received the Congressional Medal of Honor, among a host of other awards, for his heroism in Europe. During his 20-plus years as an actor, he made more than 40 feature films and a television series.

Jimmy Stewart was a household name during his era in show business. Stewart was the pilot of a B-24 in Europe as a member of the U.S. Army Air Corps. Due to his heroism, he received two Distinguished Flying Crosses and four Air Medals. In his very first film after the war—*It's a Wonderful Life*—he was nominated for the Academy Award as Best Actor. By 1954, he was nominated as the most popular Hollywood actor in the world.

This book profiles a number of Hollywood's famous personalities who were decorated war heroes, including Eddie Albert, James Arness, Jackie Coogan, Charles Durning, Douglas Fairbanks, Jr., Henry Fonda, Sterling Hayden and Rod Serling. All the others included also put themselves in harm's way.

The profiles include a lot of facts generally not known about these heroes, including their wartime experiences. For some time afterwards, World

World War II Veterans in Hollywood

War II was just referred to as "the war." It was life-changing for many and turned the United States into the world's greatest power.

Before the war, the U.S. was a much different country. The two decades between World War I and World War II were radically different from each other. The twenties were called the Roaring Twenties. The economy was great, and everyone thought the good days would last forever. Anyone who had an extra dime invested in stocks, some not so great. But then there was the crash. Everything came down, and we dropped into the Great Depression, which lasted until the start of World War II. The thirties saw some of the hardest times ever.

But then came December 7, 1941, and the U.S. experienced a radical change. Many thousands of eligible men voluntarily enlisted or were drafted. Factories were left short-handed, so women stepped in. Americans at home experienced many shortages, including gasoline, so rationing was instituted. At the beginning of the war, it seemed as if it would never end and the U.S. and Allies might lose. But then as it ground on and on, the superiority of the U.S. in terms of men, supplies and factory output turned the tide.

After the war ended, the GIs who had served their country returned to their civilian lives, and some went on to fame and fortune during the Golden Age of Hollywood.

1

Audie Murphy

Audie Murphy led an amazing life. He was a movie star, a poet, a songwriter and an author. During his 25-year Hollywood career, he starred in a large number of films, most of them Westerns, as well as in an NBC television series. But before that, Murphy served in the U.S. Army during World War II. He was the most decorated American soldier in history, winning every U.S. Army combat medal available, including the Congressional Medal of Honor, as well as top French, Belgian, and Italian medals.

Audie was a member of that Greatest Generation, those who faced the deprivations of the Great Depression and went on to help win the war against tyranny. Audie Leon Murphy was born on June 20, 1925, in Kingston, Texas. His parents, Emmett Berry Murphy and Josie Bell Killian, were poor sharecroppers farming other people's land. Audie's birth followed six older siblings, with two more to follow. The family represented the poorest of the poor during the Dust Bowl depression years.

Audie was a small, baby-faced boy, and being treated like a child filled him with a determined resolve to do manly things. In his early teens, his father deserted the family, and Audie quit the fifth grade to help his mother and siblings. He developed a special skill with a rifle in order to put meat on the table. It required hunting, stalking, and marksmanship skills that would later make him an American legend. Remembering that time, Audie said, "I can't remember ever being young in my life." During his many forays into the Texas outback, he thought not of meat but rather fantasized about being a soldier protecting his country. The December 7, 1941, Japanese attack on Pearl Harbor sparked the 16-year-old Murphy to pursue his dream of being a soldier.

Soon after World War II started, Murphy tried to enlist in the Army, then the Navy and finally the Marines. But he was only 16 years old, so he was turned down. When he turned 17, his oldest sister, Corinne Burns (her married name), falsified a certificate showing he was 18, and with that he was able to join the Army at Dallas, Texas, on June 30, 1942. (The U.S. Armed Forces required enlistees and draftees to be 18 years old.)

World War II Veterans in Hollywood

Murphy was sent to Camp Wolters in Texas for basic training. He was such a good marksman and so skilled with infantry weapons that he qualified as an expert in every category and was awarded the Expert Infantryman Badge. He was sent to Fort Meade, Maryland, for advanced infantry training with the 59th Training Battalion.

After individual training, Audie was assigned to Baker Company, 15th Regiment of the 3rd Infantry Division, which spent months in the United States training for combat. It was the only division during World War II that fought on all of the European fronts. The division first saw action when the Americans and the British invaded North Africa. It landed at Fedala (now Mohammedia), just north of Casablanca, in Morocco on November 8, 1942. Murphy joined the division at Casablanca on February 20, 1943. The division was undergoing additional training in anticipation of the invasion of Europe.

The division landed on Sicily on July 10, 1943. Because of his size and youthful looks, Audie's commanders had tried to keep him out of the front lines. His first commanding officer had tried to send him to cook and baker's school, but he insisted on being an infantryman. In Sicily his commanding officer made Audie a runner to keep him off the line. He continued his lifelong fight to overcome being babied and was finally allowed to join a platoon on the front lines. Audie was promoted to corporal ten days after landing on Sicily. On a patrol, he shot and killed two Italian officers who refused to surrender and tried to escape. Audie remembered, "I got so scared the first day in combat, I just decided to

Audie Murphy publicity photo taken after his 1948 trip to Paris to receive the Chevalier Legion d'Honneur and Croix de Guerre with Palm. Murphy is the only actor to have been awarded the Medal of Honor. He was the most decorated American soldier of World War II (U.S. Army).

1. Audie Murphy

go along with it." In September, the division landed on the mainland of Italy at Salerno. Murphy and two others on patrol were ambushed, and German machine guns killed one of them. Audie and his buddy were able to lob hand grenades into the machine gun nest, killing five Germans.

The 15th Regiment fought its way up to Naples and, after a short rest, continued the fight up the road north to the approach to Monte Cassino. At that point they were pulled out of the line and trained for a special amphibious assault that turned out to be at Anzio. It was an easy landing that became one of the worst debacles of the war. Audie spent over four months living in a mud hole, unable to be above ground in daylight due to artillery fire from the dreaded German "88," a huge railcar-mounted canon that could cover the complete 10-square-mile beachhead.

After the initial landing at the Anzio beachhead, the division attempted a breakout to Rome and fought the first battle of Cisterna on January 29, 1944. A German tank was disabled in front of Audie's position. His platoon shot and killed the tank crew. During the night, Murphy crawled alone and approached near enough to the tank for him to destroy it with rifle grenades. For this heroism, he was awarded the Bronze Star. After the battle, Audie was made the platoon sergeant. All the men in his company were awarded the Combat Infantryman Badge. According to Audie, "Two weeks of combat can make an old man out of you. You grow up real fast in the Army and you learn not to make the same mistakes twice. Because if you do, you don't grow up at all."

During the months-long stalemate at Anzio, Murphy led numerous scouting patrols and took many German prisoners. For these actions, Audie received an oak leaf cluster for his Bronze Star. After Rome was occupied by the American Army, Murphy's company was bivouacked in a Rome park during July.

On August 15, 1944, the Army began Operation Anvil and invaded southern France at St. Tropez. On landing, Murphy led his platoon through a vineyard where it came under fire by Germans in a bunker. Audie returned fire with a machine gun, killing two and wounding another. Two other Germans in a nearby house displayed a white flag, but when Audie's best friend, Lattie Tipton, stood up to accept the surrender, he was cut down by machine gun fire and killed. Murphy charged the house alone, killing six, wounding two and taking the rest prisoners. For that action, he was awarded the Distinguished Service Cross.

The regiment continued to fight its way north and, after taking Besancon, it ran into a roadblock. Audie was standing with five other soldiers awaiting orders when a mortar shell silently dropped on them. Two were killed, three wounded and Audie was knocked unconscious. But he only suffered a foot wound.

After a few days in the hospital, Audie got a new pair of shoes, a Purple Heart, and was back with Baker Company on the road to Germany.

Near Cleurie, they came upon a fortified quarry. It was a solid rock strongpoint of the German line in the Vosges mountains. The battalion commander and another officer took four men on a reconnaissance patrol. Audie followed at a distance, and when the patrol came under machine gun fire he was able to destroy the nest with hand grenades. That earned him a Silver Star.

Three days later, he advanced alone towards Germans on a hill. While under direct enemy fire, Audie radioed instructions to his men. Eventually they took the hill; 15 Germans were killed and 35 wounded. He received an oak leaf cluster to put on his Silver Star.

Back at the command post, a colonel pinned gold bars, making him a second lieutenant, on Murphy's shoulders and sent him back to command his platoon. Months earlier, he had refused a commission because he didn't want to leave his buddies.

While his platoon was advancing on October 26, they were attacked by snipers. Audie was able to capture two of them but was shot in the hip. In retaliation, Murphy was able to shoot the sniper. He spent three months at Army hospital in Aix-en-Provence. Audie received an oak leaf cluster to his Purple Heart.

In January 1945, Murphy returned to his platoon as it was advancing toward the Rhine River in the Alsace area of France. Near the town of Holtzwihr, they were counterattacked by a strong enemy force when they tried to close the Colmar pocket. As his company regrouped to meet the attack, Audie was given command of Company B.

The Germans shot up a U.S. tank destroyer, setting it on fire. The crew jumped out and fled into a nearby forest. Murphy remained where he could see the enemy soldiers, directing artillery fire with his radio while the Germans fired at his position. He ordered his men to fall back into a wooded area while he climbed atop the partially burned tank destroyer and fired its machine gun at the advancing enemy, killing all in a group crawling towards him. For over an hour he stood there on the tank, shooting at the soldiers and tanks until he ran out of ammunition. During his stand, he was injured in his leg while killing or wounding over 50 Germans. Jumping off of the tank destroyer, he rallied his men and led them to push back the enemy. He stayed with the company while his wounded leg was treated. He was only 20 years old. As a result, Murphy was awarded another oak

1. Audie Murphy

leaf cluster for his Bronze Star, and then, the big daddy of them all, the Congressional Medal of Honor. The next month, Audie was promoted to first lieutenant and received the French Legion of Merit. On September 21, 1945, First Lieutenant Audie Leon Murphy, having won every single medal for bravery in combat the United States had to award, was discharged with a 50 percent disability. After the war, he joined the Texas National Guard on inactive duty, was promoted to major, and was finally released in 1966. Afterwards, Murphy said, "I have to admit I love the damned Army. It was father, mother, and brother to me for years. It made me somebody, gave me self-respect."

Audie was hailed as a hero when he returned to Texas after the war. But still he found it hard to land suitable employment and went from job to job. As it was before the war, it was hard times again for him.

In the July 16, 1945, edition of *Life* magazine, Audie Murphy was on the cover and proclaimed the most decorated soldier. Actor James Cagney got in touch with Audie and persuaded him to come to Hollywood for a career in acting. Even though Cagney and his brother had a production company, they never cast Murphy in a film during his contract years that ended in 1947. During those years, the brothers had him trained in acting, voice and dancing. These were hard times for Murphy; he was sleeping in an athletic club in Hollywood. It was all he could afford. "I came to Hollywood because I had no place else to go," Murphy said.

During his time at the club, Audie tried to write a book about his war years. He met a screen writer,

Murphy in the 1955 movie, *To Hell and Back*, where he played himself in the true story of his World War II experiences. The movie was based on his autobiography of the same name (publicity still).

World War II Veterans in Hollywood

David "Spec" McClure, who helped him with the book. The book, *To Hell and Back*, was published in 1949. It became a best seller. McClure was able to land him a few bit parts in movies.

Murphy's first starring role was in the 1949 movie *Bad Boy*. Its success led Universal Studios to offer Audie a seven-year contract. In his first film with Universal, he starred as Billy the Kid in *The Kid from Texas*. The year ended with the motion picture *Sierra*, in which he starred with Wanda Hendrix, an up-and-coming, 18-year-old actress.

Perhaps Murphy's best-known film was *To Hell and Back*, in CinemaScope and Technicolor, which was released in 1955 on the tenth anniversary of his Army discharge. It was an adaptation of his book of the same name. When asked, he refused to star as himself. He wanted Tony Curtis to do it. But the producer and the director eventually changed his mind. He starred as himself using the screen name of Gordon Gebert. The movie was novelized, in that it didn't follow the book exactly. It shows a young boy growing up in hardship, having lost both his father and his mother. After joining the Army, Gebert encounters a number of fellow soldiers who differ from the ones in the book. After numerous scenes of realistic combat, the film ends with the presentation of the Medal of Honor.

To Hell and Back was a very big success, both commercially and critically. With his fee for the use of the book as well as an up-front payment and a percentage of the profits, Murphy ended up with a million dollars. During his years in Hollywood he appeared in 44 feature films.

Audie wound up his prolific movie career with *A Time for Dying*, released in 1969. Retired as a millionaire, he often went back to Texas, where he owned a ranch. He bred quarter horses there and ran his horses at various racetracks.

Quite a poet, Murphy wrote "The Crosses Grow on Anzio," which was used in *To Hell and Back*. In addition, his "Freedom Flies in Your Heart Like an Eagle" was set to music by Scott Turner. Audie was a successful song writer, too. Many of his songs were recorded. In 1993, Eddie Arnold made an album called *Last of the Love Song Singers*, in which Eddie recorded Audie's "When the Wind Blows in Chicago."

Murphy led a rather troubled life. He had married Wanda Hendrix in 1949; the marriage ended only two years later. Four days after the divorce, he married Pamela Opal Lee Archer. They had two sons, Terry Michael and James Shannon, both born during the fifties. Even though Audie once was wealthy, he managed to gamble most of it away and had difficulties with the Internal Revenue Service.

Murphy experienced insomnia and depression. This illness, now known

1. Audie Murphy

Audie Murphy featured on a lobby card for the movie, *To Hell and Back* (1955), where he played himself in the true story of his World War II experiences.

as post traumatic stress disorder (PTSD), was then known as "battle fatigue." Unlike today, the Veterans Administration didn't recognize it as a sickness and wouldn't treat it. He got sleeping pills from his private doctor and eventually became addicted. Eventually deciding he didn't want to live that way anymore, he secluded himself for a week and went through a successful withdrawal.

Murphy used his experiences to help Korean and Vietnam returning veterans. He gave talks about his problems. He repeatedly urged the government to give attention to PTSD and the mental state of veterans.

On May 1971, Audie and four other passengers were aboard a private plane over mountains in Virginia during a severe storm. It crashed, with the pilot and all aboard killed. Murphy was only 46 years old, but he had led an exciting, heroic and famous, though short, life.

On June 7 of that year, Audie Leon Murphy was laid to rest with full military honors at Arlington National Cemetery. He was honored throughout Texas when June 20 (his birthday) was named Audie Murphy Day. He is still honored as America's number one soldier. His grave at Arlington is one of

World War II Veterans in Hollywood

the most frequently visited. Audie's widow, Pamela, spent the rest of her life helping veterans at the Sepulveda VA Hospital in Southern California.

According to many descriptions, Audie's persona seems to have been a combination of John Wayne and Gary Cooper, with Errol Flynn's libido, in the body of a baby-faced teenager. He didn't smoke or drink and stood ready to out-draw injustice and out-punch pretention. He willingly accepted the advances of the many women that wanted to mother him.

In that war, there were brave men who faced the enemy's guns on the front lines behind the lines, there were many with imagined bravery. Audie found that in Hollywood there were men that put their egos in front of the cameras and acted. In numerous cafes in Hollywood there were thousands of wannabes that claimed they could win an Oscar ... if only. A movie, no matter how well done, is a scripted fantasy. Real life has no script and the end is always in doubt.

"To be successful in Hollywood, you must learn to suffer fools." Audie spent two years of cold nights thinking about his 200 dead friends, and the 250 men he had killed, while wondering when his turn would come. He had trouble with frivolous fiction.

2

Sterling Hayden

Hollywood star Sterling Hayden was best known for his roles in *The Asphalt Jungle, The Godfather* and *Dr. Strangelove.* Paramount Pictures called him "The Most Beautiful Man in the Movies." But he led a dual life. His love was the sea and boats. He made movies, but, he remarked, "just to make money." The record shows that Hayden had 59 credits as an actor. These were in movies, except for four television shows, the most well-known being *Wagon Train*. During World War II, he served in the Marine Corps and the OSS (Office of Strategic Services), where he was awarded a Silver Star.

Sterling Hayden was born on March 26, 1916, in Upper Montclair, New Jersey. His parents were George and Frances Walter; they named him Sterling Relyea Walter. His father died in 1925 when Sterling was only nine. His mother married James Hayden and from then on, Sterling was known as Sterling Hayden. His legal name—Walter—is on his birth certificate.

Hayden attended a private elementary and secondary school combined—the Woosookeag School—in Dexter, Maine. In 1932 at the age of 16, he ran away from the school and got a job on a schooner. (A schooner is a ship propelled by wind in sails on two or three masts.) His first trip was from New London, Connecticut, through the Panama Canal to Newport Beach, California, and back. Starting as a ship's boy, he served on a number of vessels as a seaman and even sailed around the world. Sterling rose to become a ship's captain in 1938 when he was only 22. His first command was a square-rigged sailing ship, the *Florence C. Robinson*. Its initial voyage was from Gloucester, Massachusetts, to Tahiti, a distance of over 7,000 miles.

Sterling, however, wanted to buy his own ship. To do that, of course, he needed some significant money, more that he received from the earnings of a ship's captain. So, because of his good looks, he took up modeling for advertisements. Somehow, he met movie producer Edward Griffith, who persuaded Paramount Pictures to sign Hayden, even though he had no acting training or experience. His first movie was *Virginia*, released in 1941. Directed by Griffith, it costarred Madeleine Carroll. It's the story of a New York woman

World War II Veterans in Hollywood

(Carroll) who inherits an old mansion in Virginia and meets a handsome man (Hayden), who marries her. It received mixed reviews but grossed almost eight million. Next Sterling starred in *Bahama Passage*, which was also successful. The two films made him a star. He and Madeleine were married on February 14, 1942, with a lot of media coverage.

Hayden's new career came to a halt, however, when he joined the Marine Corps just a month after his marriage. Because of his movie celebrity, he enlisted using the name John Hamilton. Like all inductees, Hayden's first assignment was to undergo basic training; Sterling's boot camp was at Parris Island. While there, he was recommended for officer training at the Marine Corps Officer Candidate School, where, upon graduation, he received a commission as second lieutenant.

Hayden in the 1950 crime/film noir movie, *Asphalt Jungle*, where he starred as Dix Handley. Directed by John Huston (publicity still).

Then Hayden was posted to serve with "Wild Bill" Donovan in the Office of Strategic Services (OSS), which later became the Central Intelligence Agency (CIA). OSS Agent John Hamilton was assigned to the Balkans, where he helped the resistance in Yugoslavia. First, he sailed a fleet of 15 large sailboats from Italy to the Yugoslav island of Korcula with guns, ammunition and supplies for Marshal Josip Tito's guerrillas. To get there, his innocent-looking sailboats had to run through a German blockade.

In January 1944, Hayden was skippering a 45-foot motorboat at night when the water pump quit and the engine froze. Sterling and his crew had to paddle ashore on Korcula. After joining the partisans, Hayden was traveling over the island in a jeep when they drove into a German ambush. The driver

2. Sterling Hayden

was killed, but Sterling and two other men were able to shoot their way out and escape. When Tito's force abandoned the island, Hayden went with them and joined with the partisans. He spent a full year with Tito's resistance force.

Hayden and his fleet of sailboats continued to take supplies to the resistance. While doing so, they assaulted a German patrol boat, and a firefight ensued. Finally, the Germans gave up and the patrol boat was taken to the island of Vis and turned over to the partisans. Lieutenant Hayden took his boats into Albania, the Adriatic islands and mainland Yugoslavia, at times during severe storms. All the while, they were bombed by German planes and chased by German boats. Sterling was eventually promoted to the rank of captain.

The Silver Star was awarded to Captain John Hamilton "for gallantry in action while serving with the Office of Strategic Services in the Mediterranean Theater of Operations from 24 December 1943 to 2 January 1944. Captain Hamilton displayed great courage in making hazardous sea voyages in enemy infested waters and reconnaissances through enemy held areas. His conduct reflected great credit upon himself and the United States Armed Forces." He was 27 at the time.

At the end of 1944, Hayden was sent back to the U.S. for a month's leave. In early 1945, he was sent to France, arriving just after the Battle of the Bulge had been won. After the German surrender, he was assigned to photograph the damage done by Allied bombing. In Paris, he got together with his wife, Madeleine, who was there to help displaced children. On December 24, 1945, Hayden was discharged, and he returned to Hollywood.

Hayden really wanted to go back to sailing, but he didn't have the funds to do so, so he ended up signing another contract with Paramount Pictures. His first film was *Blaze of Noon*. The story is about brothers, one of whom was Hayden, who flew the mail. Released in 1947, it garnered a positive review from the *New York Times* and grossed just under $2 million. He and Madeleine were divorced on May 8, 1946. Hayden had a bit part among many other celebrities in the 1947 musical *Variety Girl*. Critics called it "slam-bang entertainment."

In 1947, Sterling and Betty Ann de Noon were married and had four children: Christian, Dana, Gretchen and Matthew. Betty Ann was a dress designer from Pasadena. The marriage ended in a bitter divorce in 1953, and Betty Ann was awarded custody of the children—whereupon Serling embarked in his schooner, *Wanderer*, along with all four children. Hayden remarked, "Voyaging belongs to seamen and to wanderers of the world who cannot, or will not, fit in." They sailed from San Francisco to Tahiti, where he had planned to make a movie financed by Republic Pictures. The film never

World War II Veterans in Hollywood

came about, and Republic sued Hayden, recovering $50,000. Hayden ended up remarrying Betty Ann in 1954 and again in 1956. Both marriages also ended up in divorce.

Sterling admired the courage and dedication of Tito's partisans who were, of course, communists. He supported the motion pictures painters' union, which was then communist controlled. This led to a short membership in the Communist Party in 1946. He even attended a few meetings, but he became bored and didn't return. Still a Marine Corps Reservist, he was concerned that he might be called up for the Korean conflict and might be asked if he was, or ever had been, a communist. In 1950 he revealed to the FBI what he had learned about communist activities in the U.S. As a result, Hayden was served with a subpoena to testify before the House Un-American Activities Committee on April 10, 1951, where he revealed the names of communist friends and colleagues. For this, he was praised by the press and even by Ronald Reagan, who sent him a personal letter congratulating him. But Hayden said, "I don't think you have the foggiest notion of the contempt I have had for myself since the day I did that thing."

Hayden in the 1954 movie, *Johnny Guitar*, a western drama film co-starring Joan Crawford, in which he played the gunslinger Johnny (publicity still).

2. Sterling Hayden

While others who had been members of the Communist Party were blacklisted in Hollywood, Hayden was not, due to his testimony before Congress. Even so, no substantive offers came his way until the 1949 Western *El Paso*, in which he starred with John Payne and Gail Russell. He was in another 1949 film, *Manhandled*, co-starring Dorothy Lamour.

Then came John Huston's 1950 classic hit, *The Asphalt Jungle*. Because of his role as the leading man, the critically acclaimed movie put Hayden on top. During the fifties, he was in a number of films, mostly Westerns. Regarding these films, Sterling said, "Your mind flies free and you see yourself as an actor, condemned to a treadmill wherein men and women conspire to breathe life into a screenplay that allegedly depicts life as it was in the old wild west."

In the Stanley Kubrick's classic comedy, the 1964 *Dr. Strangelove*, he depicted an insane Air Force general, Jack D. Ripper, whose determination to stop the "communist threat" caused World War Three. (The complete title is *Dr. Strangelove or: How I Learned to Stop Worrying and Love the Bomb*.)

In 1960, he married Catherine Devine McConnell, and they were still married when he died. They had two children: Andrew and David. Catherine had a son, Scott, from a previous marriage.

It may be a surprise for some to learn that Sterling Hayden was also an author. His first book was *Wanderer*, published in 1963 by Knopf. In this autobiography, he recounts his voyage to Tahiti with his children, his experience with Congress and lots more. He also wrote a novel, *Voyage*, published by Putnam in 1976.

Hayden in the 1953 movie, *Suddenly*, a film noir crime drama co-starring Frank Sinatra where Sterling starred as Sheriff Tod Shaw (publicity still).

World War II Veterans in Hollywood

Called a "smash hit" by one critic, it's the story of a trip on a sailing ship in 1876.

Back in Hollywood, Hayden appeared in *The Long Goodbye*, *King of the Gypsies* and *9 to 5*. When he wasn't working in Hollywood, Sterling lived on his sailboat moored in Sausalito across the bay from San Francisco.

In 1969, Hayden traveled to Holland (the Netherlands) where he bought a boat that was actually a barge that traveled on canals. Sometime later, he motored it to Paris, where he lived for a while. He had a home in Wilton, Connecticut, where his wife, Catherine, lived with their children.

Sterling worked in movies rather infrequently during the eighties, spending most of his time on boats. One of his last appearances was in the 1982 television series *The Blue and the Gray*. His very last movie was *Venom*, a horror film released on January 29, 1982.

Sterling Hayden died on May 23, 1986, on his sailboat while moored in Sausalito. He was 70 years old. He had been ill with cancer for some time, and it was said that he frequently smoked hashish. Summing up his life, he once said, "I always hated acting, but I kept on acting." The reason was that he needed money for sailing.

3

Eddie Albert

Eddie Albert must be one of the most prolific of Hollywood stars. Between 1938 and 1994, he appeared in 85 movies and was seen many times on television. He was nominated for an Academy Award in 1954 for Best Supporting Actor in *Roman Holiday* and again in 1973 for *The Heartbreak Kid*. He played Ali Hakim in *Oklahoma!* and had his own television program, *The Eddie Albert Show*, as well as being the host of *Saturday Night Revue*. Even before World War II started, he worked for U.S. Army intelligence and went on active duty in the Naval Reserve, where he was awarded a Bronze Star for heroism.

Eddie Albert (left) as Col. Thompson of the 29th Infantry Division, with Robert Mitchum (right) as Brig. Gen. Norman Cota, in the 1962 World War II epic, *The Longest Day* (publicity still).

World War II Veterans in Hollywood

Albert was born on April 22, 1906, as Edward Albert Heimberger in Rock Island, Illinois. During World War I, he was sometimes made fun of due to his German last name, so he dropped the Heimberger. In addition, some mispronounced it as "Hamburger." His father was Frank Daniel Heimberger and his mother was Julia Jones. They were not married when he was born, but two years later, they got married. To hide the fact that he was born out of wedlock, his mother altered his birth certificate to read 1908.

Soon after his birth, the family moved to Minneapolis, where Eddie got his first job delivering newspapers when he was only six years old. As a teen, he had a variety of odd jobs. Noted for his excellent tenor voice, he sang in their church choir. After graduating from the Central High School where he had joined the drama club, he went on to the University of Minnesota, majoring in business and drama. He joined a song, dance and patter group there and helped pay his tuition by managing movie theatres and emceeing weekly stage shows.

Shortly before graduation, he dropped out and went to work singing in a trio, *The Threesome*, on radio. When the trio broke up, he teamed up with Grace Brandt. They became a singing duo on the NBC radio show, *The Honeymooners—Grace and Eddie Show*, which ran for three years. Albert was one of the earliest actors on television. He performed live on an RCA television test broadcast on NBC in 1936.

Eddie made his acting debut on January 8, 1936, in the play *O Evening Star*. It was a flop with only five performances. On Broadway, Albert co-starred with Ronald Reagan in a comedy play, *Brother Rat*. He and Reagan played roommates at the Virginia Military Institute. The play ran for 577 performances in 1936–1938. A critic wrote, "Albert gives a splendid performance." This led to a contract with Warner Brothers giving him the movie *Brother Rat*, which came out in 1938, again with Ronald Reagan and also Jane Wyman. Eddie and Jane became lifelong friends.

During the thirties he made two more films, both released in 1939. Eddie performed in and wrote a television show for RCA to promote their radio stations. Albert also wrote and starred in one of the first teleplays, *The Love Nest*. It was broadcast live over the NBC experimental television station W2XBS. Before this, television productions were adaptations of stage plays. Eddie acted and sang in *On Your Toes*, which was adapted from the stage hit by Rodgers and Hart. In the early forties, he appeared in fourteen more movies. Three of them were released after he enlisted in the Coast Guard in September 1942.

In California, Albert liked taking long trips down the West Coast to

3. Eddie Albert

Mexico in his sailboat. While on one of these trips, he heard about secret Japanese submarine fueling stations and Japanese "fishermen" surveying the U.S. Pacific coast, which he reported. The Army intelligence service enlisted his help and sent him to Mexico to act as a clown for the Escalante Brothers Circus. When not performing, he went sightseeing and photographed Japanese submarines in Mexican harbors.

Albert's expert seamanship was deemed to be better utilized in the Navy. The Coast Guard allowed him to be discharged and he accepted a commission as a lieutenant in the Naval Reserve. He was posted as salvage officer on the attack transport USS *Sheridan*.

As salvage officer, his principal duty was to recover usable equipment from the beach during the battle, but preliminary to that he would use a small boat to assist the boat control officer (BCO) to get the Marines ashore. The *Sheridan*'s BCO was Lt. Jack Fletcher. (The USS *Sheridan* was named after Philip Sheridan, the Civil War general.) The ship carried 1,560 Marines of the 1st Battalion, 8th Marines, and a crew of 500.

The battle for Tarawa, an atoll in the Gilbert Islands located in the mid–Pacific, was the Marines' first amphibious assault and was murderously contested on the beaches. It took place during November 20–23, 1943. After an intense naval and air bombardment, the *Sheridan* landed its battalion of Marines on the small island of Betio in the southwest of the atoll. The 4,500 Japanese, crowded on the small island, fought to the last man.

To commence the landing, Lt. Fletcher and Albert organized the landing craft into waves and at the commander's signal, sent them off. The plan was to press over the reef into the lagoon and land on the beach. The control officers were returning to the ship when they realized their boats were getting hung up on the reef because of an unexpected low tide and were under heavy fire from the shore and from a long pier adjacent to the landing beach. Marines were waist deep in the water hundreds of yards from the beach. Albert and Fletcher came about and headed into the firestorm to pick up the wounded and take them out to the larger landing crafts mechanized (LCMs). After three or four trips, Albert's salvage boat number 13 had damaged its propeller and Lt. Fletcher had taken a large load of wounded to the *Sheridan*. Albert took command of a Higgins boat (a landing craft vehicle personnel—LCVP) and four sister boats and proceeded to evacuate the rest of the wounded. He was credited with six trips into harm's way and awarded the Bronze Star with "V" for valor.

The Tarawa Campaign introduced Americans to the bloody determination of Japanese to die for Emperor Hirohito. The cost was some 6,400 lives:

World War II Veterans in Hollywood

Japanese soldiers, Korean laborers, and U.S. Marines. Of these, 4,500 were dead Japanese, and for the first time, Americans at home were shocked to see pictures of dead American Marines on a beach.

Albert had contracted an ulcer and was discharged. In 1944, he was recalled by the Navy to help make training films. In 1946, he formed Eddie Albert Productions to make educational shorts. Two were about sex education for pre-teens and were still in use 40 years later. After his final discharge in 1945, Eddie married a Mexican movie actress called Margo. He had met her when on a leave while he was still in the Navy. Her full name was Maria Margarita Guadalupe Teresa Estela Bolado Castilla y O'Donnell. It was Eddie's only marriage. The two had a nightclub singing act. They had a son—Edward Jr.—who also became an actor, and they adopted a daughter, Maria. Later, as an adult, she became Albert's business manager. Margo died in July 1985 from cancer.

Eddie returned to star in films as a leading man during the fifties. At the same time, he was on the stage in *Broadway*, *Miss Liberty*, *The Seven Year Itch*, *The Music Man*, *Reuben* and *My Fair Lady*, so he had to scurry back and forth between New York and his home in Pacific Palisades, a suburb of Los Angeles. The house was Spanish style on an acre of land. Later, Albert became an enthusiastic agronomist and turned his front yard into a cornfield and the back into a vegetable garden. In 1950, he played Lucille Ball's fiancé in *The Fuller Brush Girl*, followed by *The Sun Also Rises* and *Carrie*. Next was *Roman Holiday*, which gave him an Oscar nomination for Best Supporting Actor.

Arnold appeared in 27 movies from the end of the war to 1960, including such famous films as *Oklahoma!* and *The Teahouse of the August Moon*. At the same time, he appeared in almost 90 television series as well as acting on Broadway. His career as a singer resulted in some albums. That he could fit all of this in and still have family responsibilities is almost beyond belief.

During the early fifties, Eddie and his wife, Margo, were blacklisted as being sympathetic to the communist cause. Albert was among the hundreds named. Eddie's name was cleared due to his heroism during the war, but Margo's was not. According to their son, Edward, "My mom was spat upon in the streets and had to have a bodyguard." It was an unhappy experience.

Back on the stage, Eddie acted in a reprise of *The Music Man* and in *My Fair Lady*. Such movie hits as *The Longest Day* and *Captain Newman, M.D.*, were among the 11 films he made then. On television, Eddie had a six-year run, costarring with Eva Gabor, in the acclaimed show, *Green Acres*. Albert remarked, "The show is a comment on how insane our society is." During the

3. Eddie Albert

time from the seventies until his last movie, the animated *Spider-Man*, in which he did a voice over, Albert was in 35 motion pictures and seven television shows; three of them were series and included the noted *War and Remembrance*.

In 1979, Albert had reached the age of 69; he starred in the television drama *Switch* on CBS. Right out of the box, it was a hit and ran for three years with 70 episodes. Sometimes listed as his last movie, *Brenda Starr* was actually made in 1986, six years before its release date of 1992. One of his last starring roles was in the television movie *The Girl from Mars*, shown in 1991. After guest-starring in the 1997 *Extreme Ghostbusters*, Eddie retired from acting. He was 91.

Albert in *The Longest Day* (1962), produced by Darryl F. Zanuck. This classic World War II film depicts the June 6, 1944, landings on the beaches of Normandy, France (promotional photo).

Albert was active in a number of causes, particularly environmental issues. He was involved in the creation of Earth Day, founded the Eddie Albert World Trees Foundation, and was a trustee of the National Recreation and Park Association. In addition, he was the national chairman of the Boy Scouts of America's Conservation Program. *TV Guide* magazine named him "an ecological Paul Revere."

Eddie was also concerned with the problem of hunger throughout the world. He was an envoy for Meals for Millions and a consultant to the World Hunger Conference. He even made a documentary movie about African hunger. A promoter of organic gardening, he founded City Children's Farms. About his own home in Pacific Palisades, he remarked, "People don't know how good vegetables taste until they grow their own, and

Albert with Ike Eisenmann (left) and Kim Richards (right) in the 1975 movie, *Escape to Witch Mountain*, where Albert plays a cynical widower who helps the two children escape in this fantasy/sci-fi film (publicity still).

it is comforting to know you can still provide for yourself in this day and age."

After Albert was diagnosed with Alzheimer's in 1995, his son, Edward Jr., put his own acting career aside to help care for his father. Even so, Albert exercised regularly. It was reported that three days before his death, he was playing basketball in his wheelchair with his granddaughter. Eddie Albert died of pneumonia on May 26, 2005, at age 99 at his home in Pacific Palisades with his son Edward at his side. His grave at the Westwood Village Memorial Park Cemetery is next to Margo's and close to Eva Gabor's. His funeral was private and was attended by Shirley Jones, *Green Acres* cast members and

3. Eddie Albert

close friends and family. Unfortunately, Edward Jr., only 55 years old, died a year later from lung cancer.

Summing up his life, Albert had said, "I don't really care how I am remembered as long as I bring happiness and joy to people. What's the most important thing in the world? It is love, and I look at that as an energy, not a sentiment."

4

Jimmy Stewart

Jimmy Stewart was one of the best-known actors of his time and among the most popular stars ever. After the war, he went to Hollywood and starred in *It's a Wonderful Life*. It was nominated for five Academy Awards including Stewart for Best Actor. But before that, Jimmy was a true hero in World War II. As an Army Air Corps pilot, he received two Distinguished Flying Crosses and four Air Medals, among a number of other decorations. How he ended up as a major general is a fascinating story in itself.

James Maitland Stewart was born in Indiana, Pennsylvania, on May 20, 1908. His forebears served in both the Revolutionary War and the Civil War. The son of Alexander and Elizabeth, he was born in the family home that was on top of Vinegar Hill. His father, who had served in World War I, owned and ran a hardware store there. J.M. Stewart and Co., called "the Big Warehouse," was an institution. Jimmy had two younger sisters, Virginia and Mary. Jimmy and the girls presented magic shows and plays in the basement. The kids would ride around town in a carriage drawn by horses. As a youth, Stewart anticipated eventually running his dad's store himself, but of course, that was not to be. His mother was an accomplished musician and her children inherited this skill. The three children all learned to play the piano. Stewart's father acquired an accordion but decided he didn't want to play it. Jimmy took an interest in it, became proficient and later performed in front of audiences.

Growing up, Stewart was active in the Boy Scouts, receiving the Boy Scouts of America Silver Buffalo Award. He also had a hobby of building model airplanes in the home basement and launching them from the roof. In addition, he worked on chemistry and mechanical engineering. That was when he began dreaming of becoming a pilot.

When President Harding's funeral train passed through town, Jimmy's father took him to see it. Jimmy put two pennies on the track, where they were flattened. He kept them in his desk drawer for the rest of his life.

Jimmy began his education in a primary school called the Model School, now known as Wilson Hall. It was on the Indiana University campus. After he

4. Jimmy Stewart

James "Jimmy" Stewart began flying combat missions on March 31, 1944, and was appointed Operations Officer of the 453rd Bomb Group and, subsequently, Chief of Staff of the 2nd Combat Wing, 2nd Air Division of the 8th Air Force. He ended the war with 20 combat missions and remained in the USAF Reserve where he was later promoted to Brig. General (USAF).

graduated from the ninth grade, he was sent for high school to Mercersburg Academy, a private boarding school in Mercersburg, Pennsylvania, where he graduated in 1928. He lettered in football and track and was the art editor of the school newspaper and yearbook. A very active student, he joined the choir, the glee club and the literary society. Jimmy's very first on-stage role was in a high school play, *The Wolves*.

During his time in high school, Stewart returned home during the summer to be with his family. He always got a job. The first two summers he loaded bricks on trucks and painted lines on roadways. The last two summers he was an on-stage assistant to a magician named Bill Neff. They played on the Pennsylvania–Chautauqua circuit. For some shows, Jimmy played his accordion.

Although Stewart had wanted to go to the U.S. Naval Academy, he ended up at his father's alma mater, Princeton University, in 1928. He majored in architecture and his thesis was on airport design. It was so outstanding that the university gave him a scholarship in the graduate school. While still an undergrad, he joined the drama and music clubs plus the famous Triangle Club in 1929. The Princeton Triangle Club creates an original musical comedy each year that is written and performed by students. It showcases their talents and is the university's well-loved tradition.

Stewart acted with the college's Stoney Batter drama club. First he was in *The Frog Prince*, and then in *The Golden Dog*. He also played his accordion in the university's Marshall Orchestra. Jimmy graduated from Princeton in 1932.

That same year, a fire burned the J.M. Stewart and Co. facility, and Stewart's father became engaged in rebuilding it. This resulted in hard times for the family. Before the fire, Jimmy's two sisters had been accepted at expensive private universities. During this time, the country had descended into the Great Depression. Jimmy didn't think he could find a job in architecture.

Then Stewart's acting ability came to the rescue. He was invited to join the University Players. It was an organization that played the summer stock circuit. At first, Jimmy played his accordion and appeared in a few bit parts. In addition, he worked as a stagehand and designed sets. He also made friends with Henry Fonda.

When the Players staged the play *Carrie Nation* on Broadway in 1932, Jimmy appeared in such bit parts as a constable, a gardener, a vigilante and a bystander. The Players included Fonda. The two became friends there and roomed together. But the play ran only seven weeks. Stewart remembered, "We had an apartment on the west side of Central Park. The rent was very reasonable. We found out later that it belonged to a gangster called Legs Diamond."

Stewart had received positive reviews and they led to roles in *Goodbye Again* and three other plays. Commenting about *Goodbye Again*, the *New Yorker Magazine* reported that even though Jimmy spoke only two lines, "Mr. James Stewart's chauffeur ... comes on for only three minutes and walks off to a round of spontaneous applause." In 1934, he starred as Sergeant O'Hara in *Yellow Jack*. He was so good in the role that he received a screen test from Metro-Goldwyn-Mayer; he was off to Hollywood.

The first motion picture Jimmy played in was *Art Trouble*, released in 1934. Then came *Important News* and *Murder Man*, both in 1936. After Jimmy starred in *You Can't Take It with You*, director Frank Capra remarked, "I think he's the best actor who's ever hit the screen." Through 1939, Stewart was in a total of 29 films as well as a few parts on Broadway. He also did voice-overs for movies and on radio shows. His movie roles earned Jimmy a number

4. Jimmy Stewart

of Academy Award nominations until finally he received the Oscar for Best Actor for his role in *The Philadelphia Story*.

Stewart had always been interested in flying, even as a youth. By 1935, he could afford flying lessons. He earned his private pilot's license and, in 1938, his commercial pilot's license. Flying his own airplane, he flew wherever and whenever he could, and by the time he entered the service, he had logged more than 400 hours in the air. After appearing in the anti–Nazi film *The Mortal Storm*, Jimmy took a trip to Europe to see for himself what was going on, but he returned to the U.S. when Poland was invaded by Germany in 1939.

By then war was looming in America's future, and the Army needed men to fill the ranks that had been badly depleted after World War I. In 1940 Jimmy Stewart was drafted and then rejected because he was underweight, at only 143 pounds and over six feet tall. Consequently, he embarked on a regime to gain weight. Finally, in March 1941, he was able to enlist in the Army Air Corps. He was the first Hollywood star to join the fight.

He underwent basic training and aviation training at Moffett Field in California and became an Army Air Corps pilot. The Air Corps had to enlist some 100,000 airmen, so it used Stewart in this effort. First, he spoke on a radio program called *We Hold These Truths* and was in a movie, *Winning Your Wings*; he narrated and appeared in his flight suit.

Jimmy already had hundreds of hours in the air and a commercial license, so, after passing a difficult examination, Stewart was made a second lieutenant. He was assigned to train pilots to fly B-17 and B-24 bombers. Stuck at this job for two years, Stewart continually lobbied to be sent into combat. Now a captain in 1943, he was transferred to the 8th Air Force stationed in England. The first mission for the B-24s was to bomb a Nazi submarine base at Kiel, Germany. Soon thereafter, Jimmy led his squadron to Bremen and to Ludwigshafen. After a number of other operations, Stewart was promoted to major and awarded the Distinguished Flying Cross.

Leading the 2nd Bombardment Wing, Stewart attacked Berlin on March 22, 1944. Later that month, he was assigned as the group operations officer. Jimmy was the command pilot for missions to bomb German-occupied Europe. He flew a total of 20 missions with the wing.

Major James Stewart continued to fly on numerous missions with different groups and wings. During that time, he was awarded a second Distinguished Flying Cross and three Air Medals for bravery in combat, as well as the French Croix de Guerre. By war's end, he was a colonel. When he was released from active duty in 1945, Jimmy returned to Hollywood. The 8th Air Force alone lost more men killed in combat than the total lost by the Marine Corps.

World War II Veterans in Hollywood

Stewart's first movie after the war was *It's a Wonderful Life*, released in 1946 and directed by Frank Capra. Jimmy starred as George Bailey, the lead role along with Donna Reed. Although the film was nominated for five Academy Awards with Stewart as Best Actor, many reviews were negative and it didn't do well commercially. When he looked back on his acting career, Jimmy said that *It's a Wonderful Life* was his favorite movie.

In 1948, Stewart starred on Broadway in the play *Harvey*. The critics loved it and it ran for almost three years, with Jimmy running back and forth between New York and Hollywood. Regarding his role, Stewart said, "I'd like to do *Harvey* again. I did it two years ago with Helen Hayes in New York. It was a joy. I

Stewart being awarded the Croix De Guerre with Palm in 1944 (USAF).

was so glad to do it again because I never thought I did it right the first time." It was made into a movie in 1950, also starring Stewart, who got a Best Actor nomination. The play was revived on Broadway in 1970 and in London in 1975. NBC included it in the *Hallmark Hall of Fame* in 1972, with its perennial star, Jimmy Stewart.

For the rest of the nineteen forties, Stewart appeared in virtually a film a year. These included *Magic Town* in 1947, *Rope* and *Call Northside 777* in 1948. Next, Jimmy starred with his friend Henry Fonda in *On Our Merry Way*, about two jazz musicians. There were two more movies, but none were spectacular successes.

In 1948, Jimmy met a beautiful 31-year-old, Gloria Hatrick McLean, at the home of Gary Cooper. She was not an actress. They took to each other and were married on August 9, 1949. Gloria already had two young chil-

4. Jimmy Stewart

dren—Ronald and Michael—from a previous marriage. Stewart, at 41 years old, welcomed the two children into his life. Then Gloria became pregnant and fraternal twins resulted: Kelly and Judy.

Universal Studios made a Western, *Winchester '73*, in 1950 starring Jimmy. But due to studio finances, Stewart received a percentage of the profits rather than a salary. As it turned out, the movie was a financial success and he made quite a lot of money on the deal.

Another Western followed—*Broken Arrow*—and then *The Greatest Show on Earth*, which won Best Picture from the Academy. Starring as Charles Lindbergh in *The Spirit of St. Louis* and as Colonel Robert R. "Dutch" Holland in *Strategic Air Command*, these roles were right up Stewart's alley as an accomplished pilot. On the radio, he was in *The Six Shooter* in 1953 and 1954.

A number of Westerns followed, along with Jimmy playing the title role in *The Glenn Miller Story*, which won Stewart a British Academy Best Actor Award nomination. He was the highest paid Hollywood actor in 1954. The Hitchcock films *The Man Who Knew Too Much* and *Vertigo* become classics and increased Stewart's fame.

The nineteen sixties saw Stewart in a number of films, the most success-

Jimmy Stewart with Grace Kelly, starring in the 1954 Alfred Hitchcock mystery *Rear Window* (promotional photo).

ful of which was *How the West Was Won*, which garnered three Oscars and huge box office returns. Jimmy kept at it until 1991, when he played Sheriff Wylie Burp in *An American Tail: Fievel Goes West*. He was 81 years old and this was his last performance. He voiced an old dog in this animated film and his last words on film were: "A young pups doggin' my tail.... I'm going to the dogs in a dog eat dog world, son." With that, he retired!

After the war, Stewart continued as a reservist in the Army Air Corps and later, the U.S. Air Force. In 1953, he served as the commander of Dobbins Air Reserve Base at Marietta, Georgia. During his reserve service, he remained current, flying B-36, B-47 and B-52 bombers. In 1959, he was promoted to brigadier general. On February 20, 1966, General Stewart flew in a B-52 bombing mission over Vietnam. Jimmy retired from the Air Force on May 31, 1968, when he was awarded the United States Air Force Distinguished Service Medal. In 1985 President Reagan awarded him the Presidential Medal of Freedom and Stewart was promoted to major general USAFR. After a long struggle, Gloria died from cancer in 1994.

Jimmy was active in politics. A Republican, he campaigned for Richard Nixon and particularly for Ronald Reagan. After Reagan was elected president, Stewart was a frequent visitor to the White House. He also supported Bob Dole for his 1996 bid to the presidency and Bob Braham in his run for senator.

In February 1997, Stewart was hospitalized for an irregular heartbeat. On July 2, 1997, James Maitland Stewart died at his home in Beverly Hills. He was 89 years old. His children were with him when he said, "I'm going to be with Gloria now." On being asked how he wanted to be remembered, he said, "As someone who believed in hard work, love of country, love of family, and love of community."

5

Joseph Wapner

Joseph Wapner was best known as the judge on the long-running television show *The People's Court*, where he was hugely successful. Unlike others profiled in this book, he was not an actor, nor was he ever in a movie or on a stage. Even so, his name is on the Hollywood Walk of Fame. He was a real judge with an outstanding legal career. He was also an author of books and appeared on a number of other television shows. Wapner was a highly decorated hero in World War II.

Joseph Albert Wapner was born in Los Angeles on November 15, 1919. His parents were Jewish immigrants. His father, Joseph Max, was from Romania and his mother, Fannie Friedman, from Russia. When his father arrived in California, he went to school and became a lawyer.

Wapner went to Hollywood High School. Initially he said he wanted to be an actor, but after the theater director told him he had no talent, he gave up on the idea. Wapner's most memorable event there was when he met a schoolmate, Judy Turner, in the school library. "She was the most beautiful girl I'd ever seen," he remembered. He asked her to go with him to a nearby drug store for a Coke. She accepted and they went, but he had forgotten his wallet. She had to pay, and he was humiliated. That was his only date with Judy, who later changed her first name to Lana and became a famous movie star.

After high school, Wapner went to the University of Southern California and graduated with a bachelor's degree in philosophy in 1941. He joined the Army in 1942 and after basic training was sent to the South Pacific to join the Americal Division's 182nd Regiment. The Americal Division, later named the 23rd Infantry, was formed on the island of New Caledonia in May of 1942. In October 1942 it relieved the battered First Marine Division on Guadalcanal. It was the first Army unit to go on the offensive in World War II. In 1943 the division assumed the defense of Fiji until January 1944. On the 12th of that month, the division landed on Bougainville in the Solomon Islands to relieve the Third Marine Division. The troops endured four months of vicious jungle

World War II Veterans in Hollywood

combat against suicidal Japanese soldiers. They remained on the island for the rest of 1944, training for their next assignment. Joseph Wapner, showing signs of future greatness, was promoted from corporal to second lieutenant.

On January 8, 1945, the division was landed on Leyte in the Philippines to clean out Japanese resistance, occupy the Visayas, and prepare for the assault on Cebu. On the 26th of March 1945, Lieutenant Wapner, commanding a platoon, landed on Talisay Beach and began the five-mile fight to reach and capture Cebu City. They met light resistance on the beach, but it was strewn with mines and the jungle was teeming with snipers.

Joseph Wapner in 1993 as the presiding judge of the ongoing reality court show *The People's Court* (publicity still).

Wapner remembered that one day, "I had an unbelievably lucky brush with a Japanese sniper. A bullet ripped through my knapsack and was stopped only by a can of tuna fish my mother had sent to me. Thank you, Mom!" Later he was wounded by shrapnel from a grenade and then risked his life to save another wounded soldier from machine-gun fire. The five-mile march was a two-day muddy, bloody mess through broken jungle, booby traps and suicidal snipers. Cebu City and its airfield were secured on the 28th. Promoted to first lieutenant, Joseph Wapner earned a Bronze Star for gallantry and a Purple Heart for his wound. His outfit received a Presidential Unit Citation.

The Americal Division went on to secure other islands and then returned to Cebu to train for the invasion of Japan. The fanatic emperor-worshipers that had taken to the hills did not surrender until after the collapse of Japan. With Emperor Hirohito's acceptance of defeat, Wapner's Americal Division occupied the Yokohama-Kawasaki-Yokosuka area of Japan.

5. Joseph Wapner

The judge's Asiatic-Pacific ribbon sports three little stars, signifying combat in three major campaigns. After years of Army life and jungle combat, Wapner returned home and was discharged in 1945. He was ready for civilian life.

Joseph soon met Mildred Nebenzahl on a blind date. Her nickname was Mickey. They were married only eight weeks later. They had a daughter, Sarah, plus two sons, Fred and David, both of whom later became lawyers. Fred, following in his father's footsteps, became a judge in Los Angeles.

Wapner returned to the University of Southern California and enrolled in the law school, from which he graduated in 1948 with an LLB degree. After ten years of private practice, he was appointed a judge in the Los Angeles Municipal Court in 1959 by Governor Edmond G. (Pat) Brown. Forty years old, he served for two years before being elevated to the Superior Court. He presided there for 18 years until age 60, when he retired in November of 1979.

Then, instead of enjoying his well-earned retirement, he resumed a private law practice, specializing in the arbitration of divorce cases. His most celebrated case was when he negotiated a $4.1 million settlement between Washington Redskins owner Jack Kent Cooke and Cooke's first wife.

Joseph Wapner's pastime was playing tennis, often with Ralph Edwards and Stu Billett. These two were television producers who had formulated the idea for a new program they called *The People's Court*. They envisioned a television show that featured unscripted, real-life grievances between plaintiffs and defendants. Of course, the show needed a judge, so they picked their tennis pal who had just retired. Billett noted, "Look at him, isn't he just perfect? Look at those eyebrows. Look at that hair. You couldn't ask for anything better."

Wapner handed down decisions on *The People's Court* starting in 1981 and ending in 1993. He presided over 2,340 half-hour dramas. The litigants were chosen from cases that had been heard in Los Angeles small-claims courts. The litigants had to sign a contract in which they agreed that the decision reached on the show would be final. Each was paid $250. Each story was a courtroom adventure that provided memorable lessons in law, the unpredictability of human nature and old-fashioned justice. The show's director said, "It turns out that regular people are whiny, petty, annoying folks, so Judge Wapner's crotchety grouch manner was just what we wanted—to shut them up now and then."

The program was a huge success. A 1982 survey showed that 54 percent of Americans knew the name Judge Joseph Wapner, while only nine percent could name the chief justice of the U.S. Supreme Court. Wapner's affable, no-nonsense approach attracted many fans, making his show one of the leading syndicated programs. Only a few years after it started, it was attracting some 20 million viewers. Each show included an actor playing Rusty, the bailiff, and a host who introduced each show. After the decision by Judge Wapner, the host interviewed the litigants. "When *The People's Court* came along I had an opportunity to really teach people about law. It was very important to me," Judge Joe said.

"Everything on the show is real," he said. "There's no script, no rehearsal, and no retakes. Everything from beginning to end is like a real courtroom and I personally consider each case as a real trial. Sometimes I don't even deliberate. I just decide from the bench, the outcome is so obvious. The beautiful part is that I have *carte blanche*." A critic noted, "He brings wisdom to his decisions." Because of his popularity, Wapner was asked to speak at a number of college campuses and legal groups. He turned down guest parts on other shows saying, "I'm not an actor, I'm a judge."

On June 27, 1986, Johnny Carson invited Judge Wapner to appear on *The Tonight Show*. His role was to decide a dispute between Carson and David Letterman. David had left an old beat-up truck on the street near Johnny's house. Calling it an eyesore, Carson had it towed away, and a headlight was broken in the process. He had the truck brought to the studio for all to see. Carson offered to settle by offering Letterman a box of steaks. But the judge turned it down: "Mr. Letterman, the price isn't right." So Wapner awarded David $24.95.

Wapner's book *A View from the Bench* was published in 1987. In it, he recalled some of his favorite cases. Wapner appeared as himself in a 1989 segment of the television show *The People Next Door*. In 1992, *Judge Wapner's Family Legal Guide* was published. It included eight audio cassettes and three books.

After 1993, the producers cancelled *The People's Court* because viewership had declined. They revived the show in 1997, but without Wapner. He never offered opinions regarding the judges who had replaced him on the new show and said he never watched any of the new programs. In 1995, he was in an episode of the television show *Sliders*, appearing as himself. Then came *Judge Wapner's Animal Court*, a series that ran from 1998 to 2000 on the Animal Planet channel. In it, he and his *People's Court* bailiff, Rusty, presided over real court cases that involved animals, who were usually in the courtroom too. They included everything from horses to monkeys and, more often than not, dogs and cats. Wapner did television and print advertisements for the Singer Asset Finance Company in 1999 and 2000. Rocket Fizz, a beverage company, brought out a soda they named the "Judge Wapner Root Beer." Its slogan was, "I sentence you to drink my root beer."

5. Joseph Wapner

The Wapners' daughter, Sarah, passed away due to heart failure in 2015. Joseph Albert Wapner died from a heart attack at his Los Angeles home on February 26, 2017. He was 97 years old. His widow, Mickey, survives and is living in Rancho Mirage, California.

The People's Court format has succeeded to the extent that the judges are now among the highest paid people on television.

6

Gene Autry

Gene Autry was called the "singing cowboy." He was a well-known country and Western singer who made records and appeared in movies, radio and television from the early thirties into the fifties. Autry was also a very successful businessman. He owned a number of television and radio stations plus a baseball team: the Los Angeles Angels. Gene enlisted in the Army in 1942 and, as a pilot, flew over the Himalayas from India into China, a very dangerous operation called flying over the "Hump."

Orvon Gene Autry was born on September 29, 1907, in Tioga, Texas. He was the oldest of four children. His parents, Delbert and Elnora Autry, were poor tenant farmers. Life on the farm was tough. At an early age, he worked in the fields with his dad. When he was a child, his mother taught him to sing hymns that he performed in their church choir as well as folk songs. When 12 years old, he bought his first guitar from a Sears and Roebuck catalog for eight dollars. He had saved the money he earned baling hay on his uncle's farm.

When Autry was in his early teens, his father scraped up enough money to acquire a ranch in Ravia, Johnston County, in Oklahoma. Gene attended Ravia Community School, which included both elementary and high school. While at school, he worked on his father's ranch.

After he graduated in 1925, he found work as a telegrapher for the St. Louis–San Francisco Railway in Chelsea, Oklahoma. To pass time, Autry would sing and play on his guitar. He also sang and played at local dances. One night, Will Rogers came to send a telegram and enjoyed the music he heard. An actor, comedian and columnist, Rogers was a famous Oklahoma personality. After hearing a few more songs, Rogers suggested that Autry look for a job in radio. He got his first singing job in 1927 at Tulsa station KVOO, where he performed as "Oklahoma's Yodeling Cowboy."

Autry gained a rather large following of fans while singing at the radio station. As a result, he was offered a recording contract with Columbia Records in 1929. He went to Chicago to work for four years on one of WLS

6. Gene Autry

radio station's shows, *National Barn Dance*. In 1931, he got his own show. Autry started to make his own records, singing "Do Right Daddy Blues" and "Black Bottom Blues." Then came his first million-selling record: *That Silver Haired Daddy of Mine*, in 1932. It was a duet with Jimmy Long, which Gene and Jimmy co-wrote. Other classics followed, such as the popular songs "Tumbling Tumbleweeds," "South of the Border" and "Back in the Saddle Again."

Musician and composer Jimmy Long and Gene Autry were close friends. The Long family lived in Sapulpa, Oklahoma. Through Jimmy, Gene met Long's niece, Ina May Spivey. She was 21 and he, 25. Almost at first sight, they fell in love. He told Jimmy that she was the person he'd like to marry. And marry they did, on April 1, 1932. Ina was strong-willed and intelligent and was proud and supportive of Gene. She encouraged Autry to give Hollywood a try and to stick it out when he had initial doubts. She was responsible for his recording of "Rudolph the Red-Nosed Reindeer." At first, Gene didn't like the song, but Ina thought children would enjoy it, and she was right. The recording became a world-famous Christmas song. It sold two million copies the first year and went on to become the best-selling song of all time. The marriage lasted 48 years, until her death in 1980. They had no children.

Autry's first movie was *In Old Santa Fe*, released in 1934, in which he was part of a singing-cowboy quartet. The next year, Gene was the star in *The Phantom Empire*. He was well on his way to becoming a top

Gene Autry, "the singing cowboy."

39

box-office star. Other movies included the 1935 *Tumbling Tumbleweeds*, the first musical Western film. *The Singing Cowboy, Rhythm of the Saddle* and *Sioux City Sue* followed. Theatre owners rated Autry as one of the top ten box-office attractions in the country. This continued every year until he enlisted in the Army in 1942.

Autry was at the top of his game in the movie business and had committed most of his savings to creating a travelling rodeo show, in the manner of *Buffalo Bill's Wild West*, when the Japanese bombed Pearl Harbor. At 34 years

Gene Autry on his horse, Champion, in a 1939 movie poster for *Home on the Prairie* (publicity poster).

6. Gene Autry

old, he was subject to the draft. He wouldn't accept a deferment but wanted to follow Jimmy Stewart and Clark Gable—get a commission and fly airplanes. Gene already had a private pilot's license.

Because of adverse publicity about celebrity commissions, he was allowed to enlist at the rank of technical sergeant on July 9, 1942. Because of his fame, the Army conducted the ceremony live during his radio show, *Melody Ranch*. He took basic training at Santa Ana, California, and was then assigned to special services at Luke Field, where he broadcast the weekly radio show *Sergeant Gene Autry*. A piano player on the show was young Steve Allen. For the next 18 months Autry wrangled with Army red tape, engaged in open combat with Republic Studios over contract disputes and continued to pay for private pilot training to acquire the 300 hours needed to qualify for a transfer to the Air Transport Command (ATC).

When in October 1943 he was accepted to join the ATC, his current commander wouldn't release him. Gene drew his six-shooters and fired off missives to influential friends. None other than Lyndon Baines Johnson spoke to a general, and Autry's transfer was accomplished. Later to become president of the United States, Congressman Johnson's help was ironic, because Gene's squadron leader at Luke Field had been Barry Goldwater.

The Third Ferrying Division of the Air Transport Command at Romulus, Michigan, was adjacent to the Ford Motor Company's giant Willow Run plant, which produced thousands of B-24 bombers. Ferry Command pilots delivered all types of aircraft to all parts of the world. (Col. Hal Dixon delivered a B-25 to the Russians in Vladivostok.) Gene would later fly a converted B-24 to China.

On June 21, 1944, Gene Autry finally got his wings and was promoted to flying officer, a rank equivalent to warrant officer. He was ordered to report to Love Field in Dallas, Texas, and join the 91st Ferry Squadron. At last, he was able to pilot all the airplanes of his dreams: single engine fighters, dive bombers, and four-engine, heavy bombers.

Autry's most hazardous mission was to deliver a C-109, a converted B-24, to Kunming, China. The airplane carried a load of aviation fuel over the Himalayas, the "Hump," from India into China. The gas fueled the Flying Tigers' P-40s and P-51s that were attacking the Japanese in Hanoi and Hong Kong.

To get there, the flight originated at Willow Run and proceeded over the North Atlantic to North Africa, Egypt, the Middle East and on to India. Then, loaded with fuel, it was routed over the "Hump" to Kunming, China. On this trip, near the Azores in mid–Atlantic, they were confronted with a hurricane and a misfiring engine and forced to make a tenuous five-hour return to Gander Bay, Newfoundland. The weather moved in and they were grounded for two weeks. Eventually, however, he completed the trip to China.

When the war ended, Gene was assigned to Special Services, where he toured with a USO troupe in the South Pacific. Discharged in 1946, Autry had earned the American Campaign Medal, the Asiatic-Pacific Campaign Medal and the World War II Victory Medal.

Autry resumed his singing career in 1946. That December, he recorded many Christmas songs and was the grand marshal of the annual Hollywood Christmas Parade. As he passed, parade spectators cheered in unison, "Here Comes Santa Claus!" He had composed a song with the same title that had become a classic.

Autry continued his very popular weekly radio show on CBS: *Gene Autry's Melody Ranch*. At the same time, he had a CBS television show: *The Adventures of Champion*, his horse. Starting in 1950, he had a television show, *The Gene Autry Show*, which ran for 91 episodes. The success of these shows resulted in his producing additional series: *Annie Oakley, The Range Rider, Buffalo Bill, Jr.,* and *Death Valley Days*. Additionally, during the fifties, he produced and starred in a number of movies including *The Old West, Apache Country* and *On Top of Old Smokey*.

While starring in his radio show and movies, Autry went on tours with his stage show, which featured roping, Indian dancers and comedy skits. Trick riding and horse tricks were performed by his horse, Champion, "The Wonder Horse." The small town of Berwyn, Oklahoma, changed its name to "Gene Autry."

Autry was not only a famous performer but also a savvy businessman. He produced his own line of Western-themed merchandise that was distributed to a number of outlets. Autry invested in and helped run a number of radio and television stations including Los Angeles's KMPC radio and KTLA television, KOGO in San Diego and KSFO in San Francisco, plus others throughout the country.

Gene had a lifelong love of baseball. Once, when he was young, he was offered a chance to join a minor-league team. He began his baseball career later in life with the ownership of the Hollywood Stars, a minor-league team. When the major leagues came to the Los Angeles area, he became the owner of the Los Angeles Angels. In 1995 he sold the franchise to the Walt Disney Company.

He established the Gene Autry Western Heritage Museum in Los Angeles. Many items exhibited are from Gene's own collection of memorabilia. Later, it merged with the Southwest Museum and is now known as the Autry Museum of the American West.

6. Gene Autry

Shortly before his death, Autry was estimated to be worth $320 million. He won two Grammy Hall of Fame Awards and is the only entertainer to have five stars on the Hollywood Walk of Fame. Autry made a total of 640 recordings, including some 300 songs written or co-written by him. His records have sold more than 100 million copies, with 12 gold or platinum records. His Madison Square Garden performances sold out; everything he touched seemed to turn to gold.

Gene Autry died at his home in Studio City on October 2, 1998, three days after his 91st birthday. He was America's singing cowboy. The funeral was private.

7

Neville Brand

Neville Brand was a prolific actor. He accumulated an incredible number of credits: 64 for movies, 33 on television shows and a few on Broadway stages. His appearance made him a natural for playing outlaws, gangsters and hoodlums. Some of his most memorable roles were in *Stalag 17*, *Gunsmoke* and *Rawhide*. But more than that, he was a true World War II hero.

With war looming, Brand became interested in exploring a career in the Army. Neville enlisted in the Illinois National Guard on October 23, 1939, at age 19. He had falsified his age to be 20 and became a private in Company F, 129th Infantry Regiment. The guard was part time then, just some evenings and weekends.

When the war in Europe started, Neville Brand enlisted in the U.S. Army in March 1941. Because of his service with the National Guard, he was made a corporal. He tried for Officers Candidate School but was turned down. After five weeks of training at Fort Carson in Colorado, he was sent overseas to join the 331st Infantry Regiment, part of the famed 83rd Infantry Division, called the Thunderbolt Division. His regiment landed at Normandy in June 1944. He was promoted to sergeant and led a platoon in Company B. The division landed at Omaha Beach on June 23, 1944, and participated in the breakout from Normandy. It turned east to clear Brittany and the Loire River area. With that mission accomplished, the Thunderbolts were moved to the northwest Aachen area to breach the Siegfried Line and fight their way into Germany.

When the German surprise attack through the Ardennes created the Bulge, Brand's division was brought in to aid the First Army's defense. After the collapse of the German offensive, Brand's outfit attacked northwest into Germany toward Hamburg.

In an interview in 1966, Brand remembered the time his unit came under fire from German machine guns located in a hunting lodge. "I must have flipped my lid. I decided to get into that lodge," he said. Regardless of the extreme danger and all by himself, he worked his way to the rear of the lodge,

7. Neville Brand

Neville Brand (publicity photo).

went in through a back door and killed all of the German soldiers who were there. For this action, he was awarded the Silver Star.

On April 7, 1945, only a month before Germany surrendered, Sergeant Brand was wounded in action near the Weser River in the northwestern part of Germany. He was pinned down by withering enemy ground fire when he was shot in his upper arm. As he lay there bleeding, he knew he was dying. But then he was rescued and evacuated to a military hospital in Nance, France, where he recovered. He was sent back to the U.S., where he worked on an Army Signal Corps film with Charlton Heston. This gave him the determination to pursue a career as an actor. He was honorably discharged in October 1945 at Fort Sheridan, Illinois. During his time in the Army, he was awarded not only the Silver Star, but also a Purple Heart plus six other medals and ribbons including the Combat Infantryman's Badge.

Lawrence Neville Brand was born on August 13, 1920, in Griswold, Iowa. His father, Leo, was an electrician who worked for the Red Oak Electric Company in Griswold and later put up transmission lines connecting Cumberland and Lewis. His mother's maiden name was Helen Louise Davis. He said that his mother named him Neville because that was the first name of the doctor who attended at his birth. In 1921, the family moved to Kewanee, Illinois, where Neville grew up and graduated from Kewanee High School in 1939. His parents divorced when Neville was only 13. He helped support his mother and six siblings working as a soda jerk, waiter and shoe salesman.

Back as a civilian in 1945, Brand lived in Greenwich Village in New York City. To learn acting, he enrolled in the American Theatre Wing, worked off-Broadway and appeared in a few Broadway plays. After two years, he moved to Hollywood and went to the Geller Drama School in 1947, using

World War II Veterans in Hollywood

the GI Bill. He married Jean Enfield circa 1948 and they were divorced in 1955. They had a daughter, Mary.

His first movie was an uncredited role in *Battleground*, released in 1949. That same year he was in *Port of New York*. Then he played a sadistic hoodlum in the 1950 noir classic film, *D.O.A.*, which starred Edmond O'Brien, and he also played Sergeant Zelenko in that year's *Halls of Montezuma*, starring Richard Widmark, Richard Boone, Jack Palance, Jack Webb, Martin Milne and Robert Wagner in Wagner's first role. All in all, during the fifties, Neville was credited with appearances in 34 movies and a television show, the *Screen Directors' Playhouse*. Perhaps most notably, he played an American prisoner of war in *Stalag 17*, released in 1953.

His first leading role was in the 1954 romance movie *Return from the Sea*. In the 1956 film *The Three Outlaws*, he played Butch Cassidy against Alan Hale, Jr., as the Sundance Kid. It was a precursor to the blockbuster classic film that starred Paul Newman and Robert Redford. In the Civil War drama *Love Me Tender*, released in 1956, Brand's character killed Elvis Presley. He won the Sylvania Award in 1958 for his portrayal of Willie Stark (a fictional Huey Long) in Robert Penn Warren's *All the King's Men*. On April 6, 1957, he married Laura Rae Araujo. They had two children, Michelle and Katrina.

Brand starring in the 1954 Western movie *The Lone Gun* (publicity photo).

7. Neville Brand

But at the end of the decade, they divorced. There seems to be some confusion about his marriages. One account said his third wife was Ramona (no last name listed) and that it might have overlapped the one with Laura.

During the sixties, Neville Brand turned his talents to television shows. He was in *Gunsmoke*, *The Twilight Zone*, *Wagon Train* and *Rawhide*, among others. He was best known, perhaps, for his soft-hearted, loud-mouthed, none-too-bright but tough-as-nails role as a Texas Ranger in *Laredo*. In *Combat!*, his costar Richard Peabody recalled, "He was sort of an actor's actor … his peers respected his work a great deal. He was one of the nicer guests we had on the show; extremely friendly, and very well-liked by both the cast and the crew." Brand was a guest star on ten television shows that decade, including *The Untouchables*, in which he played Al Capone. Neville was the star of *Laredo*, which ran for 56 episodes. In addition, during the sixties he played in ten movies, usually as the heavy.

Brand in the Western television series *Laredo* (1965–1967). He starred as a Texas Ranger on the Mexican border in south Texas (publicity photo).

In 1970, Brand turned 50. Nevertheless, he continued as an active actor. That year and in 1971, he was in a number of episodes of *Bonanza* and six other television shows. He was also in 11 movies, including *Cahill, U.S. Marshal*, *Marcus Welby, M.D.*, and *Tora! Tora! Tora!*

Brand had post-traumatic stress disorder that developed from his World War II service years. He was an alcoholic and battled with drugs. "The booze became medicine," he said, "Suddenly you're not drinking to get drunk anymore. And the only way you can hit the morning—I used to call that just getting even—is to grab that jug. I'd have a pint of whiskey in the morning just to make a phone call."

World War II Veterans in Hollywood

Neville was a voracious reader and had a large collection of books at his home in Malibu. According to his friend Richard Peabody, "I saw all these book cases—I couldn't believe it, I've never seen such an array of books in anybody's private home in my life—it looked like a public library.... I was amazed about what an avid reader he was. You look at the titles and his tastes were really eclectic—he was interested in everything." Then disaster struck. His Malibu home was destroyed by fire in 1978, including many of his possessions and his beloved library of some 30,000 books.

Even with his mental problems, Brand was in six movies during the eighties. Neville's father died in 1985, and Neville married for the third time, to Mae Brand. His mother died in 1991 and he became reclusive and developed emphysema.

On April 16, 1992, he was taken to Sutter General Hospital in Sacramento, where he died. He was 71 years old. He was cremated and his ashes were placed in a niche at the East Lawn Memorial Park in Sacramento.

Mae had died in 1991. Neville was survived by his brother, Bryce, two sisters, Barbara and Louise, plus his children. His daughter, Mary, said of her father's portrayals of tough guys, "He certainly enjoyed the role. It was a chance to add a little humor to the tough guy he always played." Peter Brown, who played with him, said, "When Brand was sober, doing a scene with him was as natural as having a conversation because he was so good."

8

Art Carney

Art Carney worked on the stage, radio, and television and in the movies. On the radio, his gifted voice mimicked Franklin D. Roosevelt, Winston Churchill and Dwight D. Eisenhower. He won an Academy Award for Best Actor, a Golden Globe and six Emmys. His best-known television appearance was in *The Honeymooners*. Art Carney served in the U.S. Army during World War II, landed at Normandy in 1944 and fought in France.

Carney enlisted on December 22, 1943, in New York City. At that time, he was married, 25 years old and had worked four years in the entertainment industry. After basic training, he underwent additional training as a light

Art Carney as Saun Dann in the *Star Wars Holiday Special* (1978), an American television special set in the science-fiction universe of the *Star Wars* franchise (publicity photo).

World War II Veterans in Hollywood

machine gunner and then, in July 1944, he was assigned as a replacement to the 604th Infantry Regiment, part of the 28th Infantry Division. The 28th Division is called the Keystone because of its Pennsylvania origins. It is one of the oldest U.S. Army units, dating back to the Revolutionary War. The Germans called it the Bloody Bucket because of its blood red keystone shoulder patch.

Carney landed on Omaha Beach with the 28th Division on July 22, 1944. The division, under the command of Major General Lloyd D. Brown, fought its way inland through the hedgerows of the Bocage and then village by village. In the first 21 days, the headquarters of the 28th moved 12 times.

Operation Cobra, the assault on the city of St. Lo in order to finally break out from the Normandy beachhead, was launched on July 25 with 3,000 heavy and medium bombers. The bombers were to lay a carpet of destruction one and a half miles wide by three miles long across the front of our Army. Due to weather and smoke, some bombs fell within our lines and we suffered over 100 killed and 500 wounded. The dead included Lieutenant General Lesley J. McNair, the highest-ranking officer to die in Europe.

At the successful completion of Operation Cobra on July 29, Carney's outfit was in Agneau, a village on the west side of St. Lo, after liberating five more villages. Fifteen days later, Carney was 30 miles southeast of St. Lo at the village of Sourdeval when General Brown was relieved of command and replaced with Brigadier General James E. Wharton. In the next day's action at the village of Ger, General Wharton was killed by a German sniper. Art Carney and his machine gun were blown into the air by a German mortar round. Carney's leg was shattered; the wound was his ticket home.

The division was put in command of Major General Norman D. Cota, a hero of D-Day. Under fire on Omaha Beach, General Cota stood up and told his men: "Gentlemen, we are being killed on this beach, let's go inland and be killed." After breaking out of Normandy, the general led his troops to Paris, and they were honored to march down the Champs-Élysées.

Seriously injured, Carney was sent back to Normandy and then evacuated to an Army hospital in England. Nine months later, he was sent to the McGuire General Hospital near Richmond, Virginia. Private Arthur Carney received the Purple Heart award and was honorably discharged in 1945. His wound permanently shortened his right leg by three-fourths of an inch, causing him occasional pain and a limp for the rest of his life.

Arthur William Matthew Carney was born on November 4, 1918, in the town of Mount Vernon, a suburb of New York City just north of the Bronx. His father, Edward, was a newspaperman and publicist. Art had five older brothers: Jack, Ned, Robert, Fred and Phil. The family was Roman Catholic. Even as a child, he entertained his family with impersonations of Edward G.

8. Art Carney

Robinson, Jimmy Durante, Franklin D. Roosevelt and New York governor Al Smith.

Carney was a born mimic with a talented voice. When he was in grammar school, he was the class clown and won talent contests. At the A.B. Davis High School in Mount Vernon, New York, Art entertained at school dances doing a tap-dancing routine and his imitations. He was named the "wittiest boy" in the school yearbook.

After he graduated in 1937, his brother, Jack, who was an agent for the Music Corporation of America, got him an audition with the Horace Heidt band. He got the job and was outstanding with his impressions, novelty songs and as an announcer for Heidt's *Pot o' Gold* radio program. He was on the popular radio show starting in 1939 and through 1941. Spending three years on the road, he did impersonations of famous public figures and sang novelty songs. Unfortunately, while working for Heidt, Carney began drinking, a problem that would catch up with him later. "I was an alcoholic even then," he said.

While with the band in 1940, Art married his high school sweetheart, Jean Myers, on August 15. They had dated for a year beforehand. During the next 25 years, they had three children: Eileen, Brian and Paul. Carney kept drinking and had to leave the Heidt band in 1941 after showing up too drunk to announce the radio show. He was so out of it that he couldn't spell TUMS, the product of the sponsor. Afterwards he worked now and then at nightclubs and in vaudeville.

Art was able to land his first movie role in *Pot o' Gold*, released in 1941. He appeared as a band member and a radio announcer but didn't receive on-screen credit for either. Also that year, he played the house comic on the series *Matinee at Meadowbrook*. In 1942, his brother Jack steered him to CBS, which was hiring actors for *Report to the Nation*, a weekend news program that re-created current events with actors imitating the voices of world leaders. His success on the show led to acting jobs on soap operas, comedies, dramas and children's shows. But then along came the war, and he joined the Army in 1943.

After discharge, Carney returned to CBS radio, where he became a second banana for Milton Berle, Bert Lahr, Edgar Bergen and Fred Allen. He was on the radio and television versions of *The Morey Amsterdam Show* from 1948 to 1950, playing a dumb doorman in a New York nightclub. Viewers got their first look at Carney with him wearing a thick, Chaplinesque mustache and slicked-back hair parted in the middle.

Next was the *Cavalcade of Stars* and then the smash hit *The Honeymooners*, which debuted in 1955 on CBS. It is still shown in reruns. It was a classic

World War II Veterans in Hollywood

Carney (left) with Jackie Gleason in the hit situation comedy *The Honeymooners* (1955–1956). Art played Ed Norton, best friend of Gleason's Ralph Kramden (publicity still).

television sitcom created by and starring Jackie Gleason and consisting of a series of sketches about Ralph Kramden (Gleason), a bus driver, and Ed Norton (Carney), a sewer worker. Art became famous for his portrayal. It also made him rich, plus he got five Emmy Awards. Carney recalled, "I liked it because I could be myself, make mistakes in grammar and be comfortable." Gleason said, "I give Carney 90 percent of the credit for the show's success. He has exquisite timing—and the best body language in the world." The show ran until 1956.

The next year—1957—Art Carney made his Broadway debut in *The Rope Dancers*, in which he played an alcoholic, ineffectual husband and father in turn-of-the century New York. His costar was the Irish actress Siobhan McKenna, but the show was short lived. That same year, he played a Jew who had been elected lord mayor of Dublin in the television play *The Fabulous Irishman*.

Carney starred in the television production of *Harvey* on CBS in 1958 and acted as the stage manager in an NBC rendition of *Our Town* in 1959. He played Franklin Roosevelt in *The Right Man* on CBS in 1960 and was an alcoholic character depressed over his divorce in *Call Me Back* on NBC in 1960.

Art had his own television variety show that ran from 1959 until 1961: *The Art Carney Special*. It was a comedy series starring Carney as Axel Heist

8. Art Carney

and airing on NBC. The show earned the Primetime Emmy Award for an Outstanding Comedy Series.

In 1965, he starred on Broadway in the comedy *The Odd Couple*, playing the compulsively tidy Felix Unger opposite Walter Matthau's disheveled Oscar Madison. The long-running show ran through 1967 with 964 performances, but Carney had to drop out because he was suffering a mental and physical breakdown and checked into a psychiatric center in Hartford. Carney publicly admitted his dependence on alcohol, amphetamines and barbiturates. He spent nearly six months in a sanitarium. Friends and associates maintained they could tell that Carney's stress levels were at a danger point when his behavior seemed more like Felix.

By then his marriage to Jean was in trouble. "I was not in good shape, mentally or physically," he said, "I was hurt by my troubles with alcohol. The booze and pills and the breaking up of my marriage had me about finished." He was hospitalized, and then Jackie Gleason got him out to do a *Honeymooners'* special on CBS. He and Jean were divorced in 1965.

On December 21, 1966, Carney married the sometime dancer and actress Barbara Isaac. During their ten-year marriage, she was in *Summer Wine*, *Victory at Entebbe* and, along with Art, in the television show *Lanigan's Rabbi*. They had no children.

In 1971 Carney was in his last Broadway show, *The Prisoner of Second Avenue*. During the seventies, Carney sang and danced on a number of episodes of *The Dean Martin Show* and appeared as Santa Claus in the *Muppets Christmas* television special. Art starred in the 1974 movie *Harry and Tonto*, playing the 72-year-old Harry, an old man who, after losing his job, set out on a cross-country trip accompanied by a cat. He was only 54 at the time and felt he was too young for the role. The film was a huge success and Carney won an Oscar for Best Actor as well as a Golden Globe. During the filming, Carney joined Alcoholics Anonymous and quit drinking. Then he played an old detective in *The Late Show* in 1977.

Carney divorced Barbara in 1977 and remarried his first wife, Jean, in 1980. In 1981, he acted as Harry Truman in *St. Helens*. In 1984 he was in an episode of the television show *Terrible Joe Moran*, costarring with James Cagney as an aged boxer. Starting in 1986, he starred in the CBS sitcom *The Cavanaughs* for three years. He appeared in his very last movie, *The Last Action Hero*, in 1993. It was a minor supporting role to its star, Arnold Schwarzenegger.

Art's final appearance with Gleason was in a CBS television movie, *Issy and Moe*. Carney's last appearance was on *The Ed Sullivan Show* in 2002. On November 4, 2003, Carney turned 85 years old, and then on November 9, Arthur William Matthew Carney died in his sleep at his home near Westport, Connecticut. He was survived by his wife, Jean; two sons, Brian and Paul; daughter Eileen; plus six grandchildren and one grandson. Jean died on October 31, 2012. She was 93 years old. Art had become one of the most enduringly memorable second bananas in television history and proved himself to be a versatile actor.

9

Don Adams

Don Adams was an actor, comedian and director during his five decades on television and in the movies. He was a comic icon of the sixties and is remembered for his catchphrases "Would you believe" and "Sorry about that." He had a distinctive voice described as a "nasal staccato." Adams had 38 credits as an actor, some of them "voices." Don was best known for his portrayal of Maxwell Smart in *Get Smart*. During World War II, he served in the Marine Corps.

Donald James Yarmy was born in New York City on April 13, 1923. (He later assumed the name "Don Adams.") He was the son of William Yarmy and Consuelo Deiter Yarmy. His father was of Hungarian-Jewish descent. His dad worked in New York managing restaurants. His mother, Consuelo, was of German and Irish ancestry; she was a Roman Catholic. Don had an older sister, Gloria Yarmy Burton, who became a writer. Interestingly enough, she wrote three episodes of *Get Smart*. His brother, Richard (Dick) Yarmy, was an actor/comedian who appeared in an episode of *Get Smart*. Don remembered, "Our home was filled with loud, overlapping conversations."

Don's father being Jewish and his mother a Catholic, they decided that Don would grow up as a Catholic while his brother would embrace the Jewish faith. Adams attended DeWitt Clinton High School in New York, where he entertained classmates with his impressions of movie stars. He was often a truant, spending time attending movies on 42nd Street. He worked part-time as a theater usher. "I had little use for school," he said.

When Donald Yarmy turned 18, he dropped out of school and enlisted in the Marine Corps in late 1941. He had decided that religion was illogical. When he filled out the form, under "religion," he wrote "none." Adams reported to the 1st Training Battalion at New River, North Carolina. The outfit was later renamed the 1st Battalion, 3rd Marine Regiment. After basic training, Adams was assigned to I Company of the 3rd Battalion, 8th Marines, in San Diego, California. In May of 1942, the 8th Marines were shipped to Samoa for defense of the island and to train for the Guadalcanal operation. Ameri-

World War II Veterans in Hollywood

can Samoa was administered by the U.S., and the Navy had had a station in the harbor of Pago Pago on the island of Tutuila since 1878. It was known as the United States Naval Station Tutuila.

On August 7, 1942, the Marines made an amphibious assault on Guadalcanal and on the Japanese naval base on Tulagi Island. Tulagi was a small sister island just north of Guadalcanal. A few miles across the infamous "Slot," it had a large harbor. It had been the original target of the campaign before the airfield on Guadalcanal was discovered. The landing on Guadalcanal was unopposed, but Tulagi was fiercely defended. The 863 Japanese on the island fought to the last man. Twenty Korean laborers were captured. Of the American Marines, 122 were killed and 200 were wounded in the three-day battle.

Adams was seriously wounded by a Japanese sniper and endured horrendous conditions because of limited fa-

In his five decades on television, Don Adams was best known as Maxwell Smart (Agent 86) on the Cold War spoof situation comedy *Get Smart* (1965–1970), which he occasionally wrote and directed. Adams won three consecutive Emmy Awards for his portrayal of Smart (publicity still).

cilities in the isolated battle zone. He contracted blackwater fever, a severe form of malaria with a 90 percent fatality rate. Not expected to live, he told the nursing staff, "I'm not going anyplace." He said that he returned then to the Catholic faith, as he prayed to survive. He was finally evacuated, and he slowly recovered at a Navy hospital in New Zealand, where he spent a year. Healthy again, he was sent back to the U.S., where he served as a drill instructor for Marine recruits. Ironically, and contrary to his fame as a bumbling, incompetent detective, Corporal Donald Yarmy was an expert rifleman, a drill instructor lauded by his superiors who was able to outdo his recruits at every endeavor. He was discharged in 1945, having been awarded a Purple Heart.

After leaving the Marine Corps, he went to Florida, where he did im-

9. Don Adams

personations of movie stars on the stage in a strip bar. One time, he said, "I shared the stage with such variety acts as a woman who had birds tear off all her clothes." He refused to use "blue" material, so he was fired.

In 1947, he married Adelaide Efantis, a nightclub singer. They ended up having three daughters. She had the stage name "Adams," so Don assumed the name "Adams" because he knew that auditions were often held in alphabetical order. To support the family, he worked as a commercial artist and a restaurant cashier in between night club gigs. Don began his television career when he won the *Ted Mack and the Original Amateur Hour* talent contest in 1948.

In 1954, Don Adams met Bill Dana, a comic and writer. They became lifelong friends. Bill worked with Don to refine Adams' personalities for television. Plus, Bill helped Don to perfect his unique staccato voice. That year, Adams won a contest on *Arthur Godfreys's Talent Scouts*. This got him an appearance on *The Tonight Show*, performing a comedy skit written by Dana. Next, he made a number of appearances on *The Steve Allen Show* and *The Ed Sullivan Show* and got a recurring job on Perry Como's *Kraft Music Hall* in 1948.

In 1960 Don and Adelaide divorced, and that same year, he married dancer Dorothy Bracken. He had fallen in love with Dorothy and that was the reason for the divorce. Dorothy, also an actress, appeared in an episode of *Get Smart* in 1965. They had two children.

Adams attempted a venture onto the Broadway stage, starring with Lena Horne in *Nine O'Clock Review* in 1961. It was a glorified nightclub show comprised of a series of songs. It closed on the road, having never made it to Broadway. Next, he was on the stage in the comedy *Harold*, which opened on November 29, 1962. It was a flop, closing after 20 performances. These were the only two times that Adams appeared in stage plays. The balance of his career was in the movies and on television.

Starting in 1961, he appeared a number of times on *The Perry Como Show* on NBC. Then he played the role of an incompetent house detective on *The Bill Dana Show* during 1963 and 1964. Also, he provided his voice for various characters on the television series *Tennessee Tuxedo and His Tales*. Following that, he was in three more television shows.

In 1965, Adams was offered a role by NBC in the new television show *Get Smart*. Initially he was skeptical, but when he learned it was being written by Mel Brooks and Buck Henry, he said, "I'll do it now. Right now." The show, a parody of the James Bond series that became immensely popular, ran until 1970. It was a spy spoof that was among television's 25 most watched shows. Don played the character of a bumbling secret agent, Maxwell Smart, also known as Agent 86. His costar was Barbara Feldon, who played Agent 99, Maxwell's straitlaced alter ego. The two ended up being close friends. Audiences loved it and the show won two Emmys for Best Comedy Series. Adams won three Emmys for Best Comedy Actor. The show was funnier because of Adams' delivery and distinctive voice. Don wrote a number of the scripts and directed several episodes. Even though the series was a success, Don felt it stifled his career. He really wanted to do drama. *Get Smart* was canceled in 1970 after 138 episodes.

In the 1975 show *Don Adams' Screen Test*, he directed famous stars and amateurs in scenes from classic movies. During the rest of the seventies, Adams appeared in five television movies including *The Love Boat*, released in 1976. The television series that followed was based on the movie. *The Love Boat* series ran from 1978 through 1984. For most of the time, it was in the top ten most watched, and, for two seasons, in the top five. Adams appeared in five episodes.

Adams fell in love with an actress—Judy Luciano—who was in *The Love Boat* series. He left his second wife, Dorothy, and married Judy on June 10, 1977. She was 29 years old at the time and he was 54. They had one child. The marriage ended with a divorce.

In the next decade, Don Adams appeared in various episodes of three different television series. Also, he was in two movies, *Back to the Beach* in 1978 and *Get Smart Again!* in 1989. Even in his seventies, Adams accumulated ten credits. Six of them used his very distinctive staccato voice. In 1985, Adams starred in a Canadian television sitcom, *Check It Out*, in which he played the manager of a supermarket. The show was popular enough to run for three seasons on American television. Then he got a costarring role for an episode in *NYPD Blue*. He played Chief Maxwell Smart in five episodes in a new *Get Smart* television series in 1995. His very last appearance on a television show was in a 2000 episode of the series *Pepper Ann*. He was seventy-seven. In addition, he continued making nightclub appearances and was a guest on television shows, and he starred in and directed some television commercials that won him a CLIO award. In his spare time, he played cards at the Los Angeles Playboy Mansion and gambled at various horse tracks. He closed the 20th century performing in *Inspector Gadget* in 1999, supplying the voice for a dog.

In the new century, Adams, having been divorced for the third time, lived alone at a luxury apartment in Century City. He still spent a lot of time at racetracks and played cards at the Playboy Mansion with pals Hugh Heffner, James Caan and Don Rickles.

His health declined in later years and took a turn for the worse when his daughter, actress Cecily Adams, died in 2004. Then he suffered a fall and

9. Don Adams

contracted a lung infection. Don Adams died on September 25, 2005. As he was Catholic, his funeral mass was held at a church in Beverly Hills. He was eulogized by his *Get Smart* costar, Barbara Feldon, and his best friend, Bill Dana, plus Don Rickles and James Caan. His survivors were his three daughters from his first marriage, Carolyn, Christine and Cathy; his two children with Dorothy, Stacey and Sean; a daughter from his third marriage, Beige; his sister Gloria; plus five grandchildren and three great-grandchildren.

Adams' brother, Dick Yarmy, born Richard Paul Yarmy, was ten years younger than Don. Like his brother, Dick served with the Marines, but he didn't see any action. He had 47 credits for roles in movies and television series. He even appeared in an episode of *Get Smart*. For quite a long time, he was in the "George and Marge" television commercials for Union Oil. He was also on the stage, most notably in *The Odd Couple*. Yarmy died in 1992 from lung cancer.

10

Jackie Coogan

Jackie Coogan was a Hollywood star who started when he was only a child and continued into his sixties. He became famous during the silent era as a waif in Charlie Chaplin's movie classic *The Kid*, released in 1921 when Jackie was only seven years old. He began his acting career on the stage at age four with his father and mother, who were vaudevillians. During World War II, Jackie flew with the U.S. Army Air Corps in the CBI (China/Burma/India) theater.

Before the United States got into it, war was raging in Europe. With the belief that the U.S. would get involved, Jackie Coogan enlisted in the Army on March 4, 1941. He was 27 at the time, and his Army salary was $21 a month. After basic training, he was posted to Fort Ord, near Monterey, and then to the Port of Stockton, both in California. When the Japanese attacked on December 7, Coogan, who was an experienced civilian pilot, asked to be reassigned to the Army Air Corps, where he became a glider pilot. He was trained at the Aviation Cadet Flight School at South Plains Army Airfield in Lubbock, Texas, in a ten-week course. From there he was sent to the Desert Training Center at Twenty-Nine Palms, California. For two years, he was a glider instructor.

In 1943, Flight Officer John L. Coogan volunteered for duty with the 1st USAAF Air Commando Group, led by Lieutenant Colonel Philip Cochran, a highly decorated "black sheep" fighter pilot. During the North African Campaign, Cochran developed many air combat, air transport and air assault techniques. Colonel Cochran became the model for Flip Corkin in Milt Caniff's comic strip *Terry and the Pirates*.

In December, the group was sent to India in order to airlift British troops into Japanese-held Burma. The Indian 77th Infantry, called the Chindits, was led by General Orde Wingate, who had created the long-range jungle penetration unit. Wingate was quirky and unconventional. He wore a garland of onions and garlic around his neck. He would occasionally eat a raw onion, claiming it kept the mosquitoes away. Wingate had commanded a success-

10. Jackie Coogan

ful campaign against the Italians in Ethiopia before being given the nasty little assignment in Burma. The allies were desperate to reopen the Burma Road into China. American general "Vinegar Joe" Stillwell commanded an Army in the north. The British were in India to the west. The plan was to establish and supply a commando base 150 miles behind Japanese lines in the central Burma jungle.

On March 5, 1944, American pilots flying Waco CG-4A gliders landed the British on a small jungle clearing about 100 miles behind Japanese lines in northern Burma. Jackie Coogan's glider was to land on the jungle strip

Jackie Coogan in a 1964 episode of *The Addams Family*, a television situation horror comedy, where he played Uncle Fester. The series was based on the characters from Charles Addams' *New Yorker* cartoons and aired for two seasons (1964–1966) on ABC for a total of 64 episodes.

code named "Broadway." A headline could have read "Famous Child Movie Star Lands on Broadway." Coogan's glider was the first to land. "If you think the natives were surprised when our gliders landed," he said, "you should have seen them when we opened up the mouth of a glider and out drove a jeep." Casualty and capture rates were high. Out of 100 glider pilots, 65 were killed and 15 were wounded and taken prisoner. The gliders were towed, two at a time, by Douglas C47 transports. Sometimes a tow line snapped and the glider crashed into the jungle. Sometimes overloaded gliders touched down at an excessive speed. The gliders were retrieved from the short strips by stringing the tow line between two poles. A low flying C47 would snag the line and snatch the glider into the air.

On one mission, Coogan had to crash land. As the pilot, he sat at the controls in the front of the flimsy transport glider. When the plane came to a

World War II Veterans in Hollywood

sudden stop, all the troops were shoved up against him. He was at the bottom of the pile. Japanese soldiers bayoneted almost everyone. Jackie was the only one they missed. He lay alone at the bottom of the pile of dead and dying men. Eventually, he made his way out and escaped.

After flying more missions to land and resupply the troops, Coogan was ordered back to the U.S. and discharged in December 1945. He had attained the rank of second lieutenant and was awarded the Air Medal and the Asiatic-Pacific Campaign Medal with three bronze campaign stars.

Jackie Coogan had participated in one of the toughest, most unsung campaigns in the history of war, under the command of four unconventional black sheep leaders: Major General Orde Charles Wingate, Colonel Philip Cochran, Lieutenant General Joseph Stillwell and Major General Claire Lee Chennault, whose Flying Tigers provided air cover.

John Leslie Coogan Junior was born on October 26, 1914, in Los Angeles. His father, John Henry Coogan, was a dancer, and his mother, Lillian Rita Dolliver, had been a child star billed on the stage as "Baby Lillian." Coogan made his movie debut when he was three years old in *Skinner's Baby*, which was filmed at San Rafael, California, near San Francisco in 1917. He played the baby. It was shot by the Essanay Studio, which later became Warner Brothers. Its best-known star was Charlie Chaplin, who made 14 short, comedy silent films there.

His parents toured as a vaudeville act and added Jackie when he was four years old. He danced the "shimmy" with his father. On September 6, 1919, he sailed with his parents from New York to Southampton in England. They took tons of canned milk, flour, corn syrup and clothing for refugee children. "There were some 300,000 people at the dock to greet us," Jackie recalled later. Then they went to Paris, Geneva and Italy on the same mission. In Rome, young Coogan had a private audience with Pope Pius XI as well as Benito Mussolini, who gave him an autographed photo inscribed "Al Piccolo Grande," which means "To the Little Great One."

Back home, the three-person act played at New York's famous Palace, among other venues. While they were performing at the Orpheum Theatre in Los Angeles, Jackie was noticed by Charlie Chaplin, who was looking for a child to star in his next movie, *The Kid*. Chaplin tested him with a bit part in the 1919 silent movie *A Day's Pleasure*, where Jackie proved his stage presence. *The Kid*, released in 1921, was a huge success and made Coogan a child movie star who gurgled and wept on cue.

Regarding Chaplin, young Jackie said, "He had a mustache that came on and off." When he was seven years old, his family bought a big house at the corner of Wilshire and Western in Los Angeles. The money came from

10. Jackie Coogan

Jackie's earnings. One of the first swimming pools in Southern California was installed. Coogan remembered, "I had the best swimming instructor, the Hawaiian Duke Kahanamoku, the year after Duke won at the Olympics."

In addition to *The Kid*, Coogan played in a number of other silent movies such as *Peck's Bad Boy*, *Oliver Twist* and *Johnny Get Your Gun*. He made more than $4 million while he was still in short pants. Until he was ten, Coogan had a private tutor, but then his dad insisted on a formal education. First he spent two years at the Urban Military Academy in Hollywood, then a year at Loyola High School and finally went to the Villanova Preparatory School. Later, Jackie said, "I enjoyed my learning days. All kids should." When he was 17, his parents bought a $1.5 million ranch in east San Diego County for him. Jackie said, "I drank milk from my own ranch. I had a 65 by 80-foot room filled with toy trains and had my own golf course and football field in my backyard. Other boys went to see Babe Ruth. Babe Ruth came to see me." In addition to the house, he had approximately $4 million in savings.

Coogan (The Child), with Charlie Chaplin (The Tramp) in the silent comedy/drama *The Kid* (1921). The Tramp cares for an abandoned child, but events put that relationship in jeopardy. This was 6-year-old Coogan's first film performance.

His first talkie was *Tom Sawyer* in 1930, followed by *Huckleberry Finn* and *Home on the Range* in 1935. He was 21 years old. That year, tragedy struck. Jackie, his father, a 19-year-old actor Junior Durkin (who was Jackie's best friend), ranch foreman Charles Jones, plus actor Robert Horner had gone for a day of dove hunting over the border in Mexico. Jackie's father was driving them on a mountain highway near Pine Valley in eastern San Diego County. The car was a coupe that Jackie had just purchased. Jackie and Durkin were in the rumble seat. The automobile left the road on a deceptive curve, plunged over a bank and rolled over four times before it came to a stop in the bottom of the creek. According to Jackie, "We were forced off the road by an oncoming car. We went over an embankment. The car went end over end and was spiraling. I pulled myself out of my seat and jumped out. All the others were killed." Jackie climbed back onto the road, where a passing motorist took him to a Pine Valley store where he was given first aid. Coogan had escaped with broken ribs and bruises but was greatly depressed over his losses.

Eighteen months after the death of her husband, Coogan's mother married Jackie's business manager, Arthur L. Bernstein. The new bride and groom immediately took over all of the actor's assets including his savings. During 1935, Jackie had been receiving a weekly allowance of $6.25. When he complained to his mother, she said, "You haven't got a cent. There never has been one cent belonging to you. It's all mine." The law in California at the time stated that the income of a child belonged to the parents.

In the belief he was due the millions he had earned, Coogan filed suit against his mother. In it, he alleged that his father had always assured him that all his earnings were being held in trust for him. His mother vigorously denied it and stated, "There was never a promise in any way, shape or form." But in court, actor Wallace Beery said, "Jack Coogan, Sr., told me many times he had never used or intended to use a cent the boy earned. Every penny … was being put away and saved for him." Then Jackie's attorney presented a petition written by Coogan's parents asking a court to dismiss the "guardianship" of his wealth because they planned "the creating of a trust" for it. Eventually, it was settled out of court and Jackie received $150,000.

As a consequence, Assemblyman Chester Garmon introduced legislation to prevent what happened to Jackie Coogan. The California State Legislature enacted a law requiring up to half of the net earnings of a minor be set aside in a trust fund or other savings plan. It was called "Coogan Law."

The judge appointed a receiver to account for the over $3 million Coogan had earned between 1923 and 1936. Because of the funds his mother and stepfather had made off with, the receiver reported that all that was left was $250,000. Meanwhile, Coogan went on tour with Bob Hope. To make fun of his predicament, Hope would ask Jackie for a dime. "I haven't got a dime," he replied, "But I will give you my autograph."

Coogan became enamored with young starlet Betty Grable, and they got engaged in 1935. In 1936, Coogan interceded with RKO and persuaded them to release Grable from her studio contract. A singer, she toured with him when he led his own 17-piece band. They married on November 20, 1937, when he was 23 and she was 21. Due to the fact that Jackie's mother and step-

10. Jackie Coogan

father had taken his money, Grable was the breadwinner. She paid for their wedding reception and their modest home. They starred together in the Paramount Pictures movie *College Swing*, for which she received $500 a week and he got a flat $1,000. Next the pair went on a vaudeville tour.

Coogan spent much of the next two and a half years on the legitimate stage. He toured in *What a Life* and was in the Broadway hit *Take Me Along*. "I had some good times in radio too," he said. The marriage ended in divorce in October 1939. (Betty Grable was in 42 movies during the thirties and forties that grossed over $100 million. For 12 years, she was among the top ten box office stars and the number one World War II pin-up girl.)

Having made up with his mother, Coogan went to live with her and his stepfather in a mansion they had bought with Jackie's money. In 1941, he married nightclub entertainer Flower Parry. She had been a dancer in the *Florentine Gardens Revue*. Nineteen years old, she had been working as a cigarette girl in a nightclub when she met Coogan. They had a boy, John Anthony Coogan, also known as Jackie Coogan, Jr., born in 1942. The marriage ended in 1943 when they got a divorce.

Next Coogan was in two movies, *Sky Patrol* and *Million Dollar Legs*. He also lent his voice to the CBS radio production of *Society Girl*. Then, in 1941, he enlisted in the Army. As soon as he got out in 1946, Jackie started to date night club entertainer Ann McCormack, and they were married on December 26. Married for almost five years, they had a daughter, Joann, who was born on April 2, 1948. They divorced on September 20, 1951.

When Jackie Cooper and Jackie Coogan got out of the service, they got together and did some fund raising. According to Cooper, "As an actor, Coogan was very professional and also had one of the best senses of humor that I ever ran across." The two starred together in the 1948 movie *French Leave*. When he went back to Hollywood, Coogan said, "I got big hellos and backslaps, but no jobs."

So Coogan played in the Hollywood nightclub Slapsy Maxie's, for 14 weeks. "Then I went back to New York and for two years worked the nightclub circuit and theaters," he said. Back in Hollywood, Coogan worked bit parts playing the heavy. Even after some run-ins with weed and alcohol, he starred in another movie in the late forties, *Kilroy Was Here*. Coogan was the star of his own radio show on CBS, *Forever Ernest*, which ran for three months during 1946. The next year, *The Kid* started as a television show. He was on *Pantomime Quiz* for eight years.

Probably his best showing during the fifties was for playing a comic cook in *Forbidden Area*, which got him a nomination for an Emmy. It was on a *Playhouse 90* episode. Then Jackie was on the television show *Cowboy G-Men*

World War II Veterans in Hollywood

for three episodes. In Hollywood Coogan was in a total of 14 movies. The first was *Skipalong Rosenbloom*, in 1951.

He married Dorothea Lamphere in 1952. Dorothea Odetta Hanson, whose stage name was Dorothea Lamphere, was also known as Dodie. She had danced in Chicago and New York. They had a daughter, Leslie Diane, born in 1953, and a son, Christopher Fenton, in 1967. She gave up her dancing career to be a full-time wife and mother. Dodie was with Jackie until his death and she passed away in 1999.

After appearing in three episodes in the television show *McKeever and the Colonel*, Jackie joined the classic *The Addams Family* as Uncle Fester. Starting in 1968, he had been on the show for almost three years; he said, "Television is such a fast medium to work in. You don't really have time to prepare and you're fighting time and weather." The director, John Astin, said about Coogan, "He had a great lust for life. He was as much fun to work with as anyone I have worked with in this business." During the rest of the sixties, he was in three more television shows including *The Lucy Show* and two more movies.

While 60 years of age during the seventies, Coogan made three more movies and was on a dozen television shows including *Hawaii Five-O*, *Marcus Welby, M.D.*, and *The Wild, Wild West*. During the eighties, he was in four more movies; his last was a small part in *The Prey*.

On March 1, 1984, Jackie Coogan's wife Dodie took him from their home in Malibu to the Santa Monica Hospital because he was suffering from kidney and heart problems. They arrived just before noon. He was treated in the emergency room and then transferred to the cardiac care unit. His blood pressure dropped, and he had a heart attack. Coogan died about an hour and a half later. He was 69 years old.

Coogan's funeral was held in the chapel at the Holy Cross Cemetery in Culver City, where he was buried. Held on March 5, and in accordance with his wishes, it was open to the public. The pallbearers were fellow actors and there was open-casket viewing.

11

Douglas Fairbanks, Jr.

The Fairbanks and the Barrymores were royalty on the American stage and in the film industry from the turn of the century into the 1930s. Douglas Fairbanks Senior was the undisputed "King of the Silents." Douglas Junior segued from the silents into the talkies and both acted, produced films and hob-knobbed with European royalty and politically powerful Americans. When World War II began, he was too old to enlist, so he used his influence to don a uniform and get into the fight. He had a distinguished movie career and was also a decorated naval officer during the war.

Douglas Fairbanks, Jr., spent more time in uniform and in harm's way during World War II than any other celebrity. So why do we think of Clark Gable, Jimmy Stewart, John Huston, even John Wayne, and not Fairbanks? Because what Douglas Fairbanks, Jr., did was so important that it was kept secret for 40 years after the end of the war.

Fairbanks studied the British Navy's pioneering efforts in battlefield deception and brought the technique to the U.S. Navy's attention in 1942. In 1943, the U.S. Army developed its own "ghost

Douglas Fairbanks, Jr., portrait in military uniform (U.S. Navy).

World War II Veterans in Hollywood

Army" at Fort Drum in upstate New York. The work they did funded the development of stereo sound and tape recording, among other things.

Douglas Elton Fairbanks, Jr., was born on December 9, 1909, in New York City. His father was Douglas Fairbanks and his mother was Anna Beth Sully. His parents divorced when Douglas Jr. was only nine years old. From then on, he lived with his mother in New York, Los Angeles, Paris and London.

His father was a famous movie actor during the early Hollywood days of silent films. Born in 1883, Douglas Fairbanks, Sr., was not only a movie actor but also a screen writer, director and producer. Fairbanks Sr., whose father was Jewish, starred in 29 films, of which all but two were silents. His best-known movie was *The Thief of Bagdad*. He was one of the biggest stars during the nineteen tens and twenties, so much so that he was called the "King of Hollywood."

The senior Douglas was a founding member of the Motion Picture Academy of Arts and Sciences and hosted the very first Academy Awards in 1929. He organized his own movie company, the Douglas Fairbanks Film Corp. It was announced that Douglas Fairbanks, Jr., would star in the company's first film, *The Californian*, but the plan was cancelled.

Fairbanks Senior divorced his first wife, Anna Beth, in 1920 and married Mary Pickford. He was known as "Everybody's Hero," and she, "America's Sweetheart." They built their home, the famous Pickfair Estate, in Beverly Hills. They were the first to place their hand- and footprints in the courtyard concrete in front of Grumman's Chinese Theatre on Hollywood Boulevard. Like many of the stars of silent films, with the advent of talkies, Senior's film career just faded out.

Although Douglas Fairbanks, Jr. (known as "Young Doug" in Hollywood) appeared in some 100 movies and television shows, his fame didn't reach the level of his father's. "I never tried to emulate my father," Jr. said; "Anyone trying to do that would be a second-rate copy." Nevertheless, he was not only a famous film star but also a poet, painter, sculptor, producer, artist and businessman. There is little doubt that he was truly multi-talented.

After his parents' divorce, nine-year-old Douglas remained with his mother. In New York, he attended school at the Bovee School, the Collegiate Military Academy and Knickerbocker Grays, the Pasadena Polytechnic Institute, and then in Paris, the Lycée Janson de Sailly.

Douglas's acting debut in movies was when he was seven. He had a small role in one of his father's silent films, *American Aristocracy*. Then there was another bit part when he was 12: *The Three Musketeers*, in which his dad played d'Artagnan.

11. Douglas Fairbanks, Jr.

When he was 13, Paramount Pictures signed him up to play in the 1923 movie *Stephen Steps Out*. His pay was $1,000 a week, a lot of money in those days. (In today's money, it's around $25,000.) When he appeared in the 1925 film *Stella Dallas*, he began to be noticed by the public. He was only 15.

On an October night in 1927, Joan Crawford went to the Belasco Theatre for the opening night of the play *Young Woodley*, starring Douglas Fairbanks, Jr., who captured her attention. Afterwards, Joan sent a note backstage to Douglas congratulating him on his performance, requesting an autographed photo and asking him to call her. Fairbanks later wrote, "Imagine! Me! A note from Joan Crawford!"

She was a leading lady at the time, having appeared in some 30 movies by then. Later in her career, which spanned five decades, she won the Academy Award for Best Actress in 1946, for *Mildred Pierce*. Her first movie role had been in a silent in 1925. After 91 films, her last appearance was in 1970 in the British science fiction horror film *Trog*.

Needless to say, Douglas was quick to call her. When they got together, he asked Joan for her autographed photo in return. She inscribed it, "To Douglas, may this be the start of a beautiful friendship." They related to each other on that first meeting. They began dating and the two found themselves in love. Fairbanks insisted, "It was love at first sight."

Fairbanks starred in the 1929 movie *Our Modern Maidens*. His costar was Joan Crawford. On June 3, 1929, the two were married. Douglas was 19 years old and Joan was four years older. Fairbanks later wrote, "For two youngsters already over their heads in the choppy waters of life in a huge goldfish bowl, it was a never-to-be-forgotten day. We were relieved and happy. We were truly married. And we lived happily … for a while." Crawford described the marriage: "All of our world knows I love Doug. We study together, we work together, pray together and love together." Doug Jr. and Joan starred together as a married couple in *Women Love Diamonds*.

But the marriage that was supposed to last forever didn't. Doug said, "A sort of doldrums or marital torpor seemed to be setting in." Crawford began a love affair with Clark Gable that turned out to be a not well-kept secret. Things came to a head when Crawford accused Fairbanks of having romances with other women. One day, after a long day of filming, Douglas was informed that Joan was throwing him out of the house and that all of his things had been sent to the Beverly Hills Hotel, where she had booked a room for him. On April 29, 1933, Joan Crawford filed for divorce; it was finalized a year later.

Meanwhile, Fairbanks' movie work continued. He appeared in 28 films between 1931 and 1939. One was outstanding: *Little Caesar* in 1931. Douglas's

World War II Veterans in Hollywood

role supported Edward G. Robinson. Douglas remarked, "We knew it was going to be good when we were making it, but not that it would become a classic."

In 1934, Fairbanks went to England to star as Grand Duke Peter in *The Rise of Catherine the Great*. "Hollywood was getting to be a grind," he said; "They had me making five or six pictures a year." He made another film in England, *Mimi*, in 1935, costarring with Gertrude Lawrence, with whom he had an affair.

While still in England, Fairbanks was able to raise enough money to form his own company, Criterion Productions. Criterion made three films, the best of which was *The Amateur Gentleman* in 1936. His father came to England to watch the filming. Senior was accompanied by Lord and Lady Mountbatten. Lord Louis Mountbatten would later be the keystone of Fairbanks's military career. Mountbatten, admiral of the fleet of the Royal Navy, Earl of Burma, and the uncle of Queen Elizabeth II's consort, Prince Philip, was assassinated in 1979. He was 79 years old when his fishing boat was blown up by an Irish Republican bomb.

During the film's production, Fairbanks Jr. began an affair with Marlene Dietrich. She would smuggle him into her hotel room at Claridge's. The Fairbanks/Dietrich coupling was an item of the prewar European social scene. Some of Marlene's home movies even include shots of a young John F. Kennedy on the French Riviera.

During Douglas Jr.'s prewar efforts in Europe, there was another young American aristocrat sampling English high society and getting a taste of international intrigue. Joseph Kennedy was Franklin Roosevelt's ambassador to the Court of Saint James, and his son had an open door to high places. JFK took advantage of the opportunity and wrote his first book: *Why England Slept*.

Returning to Hollywood, Fairbanks was offered a role in the 1937 film *The Prisoner of Zenda*. At first he was reluctant to accept, but his father urged him to do it. The movie turned out to be a big success.

On New Year's Day 1939, during a party given by Herbert Swope, former publisher of the *New York World*, Fairbanks met and started to date Mary Lee Hartford. They were married on April 22 of that year. His father was his best man. She was the former wife of Huntington Hartford, the A&P supermarket heir. Mary Lee turned out to be the love of his life; he was devoted to her for the rest of her life. They had three daughters: Daphne, Victoria and Melissa. Mary Lee died in 1988.

On December 12, 1939, his father, Douglas Fairbanks, Sr., the "First King of Hollywood," founder of the Motion Picture Academy, died of a heart attack

11. Douglas Fairbanks, Jr.

at his home in Santa Monica, California. He was only 56 years old. Douglas Jr. had his biggest hit in 1939's *Gunda Din*, costarring Cary Grant. The story was set in India.

Before getting involved in World War II, Fairbanks's last film was the 1941 movie *The Corsican Brothers*, in which he played one of the three brothers. Douglas was a young-looking 32. Later that year, President Franklin D. Roosevelt, who was a friend, appointed him special envoy to South America, where he was supposed to gather intelligence. It was thought that there might be Nazi influence in some of the countries. He reported back that all were pro–U.S.

In the late thirties, America was basically isolationist. Many were afraid that the U.S. would become involved in the conflict when Britain and France declared war on Germany. Fairbanks, of course, didn't agree with America's position. He was a committed Anglophile. To counter isolationism, Douglas helped Adlai Stevenson organize the William White Committee, which lobbied for U.S. entry into the war. Along with Mrs. Franklin D. Roosevelt, he co-chaired the committee. In addition, he headed and financed the Douglas Voluntary Hospitals in Britain.

Douglas Fairbanks, Jr.'s, service during World War II was exciting, glamorous, and dangerous enough to furnish scenarios for several movies. It ran the gamut from having dinner at the White House on his last day ashore to shepherding a convoy under attack through a storm-tossed Artic Sea to Russia. He had high tea with the king of England and then ran a German–Italian blockade to deliver Spitfire fighters to the besieged island of Malta. He had wartime camaraderie with Prince George, Duke of Kent, the king's brother, and worked with the admiral of the fleet, Lord Mountbatten, in order to develop American commando tactics for the invasion of first Sicily and then southern France.

Even before the U.S. entered the war, Douglas Fairbanks, Jr., had tried to enlist in the Navy. But because he was over 30, he was turned down due to his age. Eight months before December 7, Douglas called on his friend President Roosevelt, who became instrumental in having him appointed a lieutenant in the U.S. Navy Reserve on April 17, 1941. En route to active duty from his beloved home in Pacific Palisades, Douglas and his wife, Mary Lee, dined with President Roosevelt and spent the night in the White House. The next night he was aboard a decrepit U.S. Navy supply ship, sleeping on a cot stuffed into a slot in the bow among other sailors.

In October 1941 Douglas reported aboard the destroyer USS *Ludlow* to escort a convoy across the rough North Atlantic from Newfoundland to Iceland, where he was assigned to a battleship. En route, the *Ludlow* made a depth-charge attack on a submarine. Douglas served aboard the USS *Mississippi* from November 14 until January 2, 1942. He went aboard the old battleship at Reykjavik and at the end of November, she was ordered home to Norfolk, Virginia, for retrofitting. Douglas was acting communications officer when he decoded a message: "AIR RAID ON PEARL HARBOR. THIS IS NOT A DRILL."

In March 1942 Fairbanks was ordered to report aboard the USS *Washington*. She was a North Carolina class battleship, one year old, small and fast. She was the flagship of Task Force 99, which included the aircraft carrier USS *Wasp*. The task force patrolled the North Atlantic off the coast of Norway to protect convoys headed for Russia from the German super battleships *Bismarck* and *Tirpitz*.

Admiral Ike Giffen detailed Fairbanks to accompany his chief of staff on the *Wasp*'s second mission to Malta. He was to write a detailed operation report for naval historic records. The carrier shoved off on May 2, 1942, departing down the Clyde River from Glasgow, carrying 47 Spitfires and a dozen Grumman F4F Wildcats for defense. This mission was code named Operation Bowery.

Slipping through the Strait of Gibraltar under cover of darkness, the *Wasp* steamed to within range of Malta on May 9th and launched first the F4F Wildcat combat air patrol and then the Spitfires. All but two of the Spits got off. One lost power and crashed off the bow; the other made a miraculous return to land on the ship. The *Wasp* returned to Scapa Flow, Scotland, without incident.

Because of Douglas's international celebrity, he was posted to train with the Royal Navy on HMS *Tormentor* to keep him out of sight. It was not a ship, but a naval shore establishment—a collection of landing craft and beach huts near Southampton. Next, he entered advanced training and amphibious operations at the Commando Training School at Achnacarry Castle in Scotland. There he learned about naval deception, counterintelligence and psychological operations units known as Beach Jumpers. Mountbatten had Fairbanks command an amphibious raiding craft that operated with the Royal Marine Commandos on raids to Europe.

His next assignment was back to the U.S. at Virginia Beach in Virginia. Douglas was posted with Admiral H. Kent Hewitt, who was planning for the invasion of Sicily after Operation Torch, the conquest of North Africa. Fairbanks convinced Hewitt to form and employ units of Beach Jumpers. He helped Hewitt sell the concept to Navy headquarters in Washington. The Jumpers' task was to simulate a beach landing some distance away from the actual landing, thus deceiving the enemy. The Jumpers' first action was

11. Douglas Fairbanks, Jr.

during the invasion of Sicily; then, they were on to Salerno, Southern France and then to the Philippines.

Assigned to special staff duties, including serving on the planning staff for the U.S. Atlantic Fleet Amphibious Force of the Atlantic Fleet, Fairbanks was the chief staff officer for the Beach Jumpers and participated in operations during 1943–44.

The Beach Jumper deception unit was designated Task Unit 80.4. At various times, it consisted of landing craft, motor patrol (PT) boats and even—during Anvil Dragoon, the invasion of Southern France—two English river gun boats that had been used on the Yangtze River in China.

Before the assault on Italy's mainland at Salerno, the Beach Jumpers attempted to deceive the Germans into thinking the U.S. was going for Sardinia. On September 8, 1943, Mark Clark's Army landed four divisions at Salerno, south of Naples. The Germans were determined to keep Naples and drive the Americans into the sea at Salerno. In order to force the Germans to keep their reserves in Naples and away from the beachhead at Salerno, Fairbanks's Task Unit 80.4 mounted a deceptive attack on the Pontine Islands across the bay north of Naples. With their eclectic group of small boats and landing craft, they lay off the small island of Ventotene, put down a heavy smoke screen and proceded to fire rockets and broadcast loud stereo sounds of an invasion fleet from within the smoke.

The Italians on the island soon sent up three white rockets, indicating their willingness to surrender. Fairbanks and three comrades boarded a small boat and nervously went ashore. On the small pier, a German sentry ran for cover and then took several shots at Fairbanks. The Italians readily surrendered, but it turned out there were 400 Germans on the far end of the island that intended to fight. After another day of deception, the Germans, believing a massive fleet was about to attack, surrendered. Douglas Fairbanks, Jr., was awarded the Silver Star for his brave actions.

During the eight-month run up to D-Day, Task Unit 80.4 plied the sea aiding the capture of islands off the coast of Italy and France. Fairbanks was awarded a second medal, the French Croix de Guerre for aiding the Free French to capture Elba.

Operation Anvil/Dragoon was the landing in Southern France near Saint Tropez. Task Unit 80.4.1's task was to create a diversion many miles to the west near Marseilles and the major naval base at Toulon. This mission was accompanied by the destroyer USS *Endicott*, commanded by the hero of Douglas MacArthur's escape from Corregidor, Medal of Honor awardee, Commander John Bulkeley.

The *Endicott* stood offshore while the group's smaller boats went inshore to harass and deceive the enemy. During the action, two larger German boats, a corvette and large armed yacht, made a surprise appearance. Task Group 80.4 began a fight for its life. They radioed the *Endicott* and hid in as much smoke as they could generate. As in the movie *Calvary*, Commander Bulkeley arrived and sank the aggressors and captured 40 Germans.

Fairbanks was ordered back to the States and received three more awards: he was made a Knight of the French Legion of Honor and received the Royal Navy's Distinguished Service Cross and the U.S. Navy's Legion of Merit.

During the war, he rose from lieutenant to the rank of captain. He was the father of the Navy's Beach Jumpers. Due to his actions during the war, he was made an Honorary Knight Commander of the British Empire. Regarding his service, when asked what turned him from a green officer into a veteran, Fairbanks said, "It doesn't take very long once you get a good scare." He retired from the reserves in 1954.

Fairbanks promotional photo for his starring role in *Sinbad the Sailor* (1947), the daredevil adventurer who crosses the Seven Seas to find the lost riches of Alexander the Great (lobby card).

Fairbanks returned to Hollywood and starred in *Sinbad the Sailor*, released in 1947. Unfortunately, it didn't do very well at the box office. He wrote, produced and starred in *The Exile*, also released that year. It was the first of three movies he produced and appeared in. The others were *Terry and the Pirates* and *Happy Go Lucky*.

In 1950, Douglas went to live in England until 1956, where he starred in *State Secret*, that year. He made a number of half-hour shows for his own television series, *Douglas Fairbanks Presents*. While still in the U.K., he appeared in quite a number of television shows and series including *Route 66*.

11. Douglas Fairbanks, Jr.

Back in the U.S., Fairbanks returned to the theatre and toured in *My Fair Lady* during 1968 as well as *The Pleasure of His Company*. The very last movie he was in was *Ghost Story*, in 1981. Finally, he was in various television series such as *The Love Boat* and *Strong Medicine*.

Then tragedy struck and Douglas's dear wife, Mary Lee, died in 1988. They had been together for almost 50 years. They had had homes in Palm Beach, Florida, and Manhattan as well as in London. They were close friends of the royal family and with other prominent figures. Regarding these relationships, Fairbanks said, "I prefer being a fly on the wall in the corridors of power." Mary Lee died in Palm Beach at age 75.

Fairbanks (Sinbad) with Maureen O'Hara, who plays Shireen the beautiful concubine in the 1947 film *Sinbad the Sailor* (publicity still).

Douglas Fairbanks, Jr., wrote a number of books. Released in 1988 was his autobiography, *The Salad Days*. Then he told of his World War II experiences in the 1993 *A Hell of a War*. A reviewer at the *New York Times* remarked, "*A Hell of a War* reads like the script of a 1940s war movie—at once anachronistic and entertaining." Douglas also collaborated on two other books: *The Fairbanks Album* and *Douglas Fairbanks*, a biography of his father.

Fairbanks married Vera Lee Shelton on May 30, 1991, in New York, accompanied by a few close friends and family members. It was his third marriage and her first. He was 81 years old and she was considerably younger. They had long been friends, having met in 1965 at a party in Acapulco. About a year and a half before the marriage, Doug phoned Vera to ask if she would have dinner with him. This led to a romance, culminating with the marriage. At the time, Vera Lee was an executive with the QVC Network, a home-shopping cable network.

World War II Veterans in Hollywood

On May 30, 2000, Douglas Fairbanks, Jr., died of a heart attack at the Mount Sinai Medical Center in Manhattan. He was 90 years old and was survived by his wife and by three children from his first wife: Daphne, Victoria and Melissa. He was interred in the same tomb as his father. He has three stars on the Hollywood Walk of Fame; one for movies, one for television and the third for radio.

12

Charlton Heston

Charlton Heston was a dominating figure in Hollywood, with his sonorous baritone voice and well-chiseled features. A winner of the 1960 Academy Award for Best Actor in *Ben-Hur*, he was known for playing a number of historic figures including Thomas Jefferson, Andrew Jackson, Michelangelo and Moses. Heston appeared in some one hundred films during his 60-year career. He also acted on the stage and was the author of five books. He was sometimes outspoken in politics, switching from Democrat to Republican. Charlton supported his friend Ronald Reagan for president. During World War II, he served in the U.S. Army Air Forces, flying as an aerial gunner with combat missions over northern Japan.

John Charles Carter, who later took on the name Charlton Heston, was born on October 4, 1923, in No Man's Land in Illinois. (No Man's Land is not an official place name. The term refers to a small unincorporated area north of Chicago along the shore of Lake Michigan. It is now a part of the city of Wilmette, a suburb of Chicago.) His mother was Lilla (maiden name, Charlton Baines), and Russell Whitford Carter was his father. When he was very young, his mother started to call him Charlton. His father worked in a sawmill. When Charlton was an infant, his father moved the family to St. Helen, Michigan. The area was heavily wooded, so Charlton spent much of his childhood years roaming the forest. His parents had two other children: his sister Lilla and his brother Alan. The 1930 U.S. Census, when Charlton was six years old, shows his name as Charlton J. Carter.

In 1933, his parents divorced, and it was a major change in Charlton's early life. His biographer wrote, "The little boy lost everything, his dog, his beloved woods, his dad, even his real name." He didn't see his dad again for ten years.

After the divorce, his mother married Chester Heston and his new family moved to Wilmette. A few years later, he assumed the pseudonym Charlton Heston, his mother's maiden name and his stepfather's surname; later his sister and brother also took the same surname.

World War II Veterans in Hollywood

Charlton went to New Trier High School, where he "felt like a country bumpkin compared to the other children, felt awkward and out of place." Not very popular in school, he described himself as "shy, skinny, short, pimply and ill-dressed." He became interested in acting and joined the Winnetka Community Theatre. Eventually, he won a scholarship to Northwestern University. At Northwestern, where he was a drama major, he acquired the nickname Chuck. Heston and his drama classmates decided to make their own movie. They chose to produce *Peer Gynt*, based on the Henrik Ibsen play; they shot it in 16mm, finishing it in 1941 with Chuck, who was 18 years old, playing the lead. His brother, Alan Carter, had a small role.

Charlton Heston in 1963 at the Civil Rights March in Washington, D.C. Heston was known for his political activism. In the 1950s and 1960s he was one of a few Hollywood actors to speak openly against racism and was an active supporter of the Civil Rights Movement (National Archives).

While at Northwestern, Charlton Heston dated a fellow student, Lydia Marie Clarke, who was to be his lifelong partner. Expecting to be drafted, he married Lydia on March 17, 1944. They had two children, Fraser and Holly. Shortly after the marriage, Heston enlisted in the U.S. Army. Trained as an aircraft radio operator gunner, he was posted to the 77th Bombardment Squadron in the Eleventh Air Force. The 77th was based on Attu, an island that is part of the Aleutians in Alaska. He flew for two years as a waist gunner on a North American B-25 "Mitchell" medium bomber.

The Aleutian chain of islands sweeps southwest from the Alaskan peninsula towards the Siberian peninsula of Kamchatka. The Kurile chain of Jap-

12. Charlton Heston

anese islands sweeps up northeast from the northernmost Japanese island of Hokkaido to the western tip of Kamchatka. The Kuriles enclose the Sea of Okhotsk, which is now a major area for Russian submarine operations. The shortest route to Japan from the west coast of America, a great-circle route, skirts these two island chains.

In June of 1942 the Japanese invaded Kiska and Attu Islands and also bombed Dutch Harbor, Alaska, as part of their move into Hawaiian waters. Their main thrust was to capture Midway Island in the Central Pacific. The Alaskan operation was part of a two-pronged attack that was meant to draw the U.S. Navy north and leave Midway vulnerable.

Commander Joseph Rochefort, a Japan expert who commanded the Navy's radio intercept station at Pearl Harbor, determined that the main Japanese fleet would attack Midway. Admiral Chester Nimitz concurred with Rochefort and sent our small fleet to Midway. The Navy achieved surprise and the most significant victory of the Pacific War by sinking four Japanese carriers and killing 300 irreplaceable Japanese veteran pilots.

The Northern Pacific is the breeding ground of the storms that descend on the West Coast and then sweep across America. Aircraft operations in that area, with the equipment of the day, were a pilot's nightmare. Freezing weather, zero visibility and fog were common. Some missions meant flying 50 feet above the sea for hours.

The U.S. commanders knew the Japanese had a contingent plan to move into Alaska and then down the coast. Luckily, the Americans had sufficient air power to prevent it.

The U.S. determined to dislodge the Japanese and retake Kiska and Attu, and on August 30, 1942, landed the 2nd Battalion, 134th Infantry Regiment, on Adak Island to build an air strip. Before the war, the regiment had been the Nebraska National Guard. After Pearl Harbor, it was rushed to Hueneme, California, to defend the Ventura County coastline. With the U.S. victory at Midway, the regiment moved inland to Ojai, California, for training before the move to Alaska.

After two years of fighting, the U.S. and the weather chased the Japanese out of the Aleutians. The U.S. built an airfield at Alexai Point on Attu for the 77th Bomber Squadron. From Attu, the B-25s were able to attack the Kuriles. Yamamoto had assembled his fleet there on November 26, 1941, for the attack on Pearl Harbor. During 1944–45, Heston flew missions as waist gunner and radio operator, bombing the Kurile Navy bases.

It was thought that the Allies would have to launch an all-out invasion of Japan in order to win the war. It could have cost 500,000 American lives. Those at the base where Heston was stationed were sure they would

World War II Veterans in Hollywood

be involved in the invasion. After returning from one mission, a B-25 was caught in one of Attu's treacherous crosswinds and crashed onto the island. Charlton and some other soldiers ran to help the pilots out of the cockpit. Running on a patch of ice, Charlton slipped and fell and was run over by an ambulance. He, with some other injured, was evacuated to the Elmendorf Field Hospital in Anchorage. When he was partially recovered, and confined to a wheelchair, he was assigned to work in the base control tower.

In August 1945, the United States dropped two atomic bombs on Japan. The Japanese surrendered and the Pacific war was over. American troops, including Heston, celebrated the bombing in the belief that a half million lives were saved. Later, Heston remarked, "If we had to go through that invasion, I'm not sure I'd be standing here today."

Later that same year, Staff Sergeant Charlton Heston was discharged from the Army. Just afterward, Charlton and his wife, Lydia, moved to New York City where they worked as models for artists. Heston got his big break on Broadway when he was cast as Mark Antony in a 1950 live-on-television production of *Julius Caesar*. This led to a number of stints on a CBS television series called *Studio One Anthology*.

After going to Hollywood, Heston made his professional film debut in *Dark City*, released in 1951. He starred as a hustler, but it didn't do well at the box office. Next Charlton came to the attention of Cecil B. DeMille, who had seen him in *Dark City* and was casting for his next movie, *The Greatest Show on Earth*. Until he saw Heston, he hadn't found an actor who was handsome or masculine or commanding enough to suit him. Charlton played the lead role as the circus manager in the DeMille spectacular, which also starred James Stewart. The Motion Picture Academy named it the Best Picture of 1952 and it was also the most popular film that year.

Heston was in 11 more movies, including *The President's Lady*, in which he played Andrew Jackson, and *Secret of the Incas*, which was filmed on location in Peru at Machu Picchu. Then came one of the most successful movies of all time, the 1956 epic *The Ten Commandments*, also a DeMille production. Heston produced a blockbuster performance as Moses. He prepared himself by reading 22 books on Moses, as well as the Old Testament. Charlton's three-month-old son, Fraser, was cast as the infant Moses. DeMille thought that Heston's features resembled Michelangelo's statue of Moses. The movie was one of the biggest box-office hits of all time. A reviewer described Charlton as "splendid, handsome and princely. He is remarkably effective as both the young, princely Moses and as the patriarchal savior of his people." Heston was nominated for the Golden Globe Award for Best Actor, his first. In ret-

12. Charlton Heston

rospect, Charlton said, "I've always been proud of the chance I've had to play genuinely great men."

The 1958 thriller *Touch of Evil* starred Orson Wells. Universal wanted Heston to costar in it, but he agreed only on the condition that Wells was also the director. It is now considered a film noir classic. Charlton played Andrew Jackson in another DeMille film, *The Buccaneer*.

Heston's last film of the fifties was *Ben-Hur*, starring in the title role. In it, he commanded the screen, even during the celebrated chariot race. This epic ran for more than three and a half hours. Like *Gone with the Wind* and other three-hour movies, it had an intermission halfway through for a bathroom and snack break. Its director, William Wyler, was a perfectionist, sometime shooting the same scene over and over. For one scene, he had Heston repeat the same line sixteen times. After retirement, Charlton said, "Willy is the toughest director I've ever worked for, but I think he's the best." These movies typecast Chuck as the classic hero.

Heston in 1959 starring in *Ben-Hur* for which he won an Academy Award for best actor (publicity still).

Charlton's twelve movies that he made in the sixties continued to cast him as icons of history. He played the title role in *El Cid*, filmed in Spain, John the Baptist in the *Greatest Story Ever Told* and Michelangelo in *The Agony and the Ecstasy*.

Heston was offered the costar role with Marilyn Monroe in *Let's Make Love*, but he declined because he wanted to perform in a stage play, *The Tumbler*. His motivation was the opportunity to work with its director, Laurence Olivier. It opened in Boston but closed after five performances on Broadway in February 1960. The play was a flop, but, according to Charlton, "I learned from Olivier in six weeks things I never would have learned otherwise. I think I've ended up a better actor." He ended the decade with the *Planet of the*

Apes, in which he played a time-traveling astronaut. This led to a number of other science-fiction films. By this time, he was 46 years old.

In 1970, there was a follow-up: *Beneath the Planet of The Apes*. This time, Heston had only a small, supporting role. That same year, there was a movie version of *Julius Caesar*, in which Charlton again played Mark Antony. Next, he starred along with Edward G. Robinson in the 1973 film *Soylent Green*. Then he played in the very popular *Airport* and *Earthquake*. Using his own personal experiences, Heston starred as a naval officer in *Midway* and *Gray Lady Down*.

Always interested in politics, early on he was active in the Democratic Party and supported the Civil Rights Act of 1964. He walked on the front row with Martin Luther King in the March on Washington for Jobs and Freedom and vocally opposed the Vietnam War. He was approached to run for the U.S. Senate, but turned it down because he wanted to continue his acting career.

Usually he had supported the party's candidate for president, but when it came to George McGovern, he was for his friend, Ronald Reagan. Heston liked to quote Reagan, who said that he hadn't left the Democratic Party; it had left him. He not only voted for Richard Nixon but also supported both George Bushes as well as Reagan. He was always against the cultural and sexual changes spawned by Vietnam War protests. He served six years as president of the National Rifle Association.

During the balance of the twentieth century, Heston was in an almost unbelievable fifty movies. There was an unusual series of short videos in 1992 on the A&E cable network called *Charlton Heston Presents the Bible*. He directed, as well as starred in, *Mother Lode*. Other outstanding productions included *Behind the Planet of the Apes*, *Hamlet* and *Treasure Island*. Heston was the narrator of highly classified military and Department of Energy instructional films during 1998, some of which related to nuclear weapons. To do so, he had to get the top, or "Q," security clearance.

Heston was also an author of books. His first was *Beijing Diary*, published in 1990. It tells the story of his travel, with his wife, to China to direct a Chinese version of *The Caine Mutiny*. Next was his 1995 *The Arena: An Autobiography*, wherein the author shared some intimate stories of his life and anecdotes about some of Hollywood's biggest names. In *To Be a Man: Letters to My Grandson*, Charlton articulates his beliefs regarding political and individual causes. It was published in 1997. His next book was *Charlton Heston: The Actor's Life: Journals, 1956–1976*. For those 20 years, the actor kept journals describing his daily activities and his thoughts about them, published in 1978. His last book, *The Courage to Be Free*, came out in 2000. The first half

12. Charlton Heston

contains essays on such things as culturalism, revisionism and the Second Amendment, while the rest has reprints of speeches Heston had given.

Heston was diagnosed with prostate cancer in 1998. After extensive treatment, the cancer went into remission. On November 4, 1999, he testified before the Congressional House Government Reform Subcommittee regarding gun control due to his stint as president of the National Rifle Association.

During the new century, Charlton was in a number of theatrical productions at the Los Angeles Music Center, including *Detective Story* and *The Caine Mutiny Court Martial*. He was the voice of Ben-Hur in the animated movie *Ben-Hur* and appeared (as himself) in *Bowling for Columbine*, which grossed $21.4 million at the box office. He was in an episode of the television series *The Outer Limits* as Chief Justice Wainwright, in 2000. His very last film was *Rua Alguem 5555: My Father*, starring as Josef Mengele, in 2003.

In August 2002 Charlton Heston announced that his doctors had diagnosed him with symptoms of Alzheimer's disease. From then on, he confined himself mostly to his home in Beverly Hills.

Among his many awards he received the Kennedy Center Lifetime Achievement Award in 1997, and President George W. Bush awarded him the Presidential Medal of Freedom in 2003. Charlton Heston was married to the

Heston as Professor Walter Finley in the 2001 action-packed adventure *The Order*, shot in Israel. The movie went directly to DVD (publicity still).

same woman—Lydia Clarke—from 1944 until his death. He almost always took his family with him when he went on location. Rather than participate in the merry-go-round of Hollywood parties, he enjoyed his life at home with his wife and two children. John Charles Carter, also known as Charlton Heston, died at his home on April 5, 2008, at age 84. His wife was at his side. He was survived by his wife, Lydia, their son, Fraser Clarke Heston, and their adopted daughter, Holly Ann Heston.

Heston's funeral was held on April 12 in Pacific Palisades at St. Mathews Episcopal Church, where he was a dedicated parishioner, always sitting in the same front pew for services. More than 200 friends and relatives attended, including California Governor Arnold Schwarzenegger, plus a number of Hollywood personalities such as Olivia de Havilland, Keith Carradine, Pat Boone, Tom Selleck and Rob Reiner.

During his lifetime, Charlton was awarded a large number of awards including the Order of Lincoln by the Illinois governor, the Academy Award, two Primetime Emmy Awards, and eight Golden Globe Awards. His name is on the Hollywood Walk of Fame.

13

Jason Robards

Jason Robards was a versatile and prolific actor who was in more than 20 stage plays and more than 60 movies and appeared 54 times on television. A character actor who was best known for playing historic figures, he won a Tony, two Academy Awards and an Emmy. Jason was married four times, the third time to the famous actress Lauren Bacall. He served in the U.S. Navy for over five years during World War II.

Even though his father was an actor, Jason didn't begin his acting career until after the war. After his graduation from Hollywood High School, he enlisted in the Navy on September 16, 1940, some 14 months before the Japanese attack on Pearl Harbor. After boot camp and the completion of radio school, Seaman 2nd Class Jason Nelson Robards, Jr., shipped out aboard the heavy cruiser USS *Northampton* on March 26, 1941. He was promoted to seaman 1st class on August 1, 1941.

On November 26, 1941, he was transferred to the admiral's staff and given the petty officer rank of radioman 3rd class. In his new job he handled communications and intelligence at the flag level for the admiral. This rapid promotion demonstrated the trust and confidence the Navy had in this talented 19-year-old.

On December 7, Pearl Harbor was attacked by Japanese aircraft. At the time, and luckily for the ship, the USS *Northampton* was about 100 miles at sea off Hawaii with Admiral William Halsey's aircraft carrier *Enterprise*. They had delivered fighter aircraft to Wake Island. Two days later, the *Northampton* arrived at Pearl Harbor, where the crew witnessed the appalling devastation. After a rapid refueling, the task force set out to search for the Japanese fleet. The search was unsuccessful. During the next months, the *Northampton* participated in the Navy's hit and run raids across the central Pacific. Robards was manning the radios on April 18, 1942, when the *Northampton* escorted Halsey's carrier, the *Hornet*, as it sailed toward Japan in order to launch Jimmy Doolittle's B-25s on their way to bomb Tokyo. The *Northampton*'s radio intercepted a Japanese picket boat's warning transmission and sank the boat. Prior

World War II Veterans in Hollywood

Jason Robards as Ben Bradlee in the *All the President's Men* (1976), an American political thriller about the Watergate scandal that brought down the presidency of Richard M. Nixon. Robards won an Oscar for best supporting actor in this movie (lobby card).

to radar, a ship's radio was its most important asset. Radioman Jason Robards was a petty officer third class only a year after his enlistment. Three years later, he had achieved the rank of radioman first class.

On June 4, the *Northampton* escorted the carrier *Enterprise* for the surprise attack on the Japanese fleet at Midway. Thanks to the U.S. code breakers and intercept capability, the American victory at Midway changed the course of the Pacific war. After Midway, the war moved to the South Pacific and the defense of supply routes to Australia.

The *Northampton* participated in four more major battles: San Cristobal, Bougainville, Santa Cruz Island and Tassafaronga. At San Cristobal, a Japanese submarine torpedoed and sank the USS *Wasp*, and at the battle of the Santa Cruz Islands, an Aichi D3A "Val" torpedoed the *Hornet*, which later sank after the *Northampton* attempted to tow it.

The most significant weapon during the Pacific war was the torpedo. The Japanese type 93 "long lance" was outstanding, and our Mark 15 was defective during the first year of the war. The "long lance" was powered by a two-cylinder steam engine fueled by compressed oxygen and kerosene. The oxygen was compressed to over 3,000 pounds per square inch and extremely

13. Jason Robards

dangerous. The type 93 carried a 1,000-pound warhead and could travel 12 to 20 miles. That was over twice the range of the American torpedo. Americans thought they had been launched by undetected submarines because of the long distance.

The battle of Guadalcanal had begun in August 1942, and by November, the U.S. had achieved enough air power in the area that the Japanese had to use the cover of darkness to resupply their forces. Their method was to load a string of buoyant oil drums with food and supplies. A destroyer would tow a string of 200 drums and cut them loose close to shore.

Naval security had intercepted a message in early November that an attempt to resupply forces at Guadalcanal's Tassafaronga Point would be made on the night of November 30, 1942. The attempt used eight destroyers, six carrying supply drums and two acting as escorts. All were armed with type 93 torpedoes. The *Northampton*, along with four other cruisers and four destroyers, sortied from Espiritu Santo to intercept the Japanese. The Japanese ships steamed southeast along the coast at Tassafaronga to drop their drums as the Americans steamed northwest on a parallel line. The Americans fired twenty Mark 15 torpedoes to no effect. The Japanese launched 44 type 93 torpedoes and seriously damaged three cruisers, and at 11:48 p.m. the *Northampton* took two hits and sank three hours later. In the battle, 395 sailors were killed. Robards went into the sea and, after treading water for hours, was picked up by an American destroyer at daylight. After recovering at Pearl Harbor, he was promoted to radioman 2nd class.

For the rest of World War II, Robards served on three more cruisers. Altogether the ships he was aboard accumulated 35 stars for battles they had fought. Following the *Northampton*, he was aboard the *Honolulu* when it was hit by a torpedo July 13, 1943, at Kolombangara. The damaged ship was able to return to Mare Island in California and in December returned to Espiritu Santo and participated in all the major Pacific battles during 1944. Robards was promoted to radioman 1st class on June 1, 1944. After four years at sea, Robards was sent ashore for the duration on December 7, 1944.

Radioman 1st Class Jason Robards was discharged from the Navy in 1946. He was awarded the Asia-Pacific Medal plus a number of others. Small stars on his campaign ribbons gave him credit for 17 major battles, and a hash mark on his sleeve signified he had served over four years' active duty. At 23 years old, Robards had seen several lifetimes' worth of blood, guts and dead friends. While Jason was in the Navy, he happened to read a stage play, *Strange Interlude*, by Eugene O'Neill. O'Neill's plays became the creative influence that stimulated his desire to act. Robards became famous for his performances in O'Neill plays. After his discharge, Robards confided to his father that he had a growing interest in acting.

Jason Nelson Robards, Jr., was born on July 26, 1922, in Chicago. His father, Jason Robards, Sr., was an actor who appeared on Broadway and in silent films. His mother was Hope Maxine. They moved to New York City shortly after Junior was born. When Jason was six years old, in 1928, the family moved to Los Angeles. While he was still in grade school, his parents divorced. He attended Hollywood High School, was a B+ student and all-around athlete. During his junior year, he ran a 4-minute, 18-second mile. He played on the school's baseball and basketball teams. Because of his high school performance, he had offers to go to a university, but chose instead to enlist in the Navy after graduation.

After his discharge from the Navy in 1946, he went to New York City to attend the American Academy of Dramatic Arts on the GI Bill. His father had studied there and recommended to his son that it was an excellent place to learn the actor's craft. Although he stayed at the AADA for only eight months, he had bit parts in radio and in a number of on- and off-Broadway shows. Jason's first movie role was in *Follow That Music*, a 17-minute musical short starring the jazz great Gene Krupa, in 1947. His part was far from auspicious; he appeared as the rear end of a cow. "They didn't trust me with the front end," he remarked.

On May 7, 1948, Robards married Eleanor Pittman. He commented, "First girl you kiss, you marry." They had three children: Sarah Louise, David and Jason III. Actually, this put three actors in show business with the same first name: Jason Sr., Jason Jr., and Jason III. The marriage lasted for 10 years.

His next gig was in *Stalag 17*, a three-act play that ran on Broadway starting in 1951, for which he was an understudy and an assistant stage manager. After its New York run, he joined the national touring company of the play. His television debut was in *The Big Story*, which went on air in 1951. Robards was in two episodes; both roles were as a newspaperman. Then came his big break: the off-Broadway 1956 Eugene O'Neill play *The Iceman Cometh*. At first, he was cast in a minor role. But the director was still looking for just the right actor to play the lead. Robards, who was 34 years old at the time, asked if he could read for the part. The director was so impressed that Jason got the part. The role won the actor broad recognition and critical acclaim.

Then it was back to Broadway for another O'Neill play, *Long Day's Journey into Night*, which opened in late 1956 and continued until March 1958. Playing the lead role, Robards won a Theatre World Award and was nominated for a Tony as the Best Featured Actor in a Play. With that, his career really took off. Perhaps the most important play for Robards was *The Disen-

13. Jason Robards

chanted, which opened in December 1958, and in which he costarred with his father. "It's the best time we ever had," Jason remembered; "That show, it was like a family." From the time he was born, he and his father were best friends. Robards won a Tony for Best Actor in a Play. He always preferred to act on the stage, having said, "It's the satisfaction of saying something about the human condition through the author, with the actors acting as the instrument, and then hearing the audience response." That same year, he and Eleanor divorced.

In 1959, Robards married actress Rachel Taylor. She was known for her role in the 1956–57 television series *The Secret Storm*. The coupling wasn't a happy one, due to his constant drinking, and lasted only a little over two years. After divorcing Eleanor in 1958, Jason was always in arrears on his alimony payments; the case was finally settled with Eleanor getting $7,706.

It was off to Hollywood, where Robards made his film debut in the 1959 movie *The Journey*. He had had the lead in the Broadway production of *The Iceman Cometh*, so Jason was a natural pick to star in the 1960 television show *The Iceman Cometh*. It was very popular.

Robards with Maureen Stapleton from the 1958 CBS television anthology *Seven Lively Arts*. The presentation is "Blast in Centralia #5" (publicity still).

World War II Veterans in Hollywood

In 1961 he divorced Rachel, and that same year met and began a relationship with Lauren Bacall. Both were huge stars. When they decided to get married, the ceremony was scheduled for June 16 in Vienna, Austria. Not able to verify that they both were single, the Austrian authorities refused a marriage license. Then they went to Las Vegas, where they were again refused. Finally, they drove to Ensenada, Mexico, where they were wed on July 4, 1961. The next year, Jason's father, Robards Sr., died. He was 71.

The movie *A Thousand Clowns* made Robards a big name in 1965. He was nominated for a Golden Globe Award for Best Actor—Motion Picture Musical or Comedy. During production, he struggled with his alcoholism but stayed active all during the sixties. On the stage he acted in eight plays and was in more than ten movies.

Lauren and Jason ended their marriage in 1969. It was, she said, because of his alcoholism. They had one son, Sam Robards, who became a movie actor when he grew up. After the divorce, the two stayed close friends. In early 1970, Jason married Lois Elaine O'Connor, a union that was to last his lifetime. He was almost 50 at the time and she was 14 years younger. They had met when Robards was making *Noon Wine* and she was the assistant director. They had a daughter, Shannon, and a boy, Jake.

One day in 1972, under the influence of alcohol, Robards was driving on a treacherous road in the Santa Monica mountains near Los Angeles when he drove his car into the side of a mountain. He nearly lost his life. Every bone in his face was broken and he was in the hospital's intensive care unit for two weeks. Recovery required extensive surgery and facial reconstruction. This convinced him that he had to conquer his alcoholism. It took two years, and he said he couldn't have done it without the support of his loving wife, with her quiet strength, confidence and serenity. After recovery, Jason became a campaigner for alcoholism awareness.

Jason Robards won an Academy Award for Best Supporting Actor in the 1975 movie *All the President's Men*. The film was based on the scandalous Watergate affair that led to the end of Richard Nixon's presidency. It was based on the famous book by Carl Bernstein and Bob Woodward. Jason played *Washington Post* executive editor Ben Bradlee. Robards won four other Best Supporting Actor Awards. This led to the 1977 television miniseries *Washington: Behind Closed Doors*. Appearing in six episodes, Robards depicted a fictional president based on President Nixon. This garnered him another Emmy nomination for Outstanding Lead Actor.

Then came a second triumph: the 1977 movie *Julia*. He played Dashiell Hammett and won his second award for Best Supporting Actor and two Film Critics' awards. Now over 55, Jason went back to Broadway for *A Touch of the*

13. Jason Robards

Robards (right) as Lt. Gen. Walter C. Short in the 1970 Japanese-American biographical war film *Tora! Tora! Tora!*, which dramatizes the Japanese attack on Pearl Harbor on December 7, 1941. Gen. Short was the U.S. military commander responsible for the defense of military installations at Pearl Harbor (publicity still).

Poet, which ran for four months starting in 1978. It got him a Tony nomination for Best Actor in a Play.

The 1988 television movie *Inherit the Wind* got Robards a Primetime Emmy Award. His last stage play, *No Man's Land*, ran for two months on Broadway in 1994. During the nineties, Jason narrated a number of documentaries. One of them, *Schizophrenia: Voices of an Illness*, received a Peabody Award for Excellence in Broadcasting. He wanted to narrate it because his first wife, Eleanor, had suffered from the disease.

Robards's last movie was the 1999 film *Magnolia*, in which he portrayed a man bedridden and dying from cancer. At the same time, the actor himself was waging a losing battle with the disease. Although not a major commercial success, critics liked it and he won the Florida Film Critics Award for Best Actor. When the director had offered him the role, he said, "I don't know if

World War II Veterans in Hollywood

I can do it, I'm on oxygen." The director remarked, "Bring the oxygen bottle along—it'll save me on props."

Robards had cancer and a staph infection in 1999, which put him in a three-month coma in a hospital near his home in Bridgeport, Connecticut. Recovering to some extent, Jason made his last appearance in the made-for-television movie *Going Home*, which aired in 2000. The story is about a woman who had to choose between her career or returning home to care for her sick father. The star was Jason Robards, playing the sick father.

Jason Nelson Robards, Jr., died on December 26, 2000. He was 78 years old. During his last years, he was living with his loving wife, Lois, in what he called "a quiet life on the water," in their home in Fairfield, Connecticut. He was survived not only by Lois, but also by six children and his close friend, Lauren Bacall.

Robards had a presidential bearing and an unforgettable voice. "He was as good as an actor gets in this country," said actress Mary Steenburgen, his costar in three movies. He said to her, "We are just making faces." But underneath there was his love and respect for the craft. Robards loved his colleagues like family and his family like colleagues. And many loved him too.

His early experiences growing up during the Depression, enlisting in the Navy at 18, and earning petty officer rank before turning 19 indicate a presidential personality. As a radio operator, he was the ship's connection to the world. Through four years of death and destruction he had to perform for his admiral and for his shipmates. No wonder he said that acting is just making faces.

14

James Arness

The Hollywood actor James Arness is best known as Marshal Matt Dillon. He played the lead on the television series *Gunsmoke* for 20 years. Not only that, he appeared in 39 movies, seven of them made for television. Among his television appearances, he was in *The Lone Ranger* and *How the West Was Won*. He also starred in the television series *McClain's Law*. In the Army during the war, he participated in the famous Anzio Battle while earning a number of decorations. His younger brother, who took the name Peter Graves, was also a movie actor.

James was born on May 26, 1923, in Minneapolis, Minnesota. At birth, his name was James King Aurness. Three years later he was joined by his younger brother, Peter Duesler Aurness (Peter Graves). Their parents were Rolf Cirkler Aurness and Ruth Duesler (maiden name). The father, whose parents had emigrated from Norway, had been an Army officer in the cavalry during World War I. He was a traveling salesman of medical supplies and the mother was a journalist who later wrote a column in a Minneapolis newspaper. When he got into the movie business, James changed his name to Arness.

Aurness attended schools in Minneapolis; first the John Burroughs Grade School, next the Ramsey Junior High School. While there, he joined the glee club, which he enjoyed. But he had a problem; he started growing like a weed and in one year, he was six feet, seven inches tall, four inches taller than anyone in the junior high. Insofar as academics were concerned, he barely made it through Ramsey.

Finally, Jim went to West High School, where he had trouble getting a date because of his height. Aurness took up skiing, not only downhill but also cross-country. In 1943, the school principal warned him about skipping classes and his rather wild deportment. While in high school, James had various part-time jobs including loading and unloading railway box cars.

After graduating in June 1942, Aurness, who described himself as a drifter, hopped on freight trains and a cargo ship cruising the Caribbean.

World War II Veterans in Hollywood

Finally, he returned home and enrolled in Beloit College. But after only one semester, he went into the Army on March 20, 1943. He was 20 years old. His leaving was tough for his mother. When they said goodbye, her eyes mirrored her fear that she would not see him again.

He was sworn in with the name Aurness. Because of his love for the sport, he told the officer that he wanted to be in the ski troops. He was assured that it was possible, but it never came about. He went to Camp Wheeler, Georgia, for 13 weeks of infantry basic training. Afterwards, he went to Fort Meade, Maryland, the collecting point for those headed overseas. Jim, with lots of other soldiers, was shipped to Casablanca in French Morocco to join the Third Infantry Division. (Audie Murphy was in the same division.) After a week there, they were taken by train to Oran, Algeria. Then they were shipped across the Mediterranean to Naples, Italy.

James Arness as Marshal Matt Dillon, with Amanda Blake as Miss Kitty, in the long-running television western drama series *Gunsmoke* (1955–1975). The stories take place in and around Dodge City, Kansas, during the settlement of the American West (1955 promotional still).

The division was trained for the landing at Anzio, 30 miles south of Rome. Loaded into more than 200 landing craft, they landed at the Anzio beachhead. The beachhead was 15 miles long and seven miles deep. The engagement lasted for some four months and included the British First Infantry Division and a ranger force, some 36,000 men who landed and secured an initial beachhead two to three miles deep.

James Aurness' Second Battalion hit the beach on January 22, 1944. Aurness was the first man to leap out of the landing craft when it hit the beach. He was so tall at six feet seven inches that he could determine the depth of the

14. James Arness

water. It came up to his waist, so it was clear that it was okay for the rest of the troops to land and wade through the water.

A succession of attacks resulted in heavy casualties on both sides. After fighting about five miles inland, Jim's unit came under German artillery fire. He remembered, "If you get hit dead-on, you just explode." The fight continued, but after ten days, Aurness was severely wounded in his leg and foot by German machine-gun fire. As a result, he ended up in the U.S. Army's 91st General Hospital in Clinton, Iowa. His recovery and rehabilitation took 18 months. While there, he was visited by his younger brother, Peter, who advised him to enroll in college using the GI Bill. Peter was also in the Army but didn't see any action.

At Anzio, the allied forces had been contained by the Germans, resulting in a four-month stalemate that ended in late May when the allies finally broke out, leading to the capture of Rome on the day before D-Day at Normandy. Audie Murphy began his collection of medals and promotions at Anzio.

Aurness received a medical discharge on January 29, 1945. Taking his brother's advice, he enrolled in the University of Minnesota using the GI Bill. There, he signed up for required courses and took a class in radio announcing. "Right from the start," Jim said, "I knew that this was for me." Academics weren't "Big Jim's" forte. "In fact," as he said, "studies kind of went out the window." But he enjoyed extracurricular activities. He pledged the Beta Theta Pi fraternity and joined the college choir. With a rich baritone voice, Jim sang solos at vespers services and at college affairs. In the summer of 1945, he got a job as an announcer at a Minneapolis radio station, WLOL. He was so successful at this that it seemed as if he could pursue a career in radio.

Returning to school in the fall, Aurness was added to the WLOL staff in a part-time position. After the Christmas break, he dropped out, and he and a boyhood friend hitchhiked to Hollywood in hopes of getting work as movie extras. They arrived in January 1946. Using the GI Bill, he studied at the Bliss-Hayden Theatre School under actor Harry Hayden. Jim appeared in a play called *Small Miracle on Broadway*. Playing the role of a detective, "I really got into the part," he said. The play ran for two or three weeks. A lady in the audience, Ruth Burch, came backstage afterward and invited Aurness to meet her boss at RKO. When he arrived, she introduced him to David O. Selznick and Dore Schary. After the meeting he was asked to take a screen test.

The result was a contract to appear in the 1947 movie *The Farmer's Daughter*. Paid $150 a week, he played the role of Loretta Young's brother. He worked on the film for four or five months. At the suggestion of the director, he dropped the "u" in his name and became James Arness.

This didn't seem to lead to anything else in Hollywood, so Jim became a beach bum and spent his days at San Onofre, surfing. To get around, he bought a 1938 Buick convertible. Eventually, he got a job setting pins in a Balboa Island bowling alley. Also, Arness got payments from unemployment insurance for having worked on *The Farmer's Daughter*. Then he got a job doing broadcast work on a radio station KOWL, where he gave reports on surfing conditions.

When Arness started to receive fan mail after the release of *The Farmer's Daughter*, he decided to take his acting career seriously. At the Pasadena Playhouse, Jim was cast in the role of a minister in *Candida*. Virginia Chapman also acted in the play, and that's how Arness met his first wife. Previously, she had been married and divorced and had an 18-month-old child. When they started seriously dating, Jim decided he had to get a full-time job. What he got was a salesman's job in the classified advertising department of the *Los Angeles Examiner* newspaper.

After marrying Virginia in 1948, she wanted Jim to get back into the movie business. She assembled a resumé for him and got him some interviews. As a result, he got bit parts in two movies. But then came *Battleground* in 1949. After applying to the casting director, he was told that the director was only looking for major stars, so Virginia contacted the producer, Dore Schary. He found a minor role for Arness as a private soldier.

Arness adopted Virginia's son, Craig, from her first marriage. In January 1950, she gave birth to their daughter, Jenny. The four moved to a small house in Pacific Palisades, a suburb northwest of L.A. His brother, Pete, bought a home nearby. Arness starred in the 1950 movie *Sierra*. His costar in that film was Audie Murphy. In February 1952, the Arnesses had a second child, Rolf. That same year, Jim starred with Sterling Hayden in the movie *Hellgate*, a Civil War epic.

Jim appeared in a number of movies, most of them Westerns, between 1950 and 1953. By the time he was cast in *Island in the Sky*, his salary was $700 a week. He spent about three weeks on the movie. Then Dore Schary got Jim a year's contract at MGM for $750 a week.

In 1955, Arness was cast as Marshal Matt Dillon in the television series *Gunsmoke*. Because of time constraints, his movie acting became almost non-existent. *Gunsmoke* became his signature role, and he played it for 635 episodes. His portrayal of Dillon made him an iconic figure in television. The series became the longest running in U.S. television history.

After *Gunsmoke* started, Arness was away from home a lot of the time.

14. James Arness

Virginia and Jim drifted apart and she lived a separate life. In 1958, they were divorced, and Jim was awarded custody of the children. (Virginia died in 1975.)

Pacific Palisades is near the beach, so all during the sixties, Arness took the kids there and taught them to swim and surf. Also, Jim decided he wanted to learn to fly in 1968, so he took lessons at a flight school in Burbank. He would get up very early, take lessons and then get to work at *Gunsmoke* on time. Eventually, he bought his own plane and would fly all over. He said, "Flying gave me a great sense of freedom and once in the air, I forgot about what went on far below me."

In 1974, Jim was introduced to Janet Surtees, who worked in a boutique. After his divorce, he had dated a number of women, but nothing had gone anywhere. On his first date with Janet, they flew in his plane to Mammoth Lakes Ski Resort, where they had a great time just enjoying themselves. Soon thereafter, they became inseparable. Janet had a son, Jim, from a previous marriage. Arness and Janet were married in 1978. "It was the best thing I've done in my life," he said. "We are as one—soulmates, living each day in happiness and contentment," he said after 20 years of marriage.

Tragedy struck Arness when his daughter Jenny died of a drug overdose on May 16, 1975. She was only 25 but had been involved in the drug scene for a number of years.

Gunsmoke was cancelled in 1975, so then Jim starred in another popular television series: *How the West Was Won*. It started in 1977, and the last broadcast was on April 23, 1979. The reason it was cancelled was that Arness was having a lot of trouble with his right leg, which had been wounded during the war. While shooting the final show, he was limping a lot, so much so that he had to have surgery. After the operation, however, Jim was back in a television series called *McClain's Law*. Since he still limped, the impediment was written into the script.

During the nineties, Arness starred in four *Gunsmoke* movies, which were based on episodes featuring Marshal Matt Dillon. His last appearance was in a 2011 television show called *Pioneers of Television*, playing himself as Marshal Matt Dillon.

In retirement Arness took up sailing, which he loved. He had a number of boats, each getting larger in succession. His last was a 50-footer. He even competed in the long-distance race from California to Hawaii. Eventually he donated his catamaran *Sea Smoke* to the Sea Scouts. And he donated his 1,400-acre ranch to the Brandeis Institute.

James King Arness died of natural causes at his home on June 3, 2011. He was survived by his wife, Janet, three sons and a number of grandchildren. For heroism in World War II, he received the Bronze Star. He was an honorary U.S. Marshal, was in the National Cowboy Hall of Fame and was nominated for three Emmy Awards. He is remembered by his countless fans as Marshal Matt Dillon. In a letter he wrote that he wanted posted on his web site, he said, "I had a wonderful life and was blessed with many loving people and great friends."

15

Peter (Aurness) Graves

Peter Graves was the younger brother of James Arness. Like James, Peter was a Hollywood actor and served in the U.S. military during World War II. An actor as well as a director, he was best known for his part in the CBS television series *Mission: Impossible*. In addition, he starred in the movie *Airplane!*

Peter Graves was born on March 18, 1926, in Minneapolis, Minnesota. Four years younger than James, he shared the same parents. At birth, his name was Peter Duesler Aurness. Later he adopted the name Peter Graves so as not to be confused with his older brother.

Peter went to school in Minneapolis. When he was 12 years old, he discovered the music of jazz clarinetist Benny Goodman. He was so impressed he joined the band in junior high school. First, he played the tuba, but didn't really like it, so his father gave him a clarinet.

Following his older brother, Peter started at Southwest High School in 1941 and joined the school band, playing the clarinet as well as the saxophone. When he was only 15, he joined the Musician's Union. He was also a member of the track team. In his junior year he won the Minnesota State High Hurdles Championship. Aurness graduated from high school in June 1944. Immediately thereafter, he joined the Army. According to his wishes, he was assigned to the Army Air Corps. He looked forward to having adventures, excitement and being sent overseas. To his disappointment, however, during his two-year tour, he never left the U.S. After achieving the rank of corporal, he was discharged in 1945.

Using the GI Bill, he enrolled in the University of Minnesota, where he majored in drama. While there, he met his future wife, Joan Endress, who was also a student.

Peter had leading roles in a number of college productions, including *MacBeth* and *Of Mice and Men*. He was a member of Phi Kappa Psi, a social fraternity. He had a part-time job as a radio announcer at a radio station, WMIN. After graduation in 1949, Graves moved to Hollywood, hoping to get a job in show business. His first movie appearance was in the 1951 film *Rogue*

World War II Veterans in Hollywood

River, in which he played a confused youngster. This was followed by three more movies in 1951, all in minor roles. His first lead was in the 1952 *Red Planet Mars*. It was a science-fiction movie in which he played a scientist who got messages from Mars. One of his most famous films was *Stalag 17*, in which he played a German informer masquerading as an American prisoner of war.

Graves's first appearance on television was in 1953 on *The Ray Bolger Show* doing comedy skits, singing and dancing. Next Peter was in the series *In the Western Fury*, which ran from 1955 through 1960. His most famous series was *Mission: Impossible*, starting in 1967 and running through 1973. For playing the leading role, he was awarded a Golden Globe in 1971. His last television stint was in the 2007 *Word Girl*, which used his voice.

His very last appearance was in the 2010 television movie *Jack's Family Adventure*. In all, Graves had parts in 74 movies. He was never on screen with his brother, James Arness. But Graves did direct Arness in a 1966 episode of *Gunsmoke*.

Always active, Peter Graves collapsed on March 14, 2010, and died of a heart attack. It was four days before his 84th birthday. His brother, James Arness, died a year later. Graves was survived by his wife of 60 years, Joan, and three daughters: Kelly, Claudia and Amanda. In addition to his 1971 Golden Globe Award, he won an Emmy Award in 1997.

Peter Graves starring as Captain Clarence Oveur in the 1980 satirical disaster film *Airplane!* The Paramount Pictures' movie is a parody of the disaster film genre and was a critical and financial success. Graves is James Arness' younger brother (promotional photo).

16

Ernest Borgnine

Ernest Borgnine was the consummate character actor whose prolific career on screen and stage lasted from 1949 until his death in 2012. Ernest appeared in more than 100 feature films and many television shows. His portly physique, coarse features and gap-toothed grin made him a commanding presence. He was best known as the villainous stockade sergeant in the movie *From Here to Eternity* and the gruff but lovable captain on the television show *McHale's Navy*. Most notably, he received an Academy Award for Best Actor in *Marty*, in which he played the humble, warm-hearted butcher. Before all this, he served ten years in the Navy.

Ermes Effron Borgnino was born on January 24, 1917, in Hamden, Connecticut. His parents were immigrants from Italy. His father, Camillo, was the son of Count Paolo Boselli, a financial advisor to the King of Italy. His mother, Anna, and his father separated when Ernest was two. Anna then took Ernest to live with her mother in Italy. After more than four years in Italy, his parents reconciled in 1923 and reunited in New Haven, Connecticut, where they changed their name to Borgnine. The experience served Ernest well, as he had learned to speak Italian.

Six-year-old Ernest went to elementary school in New Haven and then on to the James Hillhouse High School, where he participated in sports, but had no interest in the theater or acting. After he graduated in 1935, Borgnine got a job selling vegetables off the back of a truck. It was all he could get in the depths of the Depression. Not happy with his circumstances, one day he saw a U.S. Navy recruiting poster and enlisted on October 8, 1935, at age 18.

After boot camp in 1936, Borgnine was posted to serve on board the USS *Lamberton*. It was a destroyer then stationed in San Diego. It towed targets for surface ships, submarines and aircraft to shoot at. In November 1940, it was re-designated as a minesweeper. After a six-year tour of duty, Borgnine was honorably discharged on October 7, 1941.

Two months later, the Japanese attacked Pearl Harbor and the United States was at war. So, on January 22, 1942, Ernest reenlisted in the Navy. From then until the end of the war, he served on the USS *Sylph*. It was a converted yacht used to seek out enemy submarines. The *Sylph* was designated a Patrol Yacht (PY12). It was 205 feet long and armed with two 3-inch cannons, depth charge launchers and machine guns. As a gunner's mate 1st class, these guns were within Ernest's purview. The ship's top speed was only 10 knots. First it operated out of Tompkinsville, Staten Island, New York, and then from New London, Connecticut, patrolling for German submarines during 1942. It was a bad year for merchantmen off the East Coast, with sunken ships outnumbering new launches.

The German U-boats patrolled the coast from Florida to Maine, spotting their prey silhouetted against shore lights, and sank 452 ships in 1942. With improved antisubmarine efforts, the losses were cut to 203 ships in 1943 and, by 1945, only 30.

Ernest Borgnine in 2004 at the U. S. Navy Memorial in Washington, D.C., showing off his Honorary Chief Petty Officer cap.

At the outbreak of America's war with Germany, the Wolf Packs, as the subs were called, headed for America's Atlantic seaboard. The German captains called 1942 "the happy times." Ernest Borgnine and his shipmates turned the happy times of 1942 into a death march in 1943.

In the fall of 1943, his ship was reassigned to Quonset Point, Rhode Island, and later to Port Everglades Naval Base in Florida. The ship was a part of the Atlantic Fleet's Antisubmarine Development Detachment. She trained sonar men as well as tested and researched new sound and antisubmarine equipment. When Ernest Borgnine was discharged in September 1945, his awards were the Navy's Good Conduct Medal, the American Defense Service Medal with Fleet Clasp, the American Campaign Medal with Bronze Battle Star and the World War II Victory Medal.

16. Ernest Borgnine

After the Navy, Borgnine returned to his parents' home in New Haven. But he was not sure what he wanted to do in life. He seriously considered reenlisting in the Navy, but his mother suggested he consider becoming an actor, since, she said, "You always wanted to make a damn fool of yourself." Taking his mother's advice, he visited nearby Yale University which, he had heard, had an excellent drama school. When he got there, he met with a professor who reviewed his record and told him he would have to complete two years as an undergraduate before he could study drama. Then 28, Ernest was not eager to be a college student. He got a job at a local factory but was not happy with that kind of work either.

Keeping in mind his mother's advice, Borgnine entered the Randall School of Drama in Hartford using the GI Bill to pay the tuition. During the six months he was there, he played a lead part in *The Trojan Women*. It was his first experience on the stage.

Looking for some real-life experience, he joined the Barter Theatre in Abingdon, Virginia, in the spring of 1946. It was called the "Barter" because the actors lived on produce donated by local farmers. He worked there doing whatever needed to be done—driving, scenery painting and various stagehand chores. Finally, during a performance, he was able to get a few bit parts on the stage. Ernest won his career-making part in the *Glass Menagerie*. Playing the "Gentleman Caller," he brought the house down and got several glowing reviews.

Borgnine's career really took off when he got the part of a male nurse in the comedy *Harvey*, which opened on Broadway in 1949. This led to the role of Guildenstern in a production of *Hamlet* that traveled to Denmark and Germany, entertaining U.S. servicemen. In 1949, his mother Anna died at age 55.

On September 2, 1949, Ernest Borgnine married Rhonda Kemins, a woman he had met while he was in the Navy. She was 27, he was 32. He decided to try for roles in movies, so they moved to Los Angeles in 1951. He soon got a part in three episodes of *Captain Video and His Video Rangers*, a science-fiction television series that began in 1949 and ran through 1955.

Borgnine made his film debut in *China Corsair*, where he had a small part as a gambling club operator. The black and white movie was released on June 2, 1951. Next came another small part in *The Whistle at Eaton Falls*, released on August 2 by Columbia Pictures. On May 28, 1952, his first child, Nancee, was born.

Ernest got his big break in the movie *From Here to Eternity* in 1953. He played a sadistic stockade sergeant who broke a chair over a prisoner's head, killing him. The prisoner was played by Frank Sinatra. When Ernest auditioned for the part, he said to himself, "I've got to be the meanest, no-goodest, dirtiest guy in the world." Starring Burt Lancaster and Montgomery Clift, the film won the Academy Award for Best Picture plus 11 more Oscars, including one for Sinatra. Next was *Marty*, a love story between Ernest Borgnine and Betsy Blair. Audiences loved the film and its romantic message. In England it was hailed as the best picture of 1955. Borgnine won an Academy Award for Best Actor, a Golden Globe and two others. When Grace Kelly handed him the Oscar, he realized he was now in the big league. "The Oscar made me a star, and I'm grateful," he said. It was released on April 11, 1955, in New York City.

Borgnine was now much in demand, and steady film work followed, including *The Catered Affair* in 1956. He played the dramatic lead with his co-star Bette Davis. He and costar Alan Ladd were in *The Badlanders*, released in September 1958. Also in the movie was Katy Jurado (a Mexican firebrand and an apple in the eyes of virile American actors), who had been in many Hollywood Westerns. Jurado and Borgnine had a torrid love scene in the film. They struck up a real-life romance, so he divorced Rhonda Kemins and married Katy in 1959 at Jurado's swimming pool in Cuernavaca, Mexico. She was from a very wealthy Mexican family. She had played Gary Cooper's ex-mistress in *High Noon*, for which she received a Golden Globe. Within a year, the volatile marriage was in trouble, and they separated after a vicious quarrel at their first anniversary party. Katy accused Ernie of kicking her and claimed that he hit her all the time.

Borgnine and Jurado formed their own movie production company, the Sanvio Corporation. In

Borgnine starring in *McHale's Navy* as Quinton McHale in Season One in 1962. The sitcom aired on ABC until 1966 (promotional photo).

16. Ernest Borgnine

1961 the two went to Italy to costar in and also produce *Barabbas*. They also costarred together in an Italian movie, *I Braganti Italiani*.

McHale's Navy was a very popular Universal television series, a World War II comedy that started in 1962 and ran into 1966. Drawing on his Navy background, Borgnine starred as Lieutenant Commander Quinton McHale, the gruff but loveable skipper. Its director, Tim Conway, said, "The show boosted ABC and Navy fortunes. There were no limits to Ernie." After trying repeatedly, Borgnine finally quit smoking in 1962. This, undoubtedly, had something to do with his 95 years of life. In 1964, a spin-off movie with the same name was made.

In 1963, Katy Jurado and Ernest Borgnine separated again, and a long, dragged-out divorce was finalized in 1964. In the divorce proceedings, Ernie accused her of being cruel to him. She later remembered, "Yes we fought. Real knock-down brawling fights. But he's Italian and I'm Mexican and that's the way we Latins behave. But I love him very much."

During a Hollywood party held during the divorce proceedings, Borgnine met Ethel Merman. An actress and singer, she was famous for her distinctive and powerful voice while starring in musical theatre. She was called "The First Lady of the musical comedy stage." Ethel was at the top of her game, had been married twice and was newly divorced from her second husband, Bob Six, founder and chief executive officer of Continental Airlines. Ernie and Ethel fell for each other and decided to get married. She was 56 and he 47. They announced their impending marriage at a famous nightclub in New York City, P.J. Clarke's. The marriage took place in Borgnine's Beverly Hills home on June 27, 1964, the minute he was free from Jurado. Ethel told everyone, "I've never really been in love before." Ernest countered by saying, "Love at first sight is no myth. Wham, that's it, I'm as happy as a bug in a rug. This will last forever. You can bet your last dime on it." The marriage occasion was topped off with 50 white doves, $100,000 worth of flowers and 38 violinists playing romantic music.

Their honeymoon was in the Far East, but everything soon unraveled. In Tokyo, Merman was angry because everyone recognized him, but nobody knew her. Furious, she refused to give him some of her Kaopectate when he got diarrhea. The trip was paid for by American Express in exchange for appearances Ernie made on the company's behalf. This also didn't set very well with Merman. Back in Hollywood, the marriage finally imploded. They separated some two months later and filed for divorce on October 21, 1964. Ernest remarked, "I was married to a lovely lady who was a star. I was married to her for 32 days and that was enough." She noted, "If you blinked, you missed it." In her autobiography, Merman included a chapter titled "My Marriage to Ernest Borgnine." It consisted of one blank page.

Ernest Borgnine married actress Donna Rancourt on June 30, 1965. She was 16 years younger than Ernest and was a stand-in for Yvonne De Carlo in *The Munsters*. On August 5, 1965, they had a daughter, Sharon. Obviously, Sharon was conceived before her parents married.

In 1965, Borgnine bought a home in Beverly Hills where he lived for the rest of his life. It was on a hilltop between Beverly Hills and the San Fernando Valley. The spacious house included a swimming pool, library and office.

The Wild Bunch was a movie that grossed $11 million at the box office. The gritty Western classic was set in 1913, filmed in Mexico and shot in Technicolor and Panavision. The star, William Holden, played the part of a criminal gang chief with Ernest Borgnine as a member. It received an award for Best Cinematography and was released in June 1969.

Borgnine's son, Cris, was born on August 9, 1969. Like his father, he went on to become an actor and producer, perhaps best known for playing in *Mission: Impossible*. The next year, Ernie's daughter Diana was born on December 29.

Between then and 1972, Borgnine was in seven movies, none of which were particularly outstanding. He was also in the television film *The Trackers*. In 1971 Donna filed for divorce, and it was finalized on January 1, 1972. She claimed Ernest plotted to murder her and that he hired two hit men to do it. She was so afraid that she hired around-the-clock armed guards.

Ernest played the role of Vince Lombardi in the 1973 television movie *Legend in Granite*, plus two other films. On February 24, 1973, Borgnine married Tova Traesnaes. She was his fifth and last wife. Twenty-five years younger, she was born in 1971 in Oslo, Norway. When she was seven, her father and mother separated, and she and her mother moved to New York. Although Tova studied acting there, she got interested in makeup and formed a company, Beauty by Tova, in 1990 to market her cosmetics. She received an award for the Women's Fragrance Star of the Year in 1998.

All Quiet on the Western Front, released in 1979, was a remake of Erich Maria Remarque's World War I movie about a young German soldier who faces profound disillusionment in the soul-destroying horror of war. The original movie starred Lew Ayres. Borgnine played the role of the soldier's commanding officer and received an Emmy nomination for Outstanding Supporting Actor.

The action-adventure television series *Airwolf* first went on the air in January 1984 and continued through 1986 on CBS. The episodes center on a high-tech military helicopter (code-named *Airwolf*) and its crew as they un-

16. Ernest Borgnine

dertook various exotic missions, some involving espionage. Costarring with Jan-Michael Vincent, Borgnine played a helicopter pilot. The series was an instant hit.

During 1995, Borgnine toured the country in his customized bus. He wanted to get close and personal with his fans and to visit the heart of the country he loved and protected. The trip was the subject of a documentary film made in 1997: *Ernest Borgnine on the Bus*. When he returned to Hollywood, he starred in *The Single Guy*, a sitcom that was an NBC series that ran into 1997.

On July 17, 1996, a TWA flight from JFK Airport in New York crashed into the Atlantic 12 minutes after taking off on its way to Paris. All 230 souls on board were killed. Ernest Borgnine appeared in the thought-provoking documentary film—*TWA Flight 800*—about the ill-fated flight.

Between 1996 and the end of the century, Borgnine was in a number of movies including *McHale's Navy*, a spin-off based on the television series. Three of the films used only his voice. In addition, he was in six episodes of the television series *All Dogs Go to Heaven* and in single episodes in two others. His wife, Tova, wrote a book published in 1998 titled *Being Married Happily Forever* about her marriage with Ernest and relationships in general.

In the movie *Hoover*, released in 2000, Borgnine played the part of J. Edgar Hoover; he was also the film's executive producer. During the filming, he expressed admiration for the character he played, but was surprised that he didn't have to wear a dress.

Katy Jurado, who had been married to Ernest Borgnine for four years, died on July 5, 2002, at her home in Cuernavaca, Mexico. She had been suffering from heart and lung ailments. The cause was kidney failure and pulmonary disease. After her divorce from Borgnine in 1963, she never married again. Upon hearing of her death, Borgnine remarked, "She was beautiful, but a tiger."

From 2002 to 2004, Borgnine was in four movies and did single episodes in four television series. Ernest was made an honorary chief petty officer at a ceremony held on October 15, 2004, at the U.S. Navy Memorial in Washington, D.C. One of his close friends, retired Navy captain Kathi Dugan, said, "When Ernie was promoted to honorary chief, there was never, of all honors—even his Academy Award—never anything that meant as much to him. He had tears in his eyes."

In a 2007 television movie, *A Grandpa for Christmas*, Borgnine played the grandpa. When the grandpa in the film discovers he has a granddaughter he didn't know about, they become great friends. He was nominated for a Golden Globe.

World War II Veterans in Hollywood

Borgnine, acclaimed Academy Award winning actor and World War II chief's gunner mate and combat veteran stopped by the Pentagon in 2004 to meet with Adm. Michael G. Mullen, Vice Chief of Naval Operations (U.S. Navy).

On January 24, 2007, Borgnine's 90th birthday was celebrated in a local bistro in West Hollywood. There to help him celebrate were Tova, Tim Conway, Bo Hopkins, Debbie Reynolds, Don Rickles and many other friends. Also, there were his son, Cris, and his grandson, Anthony.

Borgnine wrote his autobiography, *Ernie: The Autobiography*, published in July 2008. This fascinating story of his life is witty, candid and a revealing memoir. In it he tells of the trials and tribulations on his road to fame, the friendships he shared with some of the silver screen's biggest stars and the glamorous leading ladies he loved.

On April 2, 2009, Borgnine was in the very last episode of the long-running television series, *ER*. His role was that of a husband whose wife died. It got him an Emmy Award nomination for Outstanding Guest Actor in a Drama Series. He was 92 years old. On October 2, 2010, Borgnine played himself on *Saturday Night Live*. Even at that age, he was in quite a number of movies. His very last one was *The Man Who Shook the Hand of Vincente Fernandez*. The story is about a retired actor, played by Borgnine, who is forced to go to a nursing home, where he finds the respect and acclaim that eluded him during his career. His acting is a testament to his indelible screen presence and charisma. It was made when Ernest was 94 and was released in 2012.

16. Ernest Borgnine

In 2011 Borgnine received the Lifetime Achievement Award from the Screen Actors Guild and died the next year on Sunday, July 8. He passed away from kidney failure at the Cedars-Sinai Medical Center in Los Angeles. He was 95, and his family was at his side. He was survived by his wife, Tova, and children: Cris, Nancee and Sharon.

The family said they were shocked by the "sudden passing." He had been in good health until a recent checkup on the previous Thursday, July 5. His friend, Harry Flynn, said it was his 95,000-mile checkup. Borgnine joked, "It turned out to be a little more serious than we thought."

The funeral was held on July 14 at Forest Lawn Memorial Park. A Navy honor guard paid tribute with full military honors. His widow Tova noted, "Ernie, as you may know, loved and adored the Navy, and the sea, and all of you. I know Ernie is looking down on us right now and blessing all of you and your fellows across the world for all you do for our country, for our people and especially for us today."

Navy captain Kathi Dugan said that Ernie had told her before he died, "I don't know if I have earned a military funeral, but I can't think of a more appropriate way for me to leave this world than with my Navy men and women."

The ceremony was organized by Navy Chief Marco Valdovinos, who said, "This veteran has a great history of contributions to our community, to our nation and to the service. There's nothing greater for me than to render one final salute to our fallen veteran."

17

Tony Bennett

Tony Bennett must be considered one of the greatest singers of all time. As a ten-year-old, he sang popular songs, and he was still performing when this was written (the summer of 2020), at age 93. He is also a painter and an author. He served in the Army as an infantryman in the European Theater during World War II and the experience changed his life.

Anthony Benedetto (who later took the name Tony Bennett) was drafted into the Army in November 1944. He was 18. First, he was sent to Fort Dix, New Jersey, for basic training and then to Fort Robinson in Nebraska where he underwent advanced infantry training. (Fort Robinson is now Robinson State Park.)

In January 1945, he was shipped to the Le Havre Replacement Depot in France. From there, he was assigned to the 63rd Infantry Division (called the "Blood and Fire" division). The 63rd had taken heavy losses during the Battle of the Bulge and fought in the Ardennes region of Belgium. It was Hitler's last gasp offensive, in which almost 20,000 Americans were killed as well as many Germans. Anthony joined the division just after the Army had closed off the Bulge and was again fighting its way into Germany. The Army was stretched thin along the Western Front and was fed replacements into the combat units rather than replacing complete units.

Tony Bennett was a true combat infantryman. He spent several months digging holes in hard, frozen ground before he could spend a frigid night in a frozen foxhole hoping a German 88 canon shell wouldn't land on him. Days were spent clearing mine fields, clearing villages, avoiding snipers, and ducking for cover when the 88s opened fire. When they ran into a roadblock or a Panzer tank, they had to pick up their BARs (Browning automatic rifle) and bazookas and slug it out. For an 18-year-old that had been in the Army just six months, war left a decidedly bad taste in Tony's mouth.

During the harsh winter of 1945, they fought across part of France and into Germany. The front line he described as "front-row seat in hell." According to Bennett, "Nighttime was the worst. We couldn't light any fires to keep

17. Tony Bennett

Tony Bennett in 2014 in a live performance at the Rose Theater of Lincoln Center for the Performing Arts with Lady Gaga to support their collaborative studio album, *Cheek to Cheek*, which was released in September 2014. The performance was aired on PBS on October 24, 2014, as part of the network's "Great Performances" series (promotional photo).

warm; we couldn't even light a cigarette because the glow would be detected by the enemy and give away our position."

They pushed the German Army back into its homeland. At the end of March, they crossed the Rhine River while experiencing heavy resistance. By month's end, they had reached the Danube. Their last mission was to liberate a Nazi concentration camp in Landsberg, some 30 miles from Dachau. "I'll never forget the desperate faces and stares of the detainees," Bennett later wrote. The Americans immediately supplied food and water to the starving refugees, who couldn't believe the U.S. Army was there to help, not kill them. Later, it was discovered that shortly before their arrival, the Nazis had killed half the survivors. "Anyone who thinks that war is romantic obviously hasn't gone through one," Tony said.

After the surrender, Tony Bennett stayed in Germany as part of the occupation force. Men were returned to the States according to a point system. Points were awarded according to the amount of time spent overseas.

Benedetto was assigned to a Special Services band in order to entertain American troops. He sang with the band under the stage name Joe Bari. He approached each song to combine the styles of Stan Getz's saxophone and Art Tatum's piano. Tony was able to tour Europe and study music for a time at Heidelberg University. On Thanksgiving Day 1945, after months of living like a touring jazz band, Anthony ran into an old friend that had been in his high school quartet. The friend happened to be black, and when they attempted to share the Army's special Thanksgiving dinner together, an officer intervened. Blacks weren't allowed to eat in the enlisted men's mess hall. A stunned Benedetto exploded with harsh words for the officer. As a result, Anthony was demoted from corporal to private and assigned to a graves registration unit, disinterring mass graves and preparing the bodies for shipment home. Soldiers were originally buried in mass graves at the battle site where they were killed. Exhuming and identifying the bodies was a nasty business. This example of racism prompted Tony to later join the Civil Rights Movement.

Tony's good fortune prevailed when a ranking officer discovered his predicament and had him transferred back to Special Services. He spent the next six months singing with a band that had been formed to emulate the famous Glenn Miller's group.

Anthony Benedetto was returned to the U.S. in August 1946 and was discharged, a 20th birthday present. He had had a lifetime's worth of experience and still wasn't old enough to buy a drink. Ordinarily he would have been decorated due to his actions in combat, but this was not to be because of his demotion. Afterwards, Bennett said, "The war gave me a social conscience and made me a pacifist."

Anthony Dominick Benedetto was born in Queens, a borough of New York City, on August 3, 1926. His father John had emigrated from Italy. His mother Anna's parents had also come from Italy. His father died when Anthony was only ten years old, leaving a family that consisted of his wife, Anthony and two older children, John and Mary. They grew up in the Great Depression in poverty. Luckily, however, their home was surrounded by relatives and friends who had also come from Italy, part of a mass migration from that country.

Benedetto enjoyed listening to the radio, hearing Al Jolson, Bing Crosby and Louis Armstrong. Soon, he was singing himself. In 1936, he sang at the opening of the New York Triborough Bridge. After Anthony's performance, Mayor Fiorello La Guardia patted him on the head. He was just ten. Young Benedetto went to the High School of Industrial Arts in Manhattan, where he was able to sing and study painting. At the school, he was the class cartoonist and thought about a career in commercial art. As a teen, he got a job waiting on tables in an Italian restaurant, where he also sang while delivering food.

But the war came along and Bennett was drafted. When he returned to New York in 1946, he studied singing at the American Theatre Wing, a New-York-based school "Dedicated to supporting excellence and education in theatre." He paid for the tuition using the GI Bill and worked to support himself waiting tables and singing in restaurants.

17. Tony Bennett

Pearl Bailey was performing in Greenwich Village and, in 1949, she asked him to sing to open her show. Bob Hope, who was there, appreciated Joe Bari's (Benedetto's stage name then) voice and invited him to go on a concert tour with him. It was Hope who suggested he use the name Tony Bennett. The next year Tony signed with Columbia Records and sang his first hit, "Because of You." The song sold more than one million records and was number one on pop charts. This was followed by other hits: "Blue Velvet," "Rags to Riches," and "Stranger in Paradise." He kept busy performing at various venues, sometimes doing more than one a day. Often his shows were attended by screaming teens.

Tony Bennett and artist Patricia Beech were married on February 12, 1952. They had been dating for two years. The marriage ceremony took place

Early album cover photograph of Bennett (1951–1962 Singles).

at St. Patrick's Cathedral in New York. It was most unusual in that some two thousand fans were outside the church. The two had two sons: Danny, born in 1954, and Daegal, or Dae, the next year.

In 1956, Tony hosted *The Tony Bennett Show*, which consisted of five 60-minute episodes aired on NBC television. It featured a host of guests including Judy Canova, Debra Paget and the Mills Brothers. At the same time, he continued making recordings. Two hits with Count Basie, "Chicago" and "Jeepers Creepers" became wildly popular. Tony remembered, "When Frank Sinatra said, 'For my money, Tony Bennett is the best singer I've ever heard,' it changed my career completely. He was my best friend, and I was his best friend."

In his landmark concert at Carnegie Hall in June 1962, Bennett sang a total of 44 songs, accompanied by Ralph Sharon and his orchestra. Just previously, Tony had released what became his signature song, "I Left My Heart in San Francisco." When the recording was released it achieved "gold record" status. The song won Grammy Awards for Record of the Year and Best Male Solo Vocal Performance.

Tony and his wife, Patricia, were divorced in 1965. The marriage failed to work, probably due to the fact that Bennett was often on the road, making records and performing at nighttime. This didn't leave much time for family life. She sued on allegations of adultery. A firm believer in civil rights, Bennett walked in the 1965 march from Selma to Montgomery.

It may be little known that Tony Bennett was in four Hollywood motion pictures. The first, released in 1966, was *The Oscar*. Not only did he sing in a cabaret performance, he also narrated the film. Unfortunately, it was a flop, received poor reviews and had a very small box office. The next was a 1994 movie, *The Scout*, a story about baseball in which Tony played himself. In 2003, he again played himself in the smash-hit *Bruce Almighty*. A fantasy comedy, it grossed almost $500 million. His last film was *Amy*, about Amy Winehouse, in which he played a musician. Regarding Winehouse, he said, "She was an extraordinary musician with a rare intuition as a vocalist."

Bennett is a talented and celebrated artist. He was first attracted to painting as a young child and continued to paint throughout his life. The United Nations commissioned him to paint a picture to note its 50th anniversary and honored him with its Citizen of the World award. His work is on permanent display at the Butler Institute of American Art and New York's National Art Club. Three of his paintings are in the Smithsonian Museum's permanent collection. In 2009, his portrait of Duke Ellington was added to the National Portrait Gallery's collection. (A number of Tony's paintings can be seen online. Go to Benedetto Arts Gallery.) He signs his art with his real

17. Tony Bennett

name: Benedetto. About his art, Tony said, "It's everything to me. To have a view on Central Park and watch the four seasons and the great vastness of the sky—it changes every day. Rembrandt said it: 'There is only one master; that's nature.' It gives me unbelievable subjects to study and paint."

Bennett is not only an artist but also an author. He has written five published books: *Tony Bennett: What My Heart Has Seen*, in 1996, was his first book and is a collection of his artwork in various mediums. Then came *The Good Life: The Autobiography of Tony Bennett*, published in 1998. *Tony Bennett: In the Studio: A Life of Art and Music*, was published in 2007. *Life Is a Gift: The Zen of Bennett*, came out in 2012. It is another memoir and a *New York Times* bestseller. His last book, *Just Getting Started*, came out in 2016.

During the late sixties, rock music came on the scene. Columbia asked Tony to make a record of contemporary rock songs. The result was *Tony Sings the Great Hits of Today*. It did not sell well.

Tony had met actress Sandra Grant while both were acting in *The Oscar*. The relationship clicked and they moved in together. On December 29, 1971, they were married in New York. They had two daughters: Joanna, who was born before the marriage in 1970 and Antonia, born in 1974. Afterward, they moved to Los Angeles. Antonia, a singer, has been performing alongside her father since she was four years old.

In 1972, Bennett left Columbia and went to England for a short time, where he hosted a television show that was broadcast from a nightclub. On his return, Tony formed his own record company called Improv. First, he recorded *What Is This Thing Called Love*, which became a favorite. Then he made two albums with jazz pianist Bill Evans: *The Tony Bennett/Bill Evans Album* in 1975 and *Together Again* in 1976. While they were well received, there were problems distributing the records and the company went bottoms-up in 1977.

No longer involved with a record company, Bennett fell on hard times. He started using cocaine and marijuana. It was an integral part of the Hollywood celebrity scene. Tony almost drowned due to taking drugs while taking a bath. This woke him up, and he was able to overcome his bad habits.

After getting clean, Bennett's oldest son, Danny, became his personal manager. With Danny's help, Tony was able to put his personal life and professional career back together. He signed again with Columbia records and released his first studio album, *The Art of Excellence*, in almost ten years. In addition, Danny had him booked on a number of television shows.

Bennett has been and still is involved with a number of different charitable causes. In 1999, he cofounded, along with Susan Crow, the nonprofit Exploring the Arts, a program that provides resources and opportunities in the arts available to high schools in New York City and Los Angeles. In addition,

World War II Veterans in Hollywood

he supported so many humanitarian causes that he was sometimes known as "Tony Benefit." He also supports the Juvenile Diabetes Foundation and the American Cancer Society.

In 2006, Tony turned 80 years old. That same year, *Duets: An American Classic* was released. The album featured not only Bennett but also Paul McCartney, Elton John, Barbra Streisand and Sonny Bono. It inspired a television show and won seven Emmy Awards.

On June 21, 2007, Tony married Susan Crow, with whom he had been in a relationship for some time. She was 44 years old and Tony was 81 at the time. She had been a schoolteacher in New York City and, when a teen, was the head of the Tony Bennett fan club.

During the year of Tony's 85th birthday in 2011, *Duets II* was released, with a host of new singers. The featured song was Bennett singing "I Left My Heart in San Francisco" to mark the 50th anniversary of its release. Bill Clinton observed then, "Now in his seventh decade of singing, Tony Bennett has kept his unique voice with its beauty and range, strength and style."

In 2012, son Danny produced a documentary film, *The Zen of Bennett*, which was shown at the Tribeca Film Festival that year. The same year, the *Viva Duets* record was released, with Latin songs in English, Spanish and Portuguese. He sang in a number of concerts in order to promote these records.

Bennett made a cameo appearance with Carrie Underwood to sing a duet on the television season premiere of *Blue Bloods* on CBS in 2011 (publicity still).

17. Tony Bennett

Bennett's 2015 long-playing recording called *The Silver Lining: The Songs of Jerome Kern* was a top seller, followed the next year by *Tony Bennett Celebrates 90*, a Columbia album and a television special.

When this was written (during the summer of 2019), Tony Bennett was still going strong. On February 5, 2018, Tony and wife Susan hosted the 11th annual *Exploring the Arts* gala held at the Ziegfeld Ballroom in New York City. Tony rounded out the evening with a classic performance of a medley of some of his famous hits. A recording was released on September 14, 2018, by Columbia Records, with Tony and Diana Krall singing a duet, "Fascinating Rhythm." When he was 23 in 1949, "Fascinating Rhythm" was Tony's very first recorded song. It is now part of a new record called *Love Is Here to Stay*.

With millions of records sold, Tony has platinum and gold albums to his credit. He has received 19 Grammy Awards plus the Grammy Lifetime Award. He has traveled around the world singing to sold-out audiences with rave reviews. In 2002 he was presented the Lifetime Achievement Award from ASCAP. He was a Kennedy Center Honoree in 2005 and was awarded the National Education Association Jazz Master honor. In addition, in 2006, he received the National Endowment for the Arts Jazz Masters' Award and a star on the Hollywood Walk of Fame. He was the winner of the 2017 Library of Congress Gershwin Prize. The Martin Luther King Center has bestowed on him their Salute to Greatness Award. And he received the United Nations High Commissioner for Refugees Humanitarian Award.

According to Tony, "To me, life is a gift, and it's a blessing to just be alive. And each person should learn what a gift it is to be alive no matter how tough things get." A celebrated singer of this and the previous century, Bennett is a legendary showman with a passion for music. On July 10, 2019, 93-year-old Tony gave a concert at the Hollywood Bowl. It was a night of joyful, jazzy exuberance under the stars.

18

Mickey Rooney

Mickey Rooney was one of the most well-known Hollywood personalities of his era. His acting stretched from the time of silent films into the twenty-first century. His was the longest career in cinema history, lasting from 1926 to 2015. His movie debut was in *Not to Be Trusted*, when he was only four years old. His last was in a television show: *The New Adventures of the Black Stallion*, released after his death at age 93. As a film actor, Rooney had 168 credits. Also, he was a vaudevillian, a stage actor, a movie producer and an author of two books. During World War II when a soldier, he was awarded a Bronze Star.

Mickey Rooney, whose real name was Joseph Yule, Jr., was born on September 23, 1920, in Brooklyn. He first appeared on a stage when he was only 17 months old as a toddler in his parents' vaudeville act. His father, Joseph Yule, and mother, Nellie W. Carter, continued their act and included their son. They divorced in 1923. According to Joseph Jr., "I was aware, even at age three, that my father had a penchant for going out by himself after a show, then returning at dawn with a nervous grin on his face. I could only guess, from my mother's angry reactions that he was doing something that hurt her very much. She kept talking about my dad's 'floozies'—which I took to be another name for 'bartender.' You see, I thought my dad had a problem with Punch, not with Judy."

He and his mother moved to Hollywood in 1925, leaving his dad in New York. For his first film, *Not to Be Trusted*, released in 1926, Joseph Jr. received $200. The next year, he starred in the first *Mickey McGuire* movie: *Mickey's Circus*, a short film. It was so popular that it generated a series of 11 more shorts. During that time, he took on the stage name Mickey Rooney. First, his movies were two-reel silent films, but later they transitioned to talkies. Mickey received $250 for each; the last was in 1931. (The first talkie was *The Jazz Singer*, starring Al Jolson, released in 1927.)

After a number of other bit parts in movies, Rooney starred as Puck in the 1935 *A Midsummer Night's Dream*. Critic David Thomson said his perfor-

18. Mickey Rooney

mance was "one of the cinema's most arresting pieces of magic." Then, what caught everyone's attention was his role as Andy Hardy, the all–American teenager in *A Family Affair*, released in 1937. What followed were more than 20 films featuring Andy Hardy. The last was *Love Laughs at Andy Hardy* in 1946. He played a delinquent teen in the 1938 movie *Boys Town*, with Spencer Tracy, which garnered him a special Juvenile Academy Award. Even though Rooney appeared in a total of nine films in 1938, he also managed to graduate from Hollywood High School that year. Lana Turner, a later costar and early romantic interest of Mickey's, was also at Hollywood High School then. Starring in the 1939 *Babes in Arms* earned him an Academy Award nomination for an Oscar. Still a teenager, Rooney later remarked, "I was a 14-year-old boy for 30 years."

In 1938 Rooney was working at the MGM studio on *Love Finds Andy Hardy*. At the same time, Norma Shearer was working there on *Marie Antoinette*. Mickey, 18, and Norma, 38, had a torrid affair and would hole up together in Shearer's trailer. The studio kept the affair from going public, but the two were severely reprimanded.

The 1939 movie *Babes in Arms* was the first musical where Rooney teamed up with Judy Garland. It helped make Mickey the top box-office star in 1939, '40 and '41. What followed was a string of more musicals for the pair: *Strike Up the Band*, *Babes on Broadway* and *Girl Crazy*. The two became lifelong friends. In 1992, he described their relationship: "Judy and I were so close we could've come from the same womb. We weren't like brothers or sisters; there was no love affair. It's very, very difficult to explain the depth of our love for each other. It was so special; it was a forever love."

On the MGM lot, he met a then-unknown teen-

Mickey Rooney studio publicity still, ca. 1940.

World War II Veterans in Hollywood

Judy Garland with Rooney in a promo shot for *Babes in Arms* in 1939.

age actress, Ava Gardner, who was a virgin at the time, and who became his first wife. They were wed in January 1942. Due to Mickey's infidelity the marriage was short-lived, and they were divorced the following year. She discovered that he had cheated on her while she was in the hospital recovering from an appendectomy. "He went through the ladies like a hot knife through fudge," Ava said. Lana Turner, who had previously slept with Rooney, called him "Andy Hard-On."

Rooney was Ava's first husband. In 1945, she married band leader Artie Shaw, divorced him the following year and finally married Frank Sinatra in 1951. They divorced in 1957 after much tumult. Mickey, on the other hand, was married eight times. When he was asked if he would marry all eight again, he replied, "Absolutely, I loved every one of them."

After the Japanese attack on Pearl Harbor, Rooney tried to join up but was classified 4-F (unable to serve due to health issues). He had high blood pressure. Until he was finally accepted into the service, he and Judy Garland entertained troops at the USO, at bond drives and on Armed Forces Radio.

After starring with Elizabeth Taylor in *National Velvet* in June 1944, Mickey Rooney was finally inducted into the Army at Fort MacArthur in

18. Mickey Rooney

San Pedro, a harbor near Los Angeles. He was sent on a troop train to Fort Riley, Kansas, where he underwent basic training. Soon he became a squad leader. Another soldier in his squad claimed that his promotion was due to his celebrity status. "Not so," Rooney said, and the two got into a fist fight. Even though he was only 5 feet, 2 inches tall, Mickey was getting the better of the conflict when it was broken up by their sergeant. Mickey was as brash and feisty offstage as on. That night over beers in the base Enlisted Men's Club, the two made up. A great marksman, Rooney qualified as a sharpshooter. Later, he remarked that he enjoyed basic training.

After basic, Rooney was sent to Fort Sibert near Gadsden, Alabama, to train in chemical warfare. While there, he was invited to a screening of the new movie *National Velvet*, in which he had starred with 12-year-old Elizabeth Taylor. (The scenes in which Rooney appeared had been shot in Hollywood before he entered the Army.) At a party afterwards, Mickey was introduced to a 17-year-old beauty, Betty Jane Rase. She was a senior at Phillips High School in Birmingham. A talented singer, she was Miss Birmingham and Miss Alabama and was the fourth runner up in the 1944 Miss America Pageant. Mickey was smitten and, after talking with her for 15 minutes, proposed marriage. She accepted, and they were married on October 1, 1944. Due to his military orders, they had only one night together, but even so, Betty Jane became pregnant with Mickey Rooney, Jr., who was born on July 3, 1945.

Fresh from his one-night honeymoon, Rooney was reassigned to the 6817th Special Services Battalion. It was one of the units that the Army had created for front-line entertainment. The unit assembled in New York and, from there, boarded the ocean liner *Queen Mary*, bound for England. More than 7,000 troops were crammed into spaces designed for 1,000 passengers.

From England, Mickey and two other entertainers were sent to Europe. The shows they performed were called "jeep shows." Their first was only three miles from the front lines. Jeep show members ate C-rations and sometimes went for weeks without showers. They were required to carry guns and were outfitted the same as combatant infantry troops. Mustered out of the Army in 1946, Rooney was awarded a Bronze Star for "meritorious service in a combat zone." Some years later, he entertained troops in Korea.

Rooney returned to Hollywood after his discharge and starred in the 1946 movie *Love Laughs at Andy Hardy*. At the time, Elizabeth Taylor was working on a different film at the MGM studio. The authors of a 2015 book, *The Life and Times of Mickey Rooney*, claim to have interviewed Rooney shortly before his death. Mickey revealed that in 1946 his second wife, Betty Jane, had come to the studio to visit him. When she opened his dressing room door and found Mickey with 14-year-old Elizabeth, sans clothes, making love,

World War II Veterans in Hollywood

"PFC Mickey Rooney imitates some Hollywood actors for an audience of infantrymen of the 44th Division. Rooney is a member of a three-man unit making a jeep tour to entertain the troops." Photo by T5C Louis Weintraub, Kist, Germany, April 13, 1945 (National Archives).

Betty Jane immediately filed for divorce. She was pregnant at the time with their second son, Tim, who was born on January 4, 1947. During the interview, Rooney said, "I charmed women into bed with my sense of humor," and bragged about having sex with other movie stars, including Lana Turner and Judy Garland. Regarding Turner, he said that she was as oversexed as he was. Turner was married eight times, as was Rooney.

During the balance of the forties, Mickey appeared in five films, the best-known and best-received being the 1948 *Words and Music*. During the fifties, he was in a grand total of 22 movies and appeared on two television shows; one was *The Mickey Rooney Show*.

In January 1949, Lauren Bacall introduced Rooney to actress and model Martha Vickers at Ciro's nightclub on the Sunset Strip in West Hollywood. Martha had been in several movies; the most important was the 1948 film *The Big Sleep*, starring Humphrey Bogart and Lauren Bacall. Mickey asked her for

18. Mickey Rooney

a date, so she invited him to have dinner at her home, where she lived with her parents. The next night, Martha and her parents had dinner at Rooney's home. And the next day Mickey introduced Martha to his mother. That same month, January, the pair announced their engagement. But, alas, they were both still married to others. Martha started divorce procedures, and in May 1949, the divorce was final. On June 3, 1949, Rooney's divorce from Betty Jane was finalized and six hours later he married Martha.

After the marriage, Rooney told a newspaper, "I've got me a wonderful girl. If I don't make this one last, there's something wrong with me." But because of Mickey's marathon drinking, the union deteriorated. On April 12, 1950, they had a son, Theodore (Ted) Michael. At the end of 1950, Martha was fed up and asked Mickey for a divorce; they parted that December. Three months later, they reconciled, but in June 1951, she filed for divorce, charging him with cruelty while he claimed she was frigid. The divorce was finalized in September. She was awarded custody of Ted as well as a large alimony.

Rooney was in two movies in 1951: *The Strip* and *My Outlaw Brother*. In 1952 he was in *Sound Off*. In September, he made a 21-day trip to the war in Korea to entertain the troops. On his first day back, he met Elaine Devry. She had been a beauty queen at college and was previously married and divorced. After meeting Rooney, she spent every night with him for a month. Mickey proposed marriage, chartered a plane, and flew to Las Vegas, where they were married on November 15, 1952. Surprisingly, the marriage lasted for six years, and they had one child, William, whom they called Jimmy. Rooney and Elaine costarred in *The Atomic Kid*, released at the end of 1954. Mickey was in a total of 13 movies during the fifties.

In the movie made from James Michener's novel *The Bridges at Toko Ri*, released in 1954, Rooney starred with William Holden. Mickey's character was a rescue helicopter pilot, a new and dangerous occupation in those early days. There were news reports that Rooney took out his "on location frustrations" in a Tokyo hotel room.

The movie *The Bold and the Brave* was released in 1956. A World War II story, it was a smash hit that sold more than a million tickets. Mickey codirected and starred in it. He also wrote and sang the title song. Rooney received an Oscar nomination for Best Actor in a Supporting Role. The following year, *Baby Face Nelson* was released.

Mickey was introduced to Hollywood actress Barbara Ann Thomason (stage name Carolyn Mitchell) at a nightclub in 1958. Smitten, he bought her an expensive fur coat. Separated from Elaine, Rooney bought a house near Hollywood where he and Barbara lived together. Rooney, still married to Elaine, traveled to Mexico with Barbara and got a divorce there; they were

World War II Veterans in Hollywood

married on December 1, 1958. On September 13, 1959, they had a daughter, Kelly Ann.

The next year, 1960, a pregnant Barbara threatened to commit suicide if Mickey didn't get a legal divorce and remarry her in the U.S., which he finally did. Then came another daughter, Kerry Yule, on December 30, 1960. Two more children were to follow: Michael Joseph in 1962 and Kimmy Sue, the year following.

Next was the celebrated television show *Wagon Train*. Mickey was in two episodes, plus he did five other television shows. During the sixties, he appeared in 12 movies, mostly in supporting roles. Standouts were *Breakfast at Tiffany's*, in which he played star Audrey Hepburn's Japanese neighbor, *Requiem for a Heavyweight*, and *It's a Mad, Mad, Mad, Mad World*. These parts illustrated Rooney's incredible range. During that time, he received an Emmy Award and a Golden Globe.

In 1964, Mickey and Barbara were introduced to a young Yugoslavian actor, Milos Milosevic, with whom they became friends. In late 1965, when Mickey went on location to the Philippines to shoot *Ambush Bay*, he asked Milos to look after his wife. And look after her he did! He moved into the house with Barbara and also into her bed. When Mickey returned from the Philippines, he found out what Barbara and Milos had been doing and said he was filing for divorce. In January 1966, Rooney was in a hospital for treatment of a disease he had acquired on location. While there, Barbara and Milos were found dead in the home. Apparently the mentally unstable Milosevic, thinking he would lose her and afraid of what would happen to him for sleeping with the wife of a superstar, shot her dead and then himself on January 31, 1966. When told of his wife's murder, Mickey went into shock and stayed in the hospital. He said, "I died when she did. I am furious at what happened to her."

During Barbara's funeral, Rooney met Barbara's best friend, Marge Lane; both were mourning their loss. Feeling sorry for him, she moved into the Rooney home in order to help take care of the children. Next, the two started sleeping together. They were married on September 4, 1967. The marriage lasted two months until December 14, when they got a divorce. Later, Mickey said he could hardly remember her. When asked about Marge Lane in an interview with *People* magazine, he said, "I think that was her name."

At the end of the sixties, Rooney hadn't reached the end of his attempted attachments. Saying he couldn't be blamed for trying again, he whisked his secretary, Carolyn Hockett, off to Las Vegas and married her on May 27, 1969. He was 48 years old; she was 25. They celebrated the union by going on the road with the Broadway show *George M!* On January 11, 1970, they had a

18. Mickey Rooney

child, Jonelle. After hitting some rocky times, they divorced on January 24, 1975.

Rooney appeared in ten movies during the seventies and a television show, *Night Gallery*, in 1972. The last film then was *The Black Stallion*. It brought Mickey an Academy Award nomination as the Best Actor in a Supporting Role. He was on Broadway in nine shows and was nominated for a Tony Award in *Sugar Babies*.

While on Broadway, Rooney met and romanced a country and Western singer Janice Darlene Chamberlin. She had previously been married and divorced and had two children, Christopher and Mark. On July 18, 1978, Janice (Jan) and Mickey were married. She was 40 years old and he was almost 20 years older. "This time for keeps," Rooney said. The marriage did, in fact, turn out to be his longest.

From the eighties and on into the new century, Rooney remained active. He was in 13 Broadway shows, four during the eighties, six in the nineties and three after 2000. He also starred in 17 movies and 15 television shows. One of them was *The New Adventures of the Black Stallion*, for which he received a Gemini Award nomination. Mickey was given an Honorary Award for his lifetime of achievement by the Academy of Motion Picture Arts and Sciences.

In his seventies, Mickey Rooney turned to writing. His first book was his autobiography, *Life Is Too Short*, published in 1991. According to a review, "With crackling wisdom and great humor, Mickey takes us back and tells us about the early days, the wild parties and squandered fortunes. It's also about the dark days on the downside of fame ... the fabled friendships, torrid romances and legendary marriages." Then he wrote a novel, *The Search for Sunny Skies*, published in 1994. It's a tale about Hollywood and a fabulous child star of the old Hollywood system named Sunny Skies who won Oscar nominations before he was wearing long pants. Mickey had intended to write more novels but, as it turned out, this was the only one.

During his final years, things started going downhill for Rooney. He experienced elder abuse from Chris Aber, Jan Chamberlin's son from her first marriage, and Aber's wife. Mickey went to court for relief. It was alleged that Chris "threatens, intimidates, bullies and harasses" Mickey, who said he was "extremely fearful that Chris will become physically threatening and may even attempt to kidnap Mickey from his home." In February 2011, the judge ordered Chris and his wife to stay at least 100 yards from Rooney. The next month, Rooney, at age 91, went to Washington and appeared before the Senate Special Committee on Aging at the urging of Mark, the other son of Jan. He testified about his experiences as a victim of elder abuse. He said that his life was "unbearable, I felt trapped, scared, used and frustrated."

World War II Veterans in Hollywood

Rooney permanently separated from Jan in June 2012. Mark and his wife, Charlene, went to live with Mickey in order to take care of him. Mark, whose last name was actually Aber, assumed the last name Rooney. Meanwhile, there was a lot of controversy among the Aber children and Jan. But the three Rooneys, Mickey, Mark and Charlene, lived happily, focusing on healthy and peaceful living and spending some time getting together with old friends. In 2014, Rooney replayed his role as Gus in *Night at the Museum: Secret of the Tomb*. The movie honored Mickey, and it was his last.

On April 6, 2014, Rooney was taking his afternoon nap and never woke up. At that time, Mickey had three projects in which he was scheduled to perform. He had said, "There may be a little snow on the mountain, but there's a lot of fire in the furnace." His acting career lasted 89 years, the longest career in cinema history; he was the only actor to appear in at least one movie in ten consecutive decades. According to the *Guinness Book of World Records*, Mickey Rooney has the record for the longest movie career. He was honored with four stars on the Hollywood Walk of Fame: for acting in movies, television, live performances and radio.

A private funeral service for Rooney was held on April 19 at the Hollywood Forever Cemetery. Mickey left a legacy as one of the most enduring performers in show business.

19

Tyrone Power

Tyrone Power (often called Ty) was one of the most popular actors during the Golden Age of Hollywood. From the thirties through the fifties, Power, who started acting at age seven, was in 45 movies, had a number of radio appearances and was on the Broadway stage for much of his career. His classically handsome looks made him a matinee idol. He was among the 100 all-time box office stars. Descended from a long theatrical line going back more than 100 years, he served in the United States Marine Corps during World War II as a pilot in the Asia-Pacific Theater.

Tyrone Edmund Power III was born on May 5, 1914, in Cincinnati, Ohio. Both of his parents, Tyrone Power, Sr., and Helen Emma Reaume, acted on the stage. His great-great grandfather, an Irish stage comedian, made frequent trips to America. Tyrone's father, Tyrone Power, Sr., appeared in more than 20 Broadway productions during his career and played Brutus in *Julius Caesar* to critical acclaim.

During the first year of his life, Ty lived with his family in Cincinnati. He was a sickly infant, and his doctor advised them to move to a better climate for his health. The family moved to California in 1915. In August of that year, Tyrone's sister, Anne, was born.

In Southern California, his parents were in various plays on stage and in a movie together, *The Planter*, released in 1917. Senior was in several other silent films, but his stage career took him frequently back to New York. He and Helen (called Patia) drifted apart and were divorced in 1920.

Now single, Patia continued her stage acting and starred in *La Golondrina*, in the town of San Gabriel, near Los Angeles. Tyrone made his acting debut when he appeared in the play with his mother in 1921. He was seven years old. In 1923, his mother moved her family (Tyrone and Anne) back to Cincinnati.

Patia and her kids moved in with Patia's aunt, who ran a school known as the Schuster-Martin School of Drama. Patia supported her kids and herself as a drama and voice coach. Starting in 1924, Tyrone attended the Sisters

World War II Veterans in Hollywood

Tyrone Power with Ava Gardner in a publicity still for the 1957 movie *The Sun Also Rises*.

of Mercy Academy for grades four, five and six and St. Xavier Academy for grades seven, eight and nine. Finally, he attended Purcell High School, where he was active in school plays. In his senior year, Tyrone had the lead role in *Officer 666*. He worked part-time as a soda jerk at a nearby drug store and graduated in 1931.

The summer after graduation, Tyrone went to live with his father in Quebec, Canada, where his father coached Shakespearean acting. In September, he and his dad moved to Chicago. While there and still a teen, Tyrone got a job helping Don Ameche, who was a personality on NBC radio. The two struck up a friendship that lasted a lifetime. Ty's father was playing the duke of Venice in *The Merchant of Venice* at the Chicago Civic Auditorium. He got his son a small role in the play. His dad was given a part in the movie *The Miracle Man*, and the two went to Hollywood, where they took a room at the Hollywood Athletic Club. While living at the club, Tyrone Power Sr. had a massive heart attack, collapsed, and died in his son's arms on December 21, 1931. The funeral was on January 2, 1932.

Tyrone decided to stay in Hollywood and try for parts in movies. The

19. Tyrone Power

going was difficult, but he finally got a bit part in *Tom Brown of Culver*, released June 12. He kept trying for other roles, but without success, so he got involved in community theater. On May 16, 1933, he had a part in *Lo and Behold* at the Pasadena Community Playhouse. To keep going, he worked as a chauffeur for one of his father's friends. Even though he got a bit part in *Flirtation Walk*, released in 1934, he decided to go to New York to try for Broadway.

First, Tyrone was cast as an understudy to Burgess Meredith in the play *Flowers of the Forest*. Next, he got real roles in *Romeo and Juliet* in 1935 and *Saint Joan* in 1936. His work in these two plays received good reviews. This got him a screen test at 20th Century Fox and a movie contract in 1936. First Power got small parts in *Girls' Dormitory* and *Ladies in Love* that reviewers liked. *The New York Post* wrote, "Tyrone Power, Jr., is as handsome as everyone seems to think Robert Taylor is."

Power's first major role in a movie was in *Lloyds of London*, released at the end of 1936. He starred with Madeleine Carroll. This propelled him to major stardom and earned him a seven-year contract with 20th Century Fox.

Tyrone starred with Loretta Young in three romantic film comedies—*Love Is News*, *Café Metropole* and *Second Honeymoon* in 1937. This led to the two becoming romantically involved. It soon became a passionate involvement, and there was talk of marriage. Years later, Loretta said, "I was crazy about him." The studio was opposed to their romance and it came to an end.

While working on the movie *Suez* in 1938, he became involved with his co-star, Annabella (whose birth name was Suzanne Georgette Charpentier). She was a French actress, and they met during the filming on the

Power with actress Linda Darnell in a publicity still for the 1940 movie *Mark of Zorro*.

World War II Veterans in Hollywood

20th Century lot. She was a huge star in Europe and had been brought to the U.S., where she was given a big buildup. They got married on April 23, 1939.

The 1940 film *The Mark of Zorro* starred Power, Linda Darnell and Basil Rathbone. It was nominated for an Academy Award for its original score. After the movie's success, he was considered among the finest of the screen's swashbuckling heroes. His duel with Basil Rathbone was ranked among the best in movie history. From then until 1942, Power was in eight movies, some of which he was not that happy with.

In August 1942, Tyrone Power put his burgeoning career on hold and enlisted in the Marine Corps. At the request of 20th Century, he was allowed to do one more movie, *Crash Dive*, a patriotic war movie in which he was credited as Tyrone Power, U.S.M.C.R. The film served as a recruiting vehicle as much as anything else. His leading lady in it, Anne Baxter, was to become his favorite, both on the screen and the stage.

He decided to start out as a private and refused the studio's offer to get him an officer's commission. First, he was sent to boot camp at the Marine Corps Recruit Depot in San Diego. He did so well there that he was sent to Officer's Candidate School at the Marine Corps Base in Quantico, Virginia. After graduation, he was commissioned a second lieutenant on June 2, 1943.

Power's prewar hobby and pastime was flying his own airplane. When he joined the Marine Corps, he already had some 180 solo hours. With this background, and at his request, he was sent to a flight training program at the Naval Air Station at Corpus Christi, Texas. His instructor said, "He was an excellent student, never forgot a procedure I showed him or anything I told him." Tyrone got his wings there and was promoted to first lieutenant.

Power was assigned to Marine Transport Squadron VMR 352 as a transport copilot in July 1944. The squadron moved to the Marine Corps Air Station in El Toro, California, in October. Lieutenant Power was reassigned to Squadron VMR 353. This squadron was equipped with R5D airplanes, the Navy version of the Army's C-54, which in turn was the military version of the Douglas DC-4. The DC-4 is a four-engine passenger airplane that had replaced the venerable two-engine DC-3 designated C-47 by the Army. He joined his squadron on Kwajalein Atoll in the Marshall Islands in February 1945. From there, he flew missions to carry cargo into and wounded Marines out of the combat area during the battle for Iwo Jima in February and March of 1945. Then he did the same during the battle for Okinawa from April to June 1945. Undoubtedly the unarmed planes he was flying into combat zones were easy prey for the enemy, but luckily, he survived. Others who served with him commented on how well Power was respected. During his service, he tried to downplay his Hollywood stardom and be a good soldier doing

19. Tyrone Power

his duty. His diligence and respect for training and protocol was noted by his superiors.

For his services in the Pacific, Power was awarded the American Campaign Medal, the Asiatic-Pacific Campaign Medal with two bronze stars and the World War II Victory Medal. He returned to the U.S. in November 1945 and was released from active duty in January 1946. (Rather than being discharged, he chose to remain in the USMC Reserve Corps.)

Tyrone Power returned to Hollywood, where he got a starring role in *The Razor's Edge* along with Anne Baxter and Clifton Webb. The film was widely praised by critics. Power and his costars were nominated for Oscars and his costars actually received them. Next, he went on to *Nightmare Alley*, a dark and gruesome story about a con man's rise and fall. When the movie was released in 1947, Tyrone received some of the best reviews of his career.

Power as a pilot in a US Marine Corps photo.

Separated from his wife, Annabella, he began a love affair with Lana Turner in 1948. Ty started going out with her because he was lonely. "She's beautiful, appealing, lively, witty and great fun," he remarked. Widely covered by the press, the affair was called one of the great romances in the history of Hollywood. The studio executives, however, were not happy. But they realized that Lana had a terrific crush on Ty. She even flew down to Mexico to be with him while he was making a movie there. Intellectually, though, the two were completely mismatched. Lana was volatile, emotional and intuitively perceptive. Tyrone was logical and methodical. The only thing they had in common was their careers. Power purchased a home in Brentwood and asked Lana to decorate it. She spent weeks supervising the work, shopping for drapes and rugs and making sure the colors blended.

In the fall of 1948, Tyrone set out on a goodwill trip around the world, flying his own airplane. He went with his friend, Bob Buck, who was an experienced pilot. First, they visited a number of places in Europe and then South Africa. Often Power was mobbed by fans. The highlight of the trip was when he met Jan Christian Smuts in South Africa, Haile Selassie in Ethiopia and His Holiness the pope. During the trip, Tyrone decided to end the affair with Lana.

While he was in Rome, Ty met and romanced Linda Christian. She was a red-haired beauty who *Life* magazine called "The Anatomical Bomb." She had had a number of bit parts in movies but had a leading role in *Tarzan and the Mermaids* in 1948. Ty proposed, and they were married on January 27, 1949, at the Church of Santa Francesca in Rome. It attracted a lot of publicity and thousands of fans were outside the church. Lana, however, had expected a proposal of marriage when he returned.

Linda said he was "the greatest love of my life," which was really saying something, as she was notorious for having affairs. During their six-year marriage, Linda had three miscarriages before finally, in 1951, she had a girl, Romina. Another girl, Taryn, was born in 1953. The marriage came to an end after Linda accused Ty of having numerous affairs. Linda, though, also had an extramarital affair—with the actor Edmund Purdom. Ty and Linda divorced in 1956.

Power went to England in 1950 to star in *Mr. Roberts* on the stage at the London Coliseum. It had sell-out crowds and played for 23 weeks. Then it was back to Broadway for *John Brown's Body*. In addition, he did two Lux Radio Theatre episodes with Debra Paget and Linda Christian. In 1953, Power starred in *The Mississippi Gambler*. He had made a deal that gave him a percentage of the profits in addition to his salary. Consequently, he earned a million dollars from this one movie.

In 1956, Power starred in *The Eddy Duchin Story*, playing the part of the famed band leader. The next year, he was in *Abandon Ship*, for which his costar was the Swedish actress Mai Zitterling, with whom he had a love affair. He then had another affair with British actress Thelma Ruby. After two more films, he was in *Witness for the Prosecution*, released in 1957, in which he gave a great performance.

On May 7, 1958, Ty met, fell in love with and married Deborah Ann Minardos. In September the two went to Madrid because Power was to be in the epic movie *Solomon and Sheba*, costarring with Gina Lollobrigida. After completing about three-quarters of the film, he had a massive heart attack while dueling with costar George Sanders.

Power was taken to a hospital in Madrid. The doctor there diagnosed him with fulminant angina pectoris. He died on November 15, 1958, at age 44.

19. Tyrone Power

His death was probably due to hereditary heart disease. Not only that, he was a heavy smoker, smoking sometimes three to four packs a day, plus several bowlfuls of pipe tobacco.

The body was returned to Hollywood, where he was interred at the Hollywood Forever Cemetery. The memorial service was held on November 21 with full military honors and a sermon by Navy Chaplain Thomas Gibson. The pallbearers were officers of the Marine Corps. In his eulogy, Caesar Romero said, "I shall always remember Tyrone as a bountiful man, a man who gave freely of himself. It mattered not to whom he gave. His concern was in the giving. I shall always remember his wonderful smile, a smile that would light up the darkest hour of the day, like a sunburst. I shall always think of Tyrone Power as a man who gave more than himself than it was wise for him to give, until in the end, he gave his life." Among the number of celebrities in attendance were Yul Brynner, Mary Pickford, Buddy Rogers, Charles Laughton, Raymond Massey, George Cohen and Lew Wasserman. Thousands thronged outside. Henry King, who had directed Power in 11 movies, flew over the funeral procession and memorial park in his private plane. King said, "Knowing his love for flying, I felt he was with me."

Tyrone and Deborah's son, Tyrone Power (the fourth), was born on January 22, 1959, a month or so after his death. Ty would have been delighted, as he always wanted a son. Power's daughters, Romina and Taryn, plus his son, followed in their father's footsteps in show business.

20

Charles Bronson

After serving in World War II, Charles Bronson went on to become an international star. He was a favorite in both the U.S. and abroad for 50 years and created movie history. He was an example of a person who applied his talent and passion to achieve great success. His facial appearance and a muscular physique had him playing macho and macabre roles. During the sixties, he was both a leading man and a leading support actor in Hollywood movies. Bronson even starred in his own television series on CBS. But his success came after an early life of hardship.

Charles Dennis Buchinsky was born on November 3, 1921, at Ehrenfield, Pennsylvania. His father, Walter Buchinsky, was an ethnic Russian from Lithuania. Lithuania is one of the three Baltic countries that include Latvia and Estonia. They are on the Baltic Sea between Russia and Poland and were the filling in a sandwich of historic violence that existed in that area. His mother, Mary, was born in Pennsylvania, although her parents were also from Lithuania. He was the 11th of 15 children. When Bronson was a youth, the family spoke only Lithuanian and Russian. He didn't learn to speak English until he was a teen.

Ehrenfield was a company town run by the Pennsylvania Coal and Coke Co. Charles's father worked in the coal mines, as he had in Lithuania, but died when Charles was only ten years old. Without the main breadwinner, the family fell into poverty. To survive, he and his brothers had to work in the coal mines, even while attending school. They earned a dollar per ton mined. One time, Charles was caught in a cave-in and almost died before being rescued. Bronson graduated from South Fork High School in 1940, the first of his family to finish high school.

Then it was back to the coal mines full time for three years until he was 22, when he joined the Army on March 17, 1943. Buchinsky enlisted voluntarily as he was about to be drafted.

After basic training he was sent to Kingman Army Airfield in Arizona and assigned to the 760th Flexible Gunnery Training Squadron. He drove a

20. Charles Bronson

Charles Bronson in *Raid on Entebbe* (1977). Bronson has portrayed the "tough guy" in many films (publicity photo).

truck and worked in the mess hall before being trained as an aerial gunner.

Like many World War II soldiers, Charles Buchinsky came from a dirt poor and limited intellectual life. Unlike middle-class soldiers, he found the three square meals and a clean bed each day a gift from God. During his youth he had had a sense that there was more to life than digging coal. He would leave his friends to their games and go off into the woods and fend for himself. If he could catch a feral chicken, he would cook it over a wood fire and contemplate the natural world around him.

Kingman Army Airfield was part of a large gunnery range established at the beginning of World War II. Buchinsky first flew as a gunner on B-25 Mitchell bombers. As they flew over the range, they would fire live ammo at targets towed by other planes or aim gun cameras at attacking P-39 fighters.

When Buchinsky was ready for combat, he became part of Captain Ken Trow's B-29 crew flying off of Guam to attack the Japanese homeland. They were a part of the 61st Squadron of the 39th Bomb Group. The 39th Bomb Group arrived in Guam on February 18, 1945, and lived in tents while they built more permanent Quonset huts.

In addition to performing raids on Japan, the 61st aided the Army and Marines with bombing runs over Iwo Jima and Okinawa. During the first half of 1945 Buchinsky flew 25 combat missions. In an attack on Iwo Jima, he was struck in the shoulder with shrapnel from an anti-aircraft burst. He was awarded a Purple Heart for this wound. Having risen to the rank of sergeant, he was at Camp Atterbury, Indiana, when he was discharged in April 1946.

World War II Veterans in Hollywood

In retrospect, Charles remarked that joining the Army was one of the best things that happened to him. For the first time, he was well fed and well dressed. Also, he had the opportunity to improve his use of the English language.

After leaving the Army, Buchinsky returned to Philadelphia and worked at many odd jobs. Always interested in art and painting, he attended the Hussian School of Art on the GI Bill in 1947. The Plays and Players Theater employed him to design and paint scenery. The repertory company that performed there gave him some minor acting roles, so he dropped out of the art school and decided to pursue an acting career.

Buchinsky got a job at an amusement pier in Atlantic City to make some money. Later he and another actor friend, Jack Klugman, moved to New York City with the idea of trying to get acting jobs. In 1948, they rented a one-room apartment where they lived together. Klugman did better at getting jobs, but Buchinsky landed a few small parts. He said, "It seemed like an easy way to make money."

Buchinsky started dating an actress, Harriett Tendler, whom he had met in Philadelphia in 1947. He was 26 and she was 18 years old. Her father was a successful Jewish dairy farmer who was not very happy with the relationship, partly because Charles was Catholic and she Jewish. In addition, the prospective groom didn't have much of an income. Nevertheless, her father finally agreed, and they were married on September 30, 1949. She helped support the new family by working in a department store.

In November 1949, Charles and Harriett moved to Southern California, where Buchinsky enrolled in the Pasadena Playhouse. At that time, this was one of the best ways to develop your talent. While there, Buchinsky was able to get uncredited bit parts in two movies. One of his teachers at Pasadena was so impressed with Buchinsky that he recommended the budding actor to movie director Henry Hathaway, resulting in Charles being cast as a Polish American sailor in the 1951 film *You're in the Navy Now*. He said he got the part because he could belch on cue. This was also an uncredited role, as were a number of others. In four more, he was credited as Charles Buchinsky.

In 1953, he played the part of Captain Jack in the Western *Drum Beat*. This time, he changed his stage name to Bronson because he felt that Buchinsky might hinder his career. A street of that name is near Paramount Studios.

Charles's outstanding performance in *Drum Beat* led to more parts in movies. He was popular with directors because he was always on time and knew his lines. For the most part during the fifties, Bronson played Slavs, American Indians, hoodlums and convicts. He had the lead in an episode—"The Apache Kid"—on the television series *Sheriff of Cochise*. More

20. Charles Bronson

appearances on television series followed: *Alfred Hitchcock Presents, Gunsmoke, The Millionaire, M Squad* and *Have Gun Will Travel.*

The 1954 movie *Vera Cruz* was filmed in Mexico. Both Bronson and Ernest Borgnine played American gringo gunfighters. One day, the two went to a nearby town to buy cigarettes. They rode on their horses in costume with pistols on their belts. The Mexican police assumed they were bandits and took them into custody at gunpoint. Of course, they said they were actors, and they were finally released when this was verified.

In 1958, Bronson had the lead in *Man with a Camera,* an ABC weekly 30-minute series that ran through 1960. He was in all 29 episodes. In it, he played a freelance photojournalist in New York who helps police solve crime. His salary was $2,000 a week. After *Drum Beat*, 14 more movies followed during that decade. He had the leads in *Gang War* and *Showdown at Boot Hill*. Outstanding was *Machine Gun Kelly*, in 1958, where he starred as Kelly.

Charles Bronson and Harriett Tendler came to a parting of the ways in 1965. Before the high-profile divorce, they had two children: Tony and Suzanne. He had been carrying on a torrid affair with English actress Jill Ireland, his costar in *The Great Escape*, being filmed in Germany. But what became of

Bronson (left) with Lee Marvin in the 1967 WWII movie *The Dirty Dozen*, based on a novel by the same title. Many of the supporting cast members were WWII veterans (publicity still).

World War II Veterans in Hollywood

Harriett? She had put her own career on hold to be a housewife. She took care of their home, washed and ironed the family clothing and raised their children. After the divorce, Harriett pursued a career as a radio talk show hostess on a number of stations in Los Angeles. In addition, she was the author of three books including *Charlie and Me*, about her marriage to Bronson.

After the parting, Charles was in eight movies, but only one, the 1967 *The Dirty Dozen*, was a real success. Bronson and Ireland were married on October 5, 1968. She was 32 and he 47. She had started her acting career in 1955 doing bit parts. Jill had married another actor, David McCallum, in 1957. The two appeared together in a number of television series. They had three sons and divorced in 1967. Jill and Charles had two daughters, Zuleika and Katrina; Katrina was adopted. Afterward, Bronson and Ireland were in 15 movies together, some of which were hits. He turned down a role in *Firepower* because there was no part for Jill.

Bronson had a French actor friend, Alain Delon, who helped Charles get hired to costar with Alain in *Adieu l'Ami*, filmed in Europe. Released in 1968, the British-French movie was a huge success. The next year came another hit, *Once Upon a Time in the West*. This was followed by *Rider in the Rain* in 1970 and the next year, *Red Sun*, wherein he costarred with legendary Japanese actor Toshirô Mifune. This extended Bronson's popularity from the U.S. to Europe and Asia. Bronson discovered that Europeans didn't buy into the Hollywood idea that only extraordinarily good-looking guys could play the leads in movies. They liked the naturally rugged-looking tough guy, Charles Bronson. Ironically, Bronson's work in Europe made him a Hollywood Star. Also, ironically,

Bronson stars in the 1968 epic western film *Once Upon a Time in the West*, with costars Henry Fonda, Jason Robards and Claudia Cardinale (publicity still).

20. Charles Bronson

Sergio Leone was a good friend and had directed him in *Once Upon a Time in the West*, but when Sergio offered Bronson the starring roles in the spaghetti Westerns that made Clint Eastwood a star, Charles turned them down.

In 1972, Bronson starred in *The Valachi Papers*, which was his first real part as a lead actor in the U.S. He was paid a million dollars plus 2 percent of the profits. His next three films were only modest successes; then in *Death Wish* in 1974, he was cast as the avenging angel. Until then, he had never had his name on a movie marquee. He was 53 years old when it came out. In it, he gave what was arguably his best performance, although critics didn't like it. But the public did, and the picture grossed over $20 million and was the high point of Bronson's career. Four even more violent *Death Wish* sequels followed.

"We don't make movies for critics," Bronson said; "They don't pay to see them anyhow." He had told his agent, Paul Kohner, that if he became a big star, he would give Paul a Rolls-Royce. Sure enough, he delivered a new Rolls to Kohner's house.

Bronson was also a successful artist and painter. He signed his work with his real name, Charles Buchinsky. In a one-man show at a Beverly Hills gallery, every piece displayed was sold. When he was young, he liked to draw things. "I'd get butcher paper or grocery bags and draw on them. At school,

Bronson (left) stars as Paul Kersey with Stuart Margolin as Ames in the 1974 action movie *Death Wish*, where Bronson becomes a vigilante to get revenge on the streets of New York City for the murder of his wife (publicity still).

World War II Veterans in Hollywood

I was the one who got to draw on windows with soap. It just seemed I just knew how to draw."

In 1983, Charles and Jill adopted Katrina Holden after her mother, Hilary, died. Jill Ireland was diagnosed with breast cancer in 1984. As a result, she wrote two books regarding her fight with cancer. Just before she died, she was at work on a third. She was a spokesperson for the American Cancer Society, and, in 1988, she spoke before a U.S. congressional committee about the medical costs of cancer. President Ronald Reagan presented her with the American Cancer Society's Courage Award.

Death Wish 3 came out in 1985. Bronson was unhappy with the director because gory scenes were filmed with extras when Bronson was not around. For *Death Wish 4*, he made $4 million and for *Death Wish 5*, $5 million plus $6 million from his share of the profits.

Jill Dorothy Ireland died on May 18, 1990. She had been suffering from her breast cancer for six years. She was only 54 years old and the true love of Bronson's life. They had lived together in a Bel Air mansion with seven children, two from his previous marriage, three of hers, two of their own. She had appeared in 35 movies and 19 times on television. She has a star on the Hollywood Walk of Fame. Charles was very active raising funds for the John Wayne Cancer Institute.

In 1998 Bronson had hip replacement surgery. From then on, he was seldom in good health. A heavy smoker, he suffered from severe chronic obstructive pulmonary disease and retired from acting. Also, that year, he married Kim Weeks. Charles had met her when she was working at the Dove Audio Company recording Jill Ireland's production of her audiobooks.

In 1999, *Family of Cops 3* was released. It was the last of three television movies and Bronson had starred in all of them. It was his very last. (It had been filmed before he retired.)

Bronson was diagnosed with Alzheimer's disease in 2000 and died three years later on August 30, 2003. Charles, born Charles Dennis Buchinsky, was 81 years old. He left an estate worth $48 million including a house in Malibu worth $8 million, a $4.8 million beach house and a ranch in Vermont. In addition, he had homes in Lithuania and Greece.

He received a special Golden Globe Award for being chosen a world film favorite in a poll conducted in 60 countries. Famed director Sergio Leone called him "the greatest actor I ever worked with." Six books have been written about Bronson. A career of blockbuster movies and a lifetime of achievement as an actor sum up Charles Bronson's life. In summary, he was in 73 movies and 27 television shows.

21

Tony Curtis

Tony Curtis was one of the most successful actors during the fifties and sixties. Well known for his good looks, smooth charm, and dashing and debonair style, he brought tremendous charisma and energy to everything he was in. One of the most prolific stars ever, he appeared in more than a hundred movies and many television shows. His leading man appeal grew from his almost neurotic intensity. In addition, he was a book author, artist, and philanthropist and was decorated for his service in the Navy during World War II.

Bernard Schwartz (whose screen name was Tony Curtis) was born on June 3, 1925, in Manhattan, New York City. Both his parents were Jewish emigrants; his father, Emanuel, was from Hungary; his mother, Helen, from Czechoslovakia. Yiddish was the language spoken at home, and Bernard didn't learn to speak English until he was five or six years old. Bernard and his brothers, Julius and Robert, grew up in extreme poverty. Bernard was very close to Julius and helped take care of him. Their father worked as a tailor and struggled to make ends meet on his meager income. They lived in a very small area in back of the shop, all five sleeping in one room. Home life wasn't very happy. The parents were always arguing over money. His mother was frustrated, vindictive and unstable. She even beat him and was later diagnosed with schizophrenia, as was Robert. Later, Bernard said, "When I was a child, mom beat me up and was very aggressive and antagonistic." When he was just a kid, he got his first experience at acting. He got a role in a neighborhood play about King Arthur's adventures—and, because of his looks, he played the part of a girl.

When Bernard was eight, his parents took him and Julius to an orphanage because they were having trouble taking care of three boys and trouble feeding them. The two stayed there for only a month before they were returned home. When Bernard was 13, Julius was hit and killed by a truck on First Avenue and 78th Street in 1938. The parents made Bernard go by himself to identify the body. The two boys had become inseparable, the most important people in each other's lives. Despondent, Bernard joined a youth gang, skipping school and indulging in minor crime.

Bernard attended Seward Park High School in Manhattan. He graduated when he was 17 and wanted to join the Navy because of the Japanese attack. His reason for the Navy was that his film hero, Cary Grant, played a sailor in the movie *Destination Tokyo*. Because you had to be 18 to join, he forged his mother's signature and enlisted in the Navy in 1943.

After basic training, Bernard went to the Navy's Signalman School in Illinois and graduated as a signalman third class. While there and during off hours and just for fun, the students put on a stage play wherein Bernard performed as a sailor. After graduation, he was assigned to serve as a signalman aboard the USS *Proteus*, a submarine tender. The *Proteus* was one of five new tenders that reported to the Pacific Fleet in San Diego and became part of Submarine Squadron 20 in the Pacific Theater. The *Proteus* took care of 26 subs, at different times performing complete refits and repairs on them. None of the subs were lost to the enemy. The squadron submarines fired some 350 torpedoes, scoring 132 hits that resulted in the sinking of 56 enemy ships and damaging nine others.

Tony Curtis, 1958 (publicity photo).

When the Japanese surrendered on September 2, 1945, on board the USS *Missouri* in Tokyo Bay, the *Proteus* was about a mile away, so its sailors witnessed the historic event through binoculars. Bernard received an official document certifying his presence onboard the USS *Proteus* in Tokyo Bay during the formal surrender of the Japanese forces to the Allied Powers, signed by admirals Chester Nimitz, William F. Halsey and Charles A. Lockwood. Bernard actually liked being in the Navy; he said, "They were like a mother should be, they fed and clothed me. They fixed my teeth and gave me

21. Tony Curtis

a job." It's interesting to note that in the 1959 movie *Operation Petticoat*, Bernard played a naval officer opposite his boyhood hero, Cary Grant.

Signalman Third Class Bernard Schwartz received an honorable discharge from the Navy in 1945 with three medals: the World War II Victory, the Asia-Pacific and the American Area. He returned to New York and attended city college using the GI Bill and studied acting at the New School in Greenwich Village. While there, he ran into his high school classmate, Walter Matthau.

In 1947 Bernard enrolled in the New York Dramatic Workshop and appeared in a number of small parts on Broadway in plays including *Twelfth Night* and *Golden Boy*. Then he acted on the "Borscht Belt" circuit in the Catskills. Curtis was in a play about anti–Semitism and the Jewish experience in America titled *This Too Shall Pass*. He also briefly acted in the Chicago Yiddish Theater.

By then, he went by the name Anthony Curtis. He was discovered by a talent agent, Joyce Selznick (David O. Selznick's niece), who persuaded him to give Hollywood a try. When he arrived there in 1948, Joyce got him a seven-year contract with Universal Pictures. He began appearing in bit and supporting roles; the first was *Criss Cross*, in 1949. This was followed by five more films that year. Regarding his arrival in Hollywood, he was credited as saying, "I was 22 when I arrived. I had more action than Mount Vesuvius—men, women, animals! I loved it too."

Anthony had an important role in the action Western *Sierra* in 1950. He did so well that he was next cast in the big-budget film *Winchester '73*, acting

Tony Curtis (PO3 Bernard Schwartz), military portrait.

Curtis as young Houdini, with costar Janet Leigh (who became his wife) as Bess, in the 1953 Paramount Pictures movie *The Great Houdini*. The film's storyline is a fictionalized account of Houdini's life as a world-renowned escape artist and magician (publicity still).

alongside another veteran, the legendary James Stewart. He met Janet Leigh on the movie lot and, although studio executives were opposed, they eloped and got married by a judge in Greenwich, Connecticut. Jerry Lewis was his best man. Regarding the marriage, he said, "I married Janet for my career. I

21. Tony Curtis

could see that the two of us could get more attention together. We had the paparazzi wherever we went; we were on the cover of all the movie magazines. It wasn't enough for a man to be cute; he had to be connected to the right woman." What better way to get famous? The two starred together in the 1953 film *Houdini*. They had two daughters, Kelly in 1956 and Jamie Lee in 1958; both later became actresses themselves.

During the fifties, Tony was in a large number of movies; 32, in fact. They were largely forgettable dramas and genre pictures. Some were outstanding, however. For the 1957 film *Sweet Smell of Success*, he not only starred but was also the executive producer. Others were *Trapeze*, the aforementioned *Operation Petticoat* and *The Defiant Ones*. In this one, Curtis insisted that African American actor Sidney Poitier be his costar. This broke a Hollywood taboo of the time.

The classic comedy *Some Like It Hot* was filmed at the Hotel del Coronado in San Diego and starred Marilyn Monroe and Tony Curtis. Released in 1959, it was voted the number one comedy of all time by the American Film Institute, which also placed it number 14 on its list of 100 greatest movies. On meeting Marilyn, Tony said, "You could tell she'd been battered by life, and I found out that she'd been in an orphanage, as I had, and that her mother was also schizophrenic. I love her. And she loved me. I'm in love with her now. I've loved her all these years. There wasn't a guy that was safe. If she liked you, there was no man who could resist." Later, he claimed to have had two affairs with Marilyn, but this has not been substantiated.

Tony and Janet Leigh starred together in one more film, *Who Was That Lady?* It was a comedy and also had Dean Martin in a leading role. Then came a big one for Tony in 1960: *Spartacus*. It is the story of a slave revolt in antiquity. Kirk Douglas was in the title role with Laurence Olivier as a roman general and Tony Curtis as Emperor Antonius. It won four Academy Awards and became the biggest moneymaker in Universal Studio's history. It was one of five films of the era chosen as being "culturally, historically or aesthetically significant" by the Library of Congress.

During the sixties, Curtis was in a total of 24 movies as well as four television shows including *Rowan & Martin's Laugh-In* and *The Ed Sullivan Show*.

Although Tony and Janet appeared to be the idyllic picture of an attractive married couple, this was not the case. About his sexuality, he said, "I ran around with a lump in my pants, chased all the girls. It was love. I was falling in love every day." While still married to Janet, he was fooling around with Christine Kaufmann, who was his costar in the 1962 movie *Taras Bulba* and in the comedy, *40 Pounds of Trouble*. She was 18 years old. In 1962 he divorced Janet, and he married Christine the next year. They had two daughters: Alexandra in 1964 and Allegra in 1966. They were divorced in 1968 and Christine went back to acting, which she had forgone during the marriage.

Four days after the divorce, Tony married Leslie Allen, a 23-year-old actress; he was 43. The marriage lasted until 1982, during which time she appeared with Curtis in the 1976 movie *The Last Tycoon*. They had two boys, Nicholas and Benjamin.

During the seventies, Curtis struggled with his addiction to alcohol and drugs. Nevertheless, he appeared on nine television shows including *The Persuaders!* and *Vega$*, on both of which he was a series regular. In addition, he was in nine movies, all low profile. Then Tony started a second career as an artist. "I still make movies," he said, "but I'm not that interested in them anymore." His paintings were seen at a gallery in Carmel, California, and *The Red Table* was displayed in the Metropolitan Museum of Art in New York City. His work gets significant prices. He tried to cure his addictions at the Betty Ford Center in Palm Springs.

Still at it in the eighties, he was in 14 films and eight television shows. All but seven were television movies except one episode in *The Fall Guy*. In 1983 he and Leslie Allen divorced, leaving her with their two boys. Curtis and Andrea Savio got married the next year. She was 21 at the time. Andrea was an actress, having played ingénue roles in the theater as a teen. In Hollywood, she had already been in three movies when she met Tony. He made it impossible for her to continue in films, as they traveled frequently. He refused to let her audition anymore. Her marriage to Curtis was her only one, and afterward, she returned to Florida where she became involved in politics. In 1987 he founded the Emanuel Foundation for Hungarian Culture and became its honorary chairman. It works for the restoration and preservation of Hungarian synagogues.

Tony was on television a number of times during the nineties, including four episodes on *Biography* wherein he was the interviewee. Five others were television movies. He was also in ten films. In 1992 he divorced Andrea Savio; he married Lisa Deutsch, a lawyer, the next year. Although he had dated Lisa during the previous year, the union was short and sweet; he divorced her after only ten months. Curtis had heart bypass surgery after a heart attack in 1994, possibly because of all his marriages, dalliances and addictions. In 1998 he married Jill Vandenberg, 42 years younger and the last of his six marriages.

After the turn of the century, Curtis was in four television shows, mostly appearing as himself. Tony was on the stage in 2002, starring in a musical version of *Some Like It Hot* at the Fox Theater in Atlanta, Georgia. He was also in a few more movies. His very last was *David and Fatima*, released in 2008.

During the new century, Tony shifted gears and concentrated on writing

21. Tony Curtis

and art. In 1993, he wrote his first book, *Tony Curtis: The Autobiography*. This was followed in 2008 by a second autobiography, *American Prince: A Memoir* and then two the next year, *The Making of* Some Like It Hot and *Some Like It Hot: Me, Marilyn and the Movie*. Tony said he enjoys painting. In 2005 New York City's Museum of Modern Art acquired one of his canvasses for its permanent collection. He said, "Painting is more meaningful to me than any performance I've ever given." And he enjoyed playing the flute for pleasure and relaxation.

Curtis and his wife, Jill, became involved in the fate of horses. They founded the Shiloh Horse Rescue to save abused, neglected and unwanted horses bound for the slaughterhouse. By 2010, more than 550 horses had been rescued and about 150 were living on their 40-acre sanctuary. Their efforts were featured in a 2008 documentary film, *The Jill & Tony Curtis Story*. Regarding Jill, he said, "She's the only one who didn't want me to change after I married her."

Tony Curtis died in 2010; he was 85. Beforehand, he remarked, "What's the secret to a long and happy life? Young women's saliva!" At a book signing in Henderson, Nevada, on July 8, he was taken to a hospital, having fallen ill due to an asthma attack. Afterwards, he was sent home, where he suffered a cardiac arrest and died on September 29.

He left behind his wife, Jill; two daughters with Janet Leigh, Kelly Lee and Jamie Lee; two daughters with Christine Kaufmann, Alexandra and Allegra; and a son, Benjamin, with Leslie Allen.

Curtis was laid to rest at the Palm Memorial Park Cemetery in Henderson. The funeral was supposed to be a private reception at the Luxor Hotel and Casino in Las Vegas on October 4. Although only 200 were invited, more than 400 celebrities, friends and family members gathered there together to say goodbye. Honorary pallbearers included Kirk Kerkorian, Kirk Douglas and Phyllis McGuire. Rabbi Mel Hecht led the room in Jewish prayers and remarked, "He was one of the greats of our culture and our society." His widow, Jill, eulogized him: "He dismissed our 45-year age difference when friends asked if he was worried about keeping up with a younger wife. Don't dwell on his death, but on his extraordinary life. He was a once-in-a-lifetime man."

Daughter Jamie Lee Curtis said, "My dad was a little 'mashugana' [Yiddish for crazy, but full of life]. All of us got something from him. I, of course, got his desperate need for attention." The two had been estranged for much of her life, but eventually had reconciled, she said. He took pride in his daughter's onscreen acting.

Rabbi Hecht brought California governor Arnold Schwarzenegger forward to say farewell. Arnold and Tony had been friends for more than 30

World War II Veterans in Hollywood

years. When Arnold came to Hollywood, Curtis acted as his mentor. "He drove sports cars that made him feel young, always dated beautiful young women to make him feel young, and then he ended up with an extraordinary young woman, Jill, of course." The governor brought down the house when he said, "I don't know if you saw the picture of him, naked, in *Vanity Fair* magazine. He was just standing there, at the age of 80, celebrating his 80th birthday standing there by the swimming pool with Jill at his side. Who has the guts to have his picture taken at age 80, naked? He felt like he was 21 years old. Everyone else in the history of mankind put a fig leaf in front of their private parts, but his were so big they had to have two dogs standing in front of him."

When Tony Curtis's will was read, it was clear that he had left everything to Jill. He had redone the will a few months before he died. When he did so, he cut out all his children—all were listed by name, including Jamie Lee—stating that he intentionally disinherited them. No reason was given. His children were shocked and not happy.

22

Lee Marvin

Lee Marvin was an actor whose dour demeanor and gruff voice with an innate predilection towards violence made evil characters ring true. He played in more than 70 movies and television shows. Some standout films were *The Delta Force*, *The Big Red One* and *The Dirty Dozen*. But he was widely known to television viewers, from shows like *The Twilight Zone*, *Bonanza*, *Route 66* and *Wagon Train*. During World War II, he was a Marine who fought in the Pacific Theater storming beaches. His first movie was in 1951, the last in 1986.

Lee Marvin came from a fractious family that loved when sober and fought when not. He was born in Manhattan on February 19, 1924, and named after his four-times-removed cousin, Robert E. Lee. His father, Lamont Marvin, was an executive, and his mother, Courtney, was an archetypal Southern belle from Virginia, a fashion and beauty writer and editor; both worked in New York City. The father's descendants had emigrated from England and founded the city of Hartford in Connecticut. Lee had an older brother, Robert, who was also named after the Confederate general.

Marvin's parents sent him to the Manumit School, a boarding school in Pawling, New York, from which he was expelled for unruly behavior. He went to a number of other schools with the same result. As a last resort, the family moved to Lakeland, Florida, so Lee could attend St. Leo's Preparatory School, 35 miles north of Tampa. He did somewhat better there and studied violin. On weekends, he hunted wild animals in the Everglades. On August 12, 1942, he dropped out of school and enlisted in the Marine Corps at age 18. He said, "If I'm going to war, I want to be in the toughest outfit." He reported to Parris Island, South Carolina, for boot camp on August 16, 1942. The normally 13-week course had been shortened to four weeks.

On September 16, Lee Marvin was sent to New River, North Carolina, for Marine Combat Training, scoring sharpshooter with his rifle, just missing expert by three points. He applied for Quartermaster School and, after passing the entrance exam, was sent to Hadnot Point, North Carolina, on October

World War II Veterans in Hollywood

7. For a kid that couldn't deal with civilian high schools, he did all right in the Marines, and on February 8, 1943, he was promoted to corporal.

The restless and rebellious Lee Marvin found Quartermaster duties boring. He wanted to fight and requested a combat assignment. He got it with the Fighting Fourth—the Fourth Marine Division's 24th Regiment. He joined the regiment's 3rd Battalion as a squad leader. The regiment spent the remainder of 1943 undergoing intensive training at Camp Pendleton, California, 50 miles south of Hollywood. Marvin met a girl at the Hollywood Canteen and as a portent of his future, spent his liberties in Hollywood. Unable to completely rein in his rebellious nature, he lost his corporal's stripes.

The regiment boarded transports in January 1944 and sailed directly into combat at Kwajalien Atoll in the Marshall Islands. The 3rd Battalion made an amphibious assault on Roi Namur, the northern island of the atoll, on January 31. The operation was so well planned that the island was secured in four days.

Lee Marvin as The Sergeant in the 1980 epic war film, *The Big Red One*, written and directed by Samuel Fuller. The movie is based on Fuller's own experiences in WWII with the 1st Infantry Division (publicity still).

Marvin had trained as a sniper and scout and to handle "satchel" charges. As the name implies, the explosive is a satchel-sized package of TNT used to blow up bunkers. The Marine casualties on Roi Namur were 206 killed in action and 798 wounded (Marvin was not), versus the Japanese, who had 3,500 killed in action and 87 captured. In an unfortunate event, a Marine tossed a satchel charge into a bunker and the bunker itself blew up with such force that it killed 20 Marines and wounded dozens. Unbeknownst to the demoli-

22. Lee Marvin

tion teams, the bunker was a storage magazine for torpedo warheads. Each warhead contained almost a thousand pounds of TNT. A pilot radioed that it looked like the whole one-square-mile island had blown up.

After clearing the Kwajalien Atoll, which contains hundreds of small islets, the 4th Marines regrouped and prepared for the assault on the Marianas. On June 5, 1944, the division left to join the Battle of Saipan. The conflict was one of the bloodiest of the war. It started at 9 a.m. on June 15, 1944, when some 8,000 Marines aboard landing craft invaded the west coast of Saipan. They were supported by a barrage of rocket and cannon fire on Japanese defenses. Meeting heavy resistance, the Marines secured a six-mile-wide beachhead by nightfall. That night the Japanese counter-attacked but were beaten back. A sniper, Lee was sent to the beach in a small rubber boat during the night, before the rest of his platoon landed.

Six days later, on a scouting mission for Item Company, Marvin was pinned down in a gulley by a Japanese sniper. In Marvin's words, "His first shot hit my foot, his second just about three inches in front of my nose." Marvin knew he couldn't get up and run, so he tried to wiggle like a snake and crawl to cover. The next bullet caught him just below the belt line and carved a 2-inch-deep gouge that was 3 inches wide and plowed 8 inches down through his buttocks, cutting his sciatic nerve. He was able to finally crawl to cover. He was awarded the Purple Heart and spent 13 months in naval hospitals. His outfit went on fighting the Pacific War, including the bloody capture of Iwo Jima. His 133 comrades in Item Company had only nine survivors. Marvin had taken part in the invasions of 21 islands in the Pacific.

In a letter written home, Marvin wrote, "I was on Saipan and got hit. Not too bad, but bad enough to hamper me if I stayed. I was hit in my left buttocks just below the belt line. You may think it's funny to get hit in the can like that, but at the time I was very lucky that is all I got. I was pinned down and could not move an inch and then a sniper started on me. His first shot hit my foot and his second just about three inches in front of my nose. It was a matter of time, as I knew I would get hit sooner or later. If I got up and ran, I would not be writing this letter, so I just kept down." Later, Marvin said that he learned to act by trying to seem unafraid during combat.

The Americans had taken a large part of Saipan, when the Japanese attempted an attack by sea on June 19. In the resulting Battle of the Philippine Sea, a disaster for the Japanese, they lost three aircraft carriers and 650 airplanes. The air action was nicknamed "The Great Marianas Turkey Shoot." The Japanese battle plan was based on the capability of their aircraft. Japanese carrier planes had a longer range than those of the Americans. They planned to stand off out of the reach of the Americans, send their planes to attack

World War II Veterans in Hollywood

the American fleet and fly on to Guam to refuel. The U.S. intercepted their messages and slaughtered their air fleet. Thereafter, resupply of the Japanese defenders was impossible. Nevertheless, the defenders of Saipan were determined to fight to the last man. By July 7, they had nowhere to retreat to, so they made a suicidal "banzai charge." In the end, 30,000 Japanese on the island died. The victory for Americans was costly, with 2,949 killed and 10,464 wounded.

Marvin was discharged on July 24, 1945, and returned to live at home. The family members had trouble securing employment and even moved to Chicago before finally settling in Woodstock, New York. Marvin acquired an apprentice's card in the plumbers' union and found a job working for a local plumber. One day, he was sent to repair a toilet at a community theatre, the Maverick Playhouse. The artsy town had three theaters. While working at the Maverick, he was asked to replace an actor who had become sick during rehearsals. He did so well he got a job at the Playhouse at $7 a week. He quit the plumbing job the day after his first performance. This got him hooked on acting, so he moved to Greenwich Village in New York City to try to pursue a career. Using the GI Bill, he enrolled at the American Theatre Wing, the best-known place then to learn the trade. He found that his rebellious personality and stentorian voice, along with his Marine Corps training, could propel him to a satisfying career on stage and screen.

While studying there, he got small, unaccredited roles on and off Broadway. He played on stage in *Uniform of Flesh* and *The Nineteenth Hole of Europe*, both in 1949. In addition, he had some bit parts on television shows such as *Escape*, *The Big Story* and *Treasury Men in Action*. With the offer of a motion picture role, Marvin went to Hollywood in 1951.

Lee made his screen debut in the movie *You're in the Navy Now*, which appeared in 1951. Marvin's role was as a member of a ship's crew, but uncredited. It was also the debut of another veteran, Charles Bronson. The director, Henry Hathaway, liked Marvin's work, so his role was expanded. Lee did a creditable job, so it was followed by five more films that year, three of them uncredited.

In 1951, Lee met a young girl, Betty Ebeling, who had just graduated from the University of California at Los Angeles. She was a nanny for Joan Crawford's children. After a whirlwind courtship, they ran off to Las Vegas and were married in February. It was the first marriage for both; he was 27 and she was 23. She became his dependable hostess and housewife. They had one son and three daughters. It didn't turn out to be a very happy time for Betty, as she had to put up with Marvin's heavy drinking and womanizing.

His first credited movie role was in the 1952 *The Duel at Silver Creek*.

22. Lee Marvin

Then it was back to New York for *Billy Bud* on Broadway. But after a few small roles in television shows, he went back to Hollywood. After small parts in eight films, he scored big in *The Wild One*, opposite Marlon Brando, which was released in 1953 and established him as a major screen villain. To avoid using a double and not to be bettered by Brando, Marvin learned to ride a motorcycle for the film. This caused him to take up the sport, and he bought a 500cc Triumph TR5 on which he competed in desert races.

After a few more appearances in television series, he was notable as a smart-aleck sailor in the acclaimed 1954 movie *The Caine Mutiny*. After various roles in a number of fifties-era movies, Lee began a successful run in the television series *M Squad*, playing the lead as a hard-bitten but honest police detective. He got top billing in 1964 in *The Killers*. The supporting cast featured Ronald Reagan in his last movie role before going into politics.

The early sixties had Marvin appearing in a series of hit television series: *Wagon Train*, *Route 66*, *The Untouchables* and *The Twilight Zone*. Marvin came to international stardom in the Western comedy *Cat Ballou*, which came out in 1965. In it, he acted as two different characters and it made him a major star. He played a drunken gunfighter and also his evil brother. On screen he was alcohol-soaked (and off as well). His costar, Jane Fonda, remarked, "Never have I met such an outrageous personality. Lee loved to drink, and the more he drank, the more outrageous he became." When he accepted the Oscar for Best Actor, he said, "I think half of this belongs to a horse somewhere out in the San Fernando Valley." (The film featured an apparently drunken horse.) Marvin was the only actor who ever got an Oscar for playing two parts in the same film.

Lee Marvin starring in 1961 in the television series, *The Twilight Zone*—Episode: *The Grave*, October 6, 1961 (publicity still).

World War II Veterans in Hollywood

After becoming a major star, Marvin started getting fan letters. One arrived from West Berlin. It was from a girl who wrote that she was an ardent fan. She enclosed a photo of herself sitting on a couch, suggestively dressed. She wrote, "Please answer this letter." He didn't answer. A month later, another letter arrived with a photo of her sitting on the same couch, but with a little less clothing. This went on for three or four letters. Finally it reached the point where she was completely nude, sitting on the couch with her legs spread.

Even though still married, he left his wife Betty and his children and went to live with Michelle Triola in 1965. She and Marvin had met when she

Marvin in the 1965 western musical comedy *Cat Ballou* with Jane Fonda as Catherine "Cat" Ballou. Lee Marvin won a Best Actor Academy Award for playing dual roles of Kid Shelleen and Tim Strawn in this movie (publicity still).

22. Lee Marvin

had a bit part on a film that starred Lee, *Ship of Fools*. Having been in the 1958 Broadway show *Flower Drum Song* and having acted in other minor roles, she was also a cocktail lounge singer and dancer. Although never married, they cohabited for over five years and she legally changed her last name to Marvin.

While still with Michelle, Marvin continued having problems with alcoholism. Now and then he got stopped for drunken driving, but he got away with it by signing autographs for the officers. Lee remarked, "Tequila straight; there's a real polite drink. You keep on drinking until you finally take on more and it just won't go down. Then you know you've reached your limit. I quit drinking every morning and I start again every evening." In addition, he smoked up to six packs of cigarettes a day.

After he left, Betty filed for a divorce that was finalized on January 5, 1967. That year, Marvin and Angie Dickinson played together in *Point Blank*. He was a small-time criminal out for revenge against his wife (played by Dickinson). It didn't do very well when it was released but later became a cult favorite, hailed as a paradigm of nihilistic violence.

In 1969 Lee and Clint Eastwood costarred in *Paint Your Wagon*. The two sang a duet of the song "Wandering Star" in the movie, which was a version of the classic Broadway musical set against the backdrop of the California Gold Rush. It became a surprise hit, earning a gold record for a million copies sold that year. His singing voice was called "rain gurgling down a rusty pipe."

Marvin's mother had died, and his father still lived in Lee's postwar home in Woodstock, New York. In late 1970, his father became ill, so Marvin went to spend some quality time with him. While there, he got together with his high-school girlfriend, Pamela Feeley, and they ended up getting married in October of that year. She was 40 years old, having never left Woodstock, with three previous husbands and four children. When she was 15 years old at Kingston High School in 1945, her boyfriend was 21-year-old returned veteran Lee Marvin. They had parted in 1948 when he left home to pursue his acting career. Pamela wrote the definitive biography of her husband, titled *Lee*.

After appearing in six films during the early seventies, Marvin went into semi-retirement after filming *The Great Scout & Cathouse Thursday*, which was released in 1976. In 1975, he and his family had left Hollywood and moved to Tucson, Arizona.

The jilted Michelle Triola, feeling that she had been everything but a legal wife to Marvin for a number of years, brought suit against him for alimony in 1976. At that time, she was living with, but not married to, actor Dick Van Dyke. The suit claimed financial compensation available to spouses under

World War II Veterans in Hollywood

California community property laws. The case went to trial in 1979; the judge ordered Marvin to pay $104,000 to Triola for "rehabilitation purposes," but denied her community-property claim for half of the $3.6 million Marvin had earned during their time living together. But Marvin appealed the decision to the California Court of Appeals in August 1981. The court ruled that, since Triola couldn't come up with a contract between the two that would justify any payment, no money was due from Marvin to Triola.

The cases were widely covered by the media at the time. Her claim was referred to as palimony, and was highly publicized, particularly by the magazines that reported Hollywood goings-on. Michelle continued to live with Van Dyke until her death in 2009.

Marvin returned to acting during the eighties with roles in *The Big Red One*, *Death Hunt* and *The Iceman Cometh*, costarring with Robert Ryan. A member of the cast, Jeff Bridges, remembered that Lee and Robert, despite their obvious tough-guy personas, were unusually kind and giving personally. Marvin's very last performance was in the 1986 film *The Delta Force*. By then his health was rapidly declining. In December he was sent to the hospital in Tucson where he underwent intestinal surgery after suffering abdominal pains. On August 29, 1987, drinking and smoking caught up with him and he died at age 63. Lee Marvin was laid to rest at Arlington National Cemetery with full military honors.

23

Rod Serling

Although Rod Serling was an occasional actor, he is best known as a gifted writer. He wrote scripts for the popular television show *The Twilight Zone*. Serling also wrote scripts for the movies *Seven Days in May* and *The Planet of the Apes*. In addition, he was the author of eleven books. Rod received many awards for his writing and is considered to be one of the most influential writers in television history. His work made him an American icon, and the many skirmishes with network executives and sponsors who tried to censor his work led to his reputation as "The Angry Young Man of Television." Serling was a hero during World War II, serving in battles for the Philippines and winning the Bronze Star, a Purple Heart, a Combat Infantry Badge and a Parachutist Badge.

Rodman Edward Serling was born in Syracuse, New York, on Christmas Day, 1924. His father was Samuel Lawrence Serling, his mother, Esther Cooper. His Jewish parents had two boys, Robert and then Rodman. Robert was six years older than Rodman and preceded him in the Army and as a writer, later becoming a novelist and aviation writer. Their father worked as a butcher during the Great Depression.

* * *

In 1926, the family moved to Binghamton, New York, south of Syracuse, where his father opened a grocery. As he grew older, his parents encouraged his talents as a performer. His dad built a small stage in the basement where Rod put on plays, sometimes with neighborhood children.

Rod went to elementary school there, where he was known as the class clown. He was said to be extremely talkative and would go on for hours without stopping. Next, he went to Binghamton Central High School in 1940. Interested in sports, he played tennis. When he tried to join the football team, he couldn't because he was too small. He wrote for the school newspaper, was on the debate team and spoke at the 1943 graduation ceremony. Even though he had been accepted into a college in his senior year, he decided to join the Army instead.

World War II Veterans in Hollywood

During basic training, Serling took up boxing as a hobby, competing as a flyweight in 17 fights. He lost in the second round of the Army Division finals. After basic training, Rod was assigned to the 511th Parachute Infantry of the 11th Airborne Division at Camp Toccoa, Georgia, where he underwent a year of paratrooper training. The grueling and harsh training at Toccoa is portrayed in the television series *Band of Brothers*.

* * *

In April 1944, Serling and his division were sent to California, where they loaded aboard the troop transport ship USS *Sea Pike* headed for the Pacific Theater. The 11th Airborne Division's first action was in the Philippines but, rather than going in via parachutes, they served as light infantry, making an amphibious assault by boat on the island of Leyte. The battle for Leyte saw some of

Rod Serling as the writer/creator of the classic television series *The Twilight Zone* which premiered on CBS, October 2, 1959. Serling drew on his own experiences for many episodes, frequently about boxing, military life and airplane pilots (publicity still).

the fiercest fighting of the war. Rod was transferred to the 511th demolition platoon, a dangerous assignment during which he was wounded on his kneecap and wrist. He partially recovered, well enough that he returned to his unit.

On February 3, 1945, the 511th parachuted onto the Tagaytay Ridge, a high plateau overlooking the city of Manila. The ridge was an open space that had been mostly cleared of Japanese troops by local Filipino guerrillas. After meeting up with its two other regiments, the entire 11th Airborne Division began advancing towards Manila. As it approached the city, there was stiff resistance from 17,000 Japanese defenders with artillery, machine

23. Rod Serling

gun nests and booby-traps. Japanese Army general Tomoyuhi Yamashita had abandoned the city but naval admiral Sanji Iwabuchi disobeyed the order. He ordered his Marines to fight to the death and subjected the Manila civilians to terrible atrocities. For a month, the Americans fought block by block for control of Manila. When parts of the city were liberated, civilians showed their appreciation by throwing parties for the troops. Japanese artillery started firing on one of the parties, injuring a civilian. Serling ran into the area of exploding shells and rescued him. This earned him a Bronze Star. After the war, General Yamashita was blamed for the atrocities and he was hung as a war criminal.

As the Americans moved into other parts of the city, Serling's regiment had a 50 percent casualty rate with more than 400 killed. It was a vicious house-to-house fight. Rod was injured by shrapnel. After recovering again, he rejoined his regiment. By March 3, all Japanese resistance had ended.

In early August 1945, the atomic bombs were dropped and on the 15th of August the Japanese surrendered. The 11th Airborne Division, the first to land in Japan, was airlifted to Atsugi Airbase 30 miles south of Tokyo to secure the area in anticipation of General MacArthur's arrival. The division's band was on the Yokohama docks on September 2, belting out a blaring rendition of the "Old Gray Mare She Ain't What She Used to Be" to serenade the Army's 1st Cavalry Division on their arrival ashore in Japan.

After informing Serling that his father, Sam, had died on September 1, 1945, of a heart attack at age 52, the Army failed to grant emergency leave to Serling because of a totally jammed up transportation system. His daughter Anne said, "It was a loss of such magnitude that he never truly recovered." After serving as an occupation force, the regiment returned to the U.S. Serling was sent to a rehabilitation hospital for therapy for his leg wound. As it turned out, his knee continued to bother him for years. During his time there, he worked at the hospital.

Technician Fifth Grade (same as sergeant) Rod Serling, during his three years in the Army, had received the Bronze Star, the Purple Heart, the Philippine Liberation Medal, the Occupation of Japan Medal, plus four other medals and two badges. He took his combat experiences home with him and had nightmares and flashbacks for the balance of his life. He said, "I was bitter about everything and at loose ends when I got out of the service. I think I turned to writing to get if off my chest." His experiences made him antiwar from then on. His daughter Anne said, "What I vividly recall is my dad having nightmares, and in the morning, I would ask him what happened, and he would say he dreamed the Japanese were coming at him."

Upon his discharge from the hospital, he enrolled at Antioch College in

World War II Veterans in Hollywood

Yellow Springs, Ohio, taking advantage of the GI Bill. At first, Rod majored in physical education, but he quickly changed to literature. He soon had an opportunity to work part-time at a local radio station writing, directing and acting in weekly productions. Still a student, he sold three scripts for $100 each for the television series *Stars Over Hollywood*, which aired on NBC during 1950 and '51. He found an unusual way to supplement his income and took another part-time job testing parachutes for the Army at $50 a jump.

While attending college in 1946, Rod met a seventeen-year-old student, Carolyn Louise Kramer, who was an education major. They started dating and the relationship led to their marriage on July 31, 1948. They honeymooned at Carolyn's grandmother's vacation house on Cayuga Lake in Interlaken, New York. After the marriage, she worked as an actress in and a producer for some of Serling's shows. They had two daughters, Jodi, born in 1950, and Anne in 1955. Theirs was a lifelong union and their permanent home was on Cayuga Lake.

Serling graduated in 1950 with a bachelor of arts degree in literature. With his new degree in hand, Serling began his career in radio. He had worked at the New York station WNYC as an actor and writer during his college summer break in 1946. He had a dramatic voice with a clipped manner of speaking. In 1950, Rod got a job as a junior staff writer at radio station WLW in Cincinnati, Ohio. Not satisfied with the demands of this work, he started writing stories in his free time. He submitted them and received 40 rejection slips. Finally, in 1951, he sold some scripts and earned $5,000, so he left the radio station and wrote teleplays full time. More than 70 of his television scripts were produced, winning both public and critical acclaim. To create such a number, he would dictate them to his tape recorder and have his secretary type them. Some of his scripts explored the trauma of war.

Serling's big break came in January 1955 when his 72nd television script was aired, a play called *Pattern* that centered on cutthroat corporate politics. It was a play in that it was aired live from beginning to end. It was a live broadcast shown on the Kraft Television Theatre. It was aired a second time the next month. Critics called it a creative triumph. It won Rod his first Emmy Award. (Five more were to follow.)

Rod continued to work on screenplays for MGM and as a scriptwriter for the CBS *Playhouse 90*. He wrote *Requiem for a Heavyweight*, shown in 1956 on *Playhouse 90*. It was a huge success, winning him his second Emmy, the Television-Radio Writer's Annual Award, the Sylvania Award and the George Foster Peabody Award. The show later became a feature film and a

23. Rod Serling

Broadway play. Next he wrote another *Playhouse 90* script, *The Comedian*, that starred Mickey Rooney. This got him another Emmy.

The Serling family moved to Hollywood in 1957. That year, a script he had written in 1950 called *The Twilight Zone* was submitted to CBS. That was the birth of the famous television show. Rod was not only the *Twilight Zone's* most important writer; he was also the producer and narrator. On October 2, 1959, the first episode went on the air. Of the 156 segments that were shown, Serling wrote 92. *The Twilight Zone* continued on the air through 1964. As the producer, he kept control of all of the episodes and hired other writers for those he didn't write himself. They included noted authors such as Ray Bradbury and Richard Matheson. Rod's own favorite episode was called "Time Enough at Last." It was the story of a bank teller who loved books but lived in a science-fiction world where he was prevented from reading them. Many *Twilight Zone* episodes were based on Serling's own experiences such as the Army, war, airplanes and boxing. Rod also wrote about the human condition, politics, life and death.

The Twilight Zone episodes written by Serling are considered by some to be the finest work television has ever seen. The show was acclaimed by critics as well as its viewers and had a cult following. It garnered two Emmy Awards for Outstanding Writing Achievement in Drama, and a Golden Globe for Best TV Producer/Director. Later, CBS revived the series, but without Serling. The latest installment came 60 years after the first 1959 episode. It resurfaced on April 1, 2019.

Serling started teaching at Ithaca College in upstate New York in 1967. He screened his own work and mentored students by providing feedback on their scripts and projects. He even occasionally hosted some students at his family home on Cayuga Lake. His wife Carol was a longtime Ithaca College trustee. After his death, she donated some of his work to the college. This resulted in the Rod Serling Archives there, the largest single collection of his scripts and screenplays.

During the sixties and seventies, Rod Serling wrote eleven published books. In 1962, he came out with *Requiem for a Heavyweight: A Reading Version of the Dramatic Script*. The following year he wrote *Rod Serling's Triple W: Witches, Warlocks and Werewolves; A Collection*, and two more followed in that decade. During the seventies there were three more: *Night Gallery, Night Gallery 2* and *Rod Serling's Other Worlds*.

After *Twilight Zone* went off the air, Serling wrote a script for *A Carol for Another Christmas*. It was a television movie based on *A Christmas Carol* by Charles Dickens and was shown only one time. Then he wrote for *The Loner*, a CBS series that ran for almost a year. Rod started writing for a new series,

World War II Veterans in Hollywood

Night Gallery, in 1969. He also starred in it, playing the curator of a museum. Its themes were the macabre, horror and suspense. It ran on NBC until it was cancelled in 1973. It was rumored that Serling was paid $100,000.

During the seventies, Rod recorded commercials for Ford and Mazda. In 1972, he acted in an episode of the *Ironside* series called "Bubble, Bubble, Toil and Murder." The next year, he went back to radio on the drama series *The Zero Hour*. He hosted a rock concert, *Fantasy Park*, in 1975. It was his last.

* * *

In May 1975 Rod Serling was taken to the Tomkins County Community Hospital because of a mild heart attack. On June 26, he had a coronary bypass, but the operation went wrong and he died on June 28, 1975, at the Strong Memorial Hospital in Rochester, New York. He was only 50 years old but had been smoking three to four packs of cigarettes a day. His private funeral was on July 2. There was a memorial service held at Cornell University on July 7.

Among others, his daughter, Anne, who had just turned 20, spoke about him. "He was literally the funniest person I ever met, and he would do anything for a laugh. He was devoted to his family and was always there for us."

Serling in 1970 featured on the set of the television series *Night Gallery* in a dimly lit museum where he was the on-camera host (curator) (publicity still).

24

Kirk Douglas

Kirk Douglas is one of the most active members of the Greatest Generation. Notice the "is," not "was." He is still living and, at this writing, is 103 years old. Multi-talented, he has acted in many Hollywood movies and television series plus Broadway and radio shows. Not only that, he produced and directed some of them. He is a published author with ten novels to his credit. During World War II, he served in the Navy for three years and was awarded the Purple Heart.

* * *

Douglas's real name is Issur Danielovitch Demsky. He was born on December 9, 1916, in Amsterdam, 35 miles north of Albany in upstate New York. His father, Hershel Danielovitch, and mother, Bryna, were Jewish refugees from Russia who came to America in 1912. His father's brother had come to the U.S. beforehand and used the name Demsky, so his father changed his family's name from Danielovitch to Demsky. Kirk was the only boy among six sisters: Pesha, Kaleh, Tamara, Rachel and twins: Haska and Siffra. They grew up in abject poverty. "There was nowhere to go but up," he once remarked.

Douglas remembered, "My father, who had been a horse trader in Russia, got himself a horse, a small wagon and became a ragman buying old rags, pieces of metal and junk. Even on Eagle Street [where the family lived], in the poorest section of town [Amsterdam], where all the families were struggling, the ragman was on the lowest rung of the ladder. And I was the ragman's son." He went on to say, "I was a ragamuffin kid trying to cope with a neighborhood filled with gangs."

Douglas was raised an observant Jew; his parents spoke Yiddish at home and he had his Bar Mitzvah when he turned 13. As a youth, Douglas had to work in order to help his family. He had a number of different jobs such as delivering newspapers and waiting on tables in restaurants. In school he excelled in Hebrew studies. Some of those in the Jewish community wanted to send him to rabbinical school, but he refused: "I wanted to be an actor ever

World War II Veterans in Hollywood

Kirk Douglas as Colonel Dax in the 1957 anti-war film *Paths of Glory*, set during World War I. Photo is a behind the scenes publicity shot with director Stanley Kubrick to the left of Douglas. In 1992 this film was deemed "culturally, historically or aesthetically significant" by the Library of Congress and selected for preservation in the U.S. National Film Registry.

since I was a kid. In the second grade I was in a play. My mother made a black apron, and I acted as a shoemaker. After the performance, my father gave me my first Oscar, an ice cream cone. I've never forgotten that."

Douglas went to the Wilbur H. Lynch High School in Amsterdam, graduating in 1934. In school, he was active in the drama department and auditioned for and secured roles in as many plays as he could handle. Kirk wanted to go to the St. Lawrence University in Canton, New York, because he had a friend there. Canton is about 185 miles north of Amsterdam, near

24. Kirk Douglas

the Canadian border. Kirk and his buddy hitchhiked to the school. But he didn't have money for tuition, so he got an appointment with the university dean and showed him a list of his high school activities. Impressed, the dean loaned him the funds for the tuition. He paid it back by working part-time as a gardener and janitor at the school. Douglas was a good student and was on the wrestling team. One summer, he even wrestled in a carnival. On the last summer before his graduation in 1939, Kirk got a job at a stock playhouse. He and a fellow actor—George Sekulovich—became friends. George changed his name to Karl Malden to further his career. He suggested that Issur (nickname: Izzy) Demsky change his name to Kirk Douglas, which he did.

After graduation, Douglas went to New York City. He had won a scholarship to the American Academy of Dramatic Arts to further his education as an actor. While there, he had minor roles in a number of Broadway plays. He and a classmate—Betty Joan Perske—became friends. They dated and she wrote, "I had a wild crush on Kirk." Later, when she went to Hollywood, she changed her name to Lauren Bacall. One time she was especially kind to Kirk. He recalled, "I had a thin coat that someone had given me. I wore it for two years. It was winter and Betty thought I must be freezing. So, she went to her uncle, talked him out of an overcoat, and gave it to me. I wore it for another two years."

The dating was casual, however, because Kirk thought Betty was too young for him. (She was only 15, eight years younger.) Nevertheless, she fantasized about someday sharing her life with him. "Kirk didn't really pursue me," she said; "He was friendly and sweet and enjoyed my company." Bacall introduced Kirk to another classmate—Diana Dill—whom Douglas would later marry.

Kirk Douglas completed his two-year course at the American Academy and contemplated a career on Broadway. But then the United States entered World War II.

With his country at war, Douglas enlisted in the Navy in 1941 at age 25. Early in 1942, he was sent to the Naval Reserve Midshipmen's School at Notre Dame. After receiving his commission, Ensign Douglas went to the Submarine Chaser School. To celebrate his graduation, Kirk married Diana Dill on November 2, 1943. They had two sons: Michael, born in 1944, and Joel in 1947. When Douglas completed the sub chaser course in late 1943, he was assigned as a gunnery and communications officer aboard the Sub Chaser PC-1139. (Sub chasers were numbered, not named.)

This PC-461 class vessel was steel-hulled, 173 feet long, and manned by a crew of 65. It was armed with a three-inch cannon, a 40 mm Bofors and two 20 mm guns. For attacking submerged U-boats, it had four mousetrap

World War II Veterans in Hollywood

launchers on the bow and two depth charge roll-off racks astern. The mousetraps could toss small depth charges that would explode on contact. PC-1139 also had a considerable amount of detection and ranging gear to find and locate submarines.

While on patrol in the South Pacific on February 7, 1944, PC-1139 picked up sonar pings. The crew began an exploratory attack, launching a pattern of small bombs with their mousetraps. When one of them exploded, excitement aboard followed. The captain moved the ship over the spot of the explosion and ordered a marker released to prepare for a depth charge attack. Instead of the marker, the sailor in charge rolled off a depth charge that, because the ship was barely moving, exploded under the stern. The ship was raised out of the water, with people and equipment tossed about. Kirk was slammed into a bulkhead and his stomach was injured by a piece of equipment. In the hospital it was discovered that he had chronic amoebic dysentery, an infection of the bowel caused by amoebae. After recovery from his wounds, Douglas was discharged with the rank of lieutenant junior grade in 1944.

After the war, Douglas returned to New York and played on Broadway in *Kiss and Tell* and *The Wind Is 90*, for which he was reviewed favorably. He also worked on radio, doing some commercials, and used his voice on several network soap operas. Kirk thought his radio experience was valuable because vocal skills are essential to an aspiring actor.

His Broadway acting led to more stage offers. But his friend Lauren Bacall recommended him to movie producer Hal Wallis. Douglas relocated to Hollywood, where his first film was *The Strange Love of Martha Ivers*, starring opposite Barbara Stanwyck. He got rave reviews and it was noted that "he was a natural film actor." This led to seven more movies during the forties, including his role as Peter Niles in *Mourning Becomes Electra*. He received his first Oscar nomination for playing a boxer in 1949's classic movie *Champion*. This role established Kirk as a movie tough guy. *Sports Film* historian Frederick Romano wrote, "Douglas shows great concentration in the ring. His intense focus on his opponent draws the viewer into the ring. Perhaps his best characteristic is his patented snarl and grimace."

In 1950, Kirk starred in *Young Man with a Horn*, playing opposite Hoagy Carmichael, Doris Day and Lauren Bacall. The film is about jazz musician Bix Beiderbecke, who was a friend of Douglas. In the coming years, Kirk and Lauren would star in three more movies together.

During the next two decades, Kirk Douglas was a major Hollywood star, scoring at the top of the box office. In the fifties, he was in more than 20 movies as well as a television series, *The Jack Benny Program*, where he played

24. Kirk Douglas

himself as a musical guest. Douglas received two more Oscar nominations for *The Bad and the Beautiful* and *Lust for Life*.

Kirk and Diana divorced in 1951. While filming the 1953 movie *The Story of Three Loves*, he got engaged to his costar, Pier Angeli, but the relationship didn't go beyond that. It was probably ill-fated from the beginning due to religious differences. After the relationship with Kirk, Angeli had an affair with Jimmy Dean that, according to Pier, her mother broke up because Dean wasn't Catholic. In 1954 Kirk married Anne Buydens on May 29. An occasional actress and producer, she worked with Douglas on various charities. They had two sons: Peter, born in 1955, and Eric in 1958.

Douglas played a sheriff in the Western *Along the Great Divide*, released in 1951. Many more Westerns followed. His favorite movie is *Lonely Are the Brave*, which was a flop at the box office. Then, *Ace in the Hole* followed, which was a flop in the U.S. but won a best foreign film award at the Venice Film Festival. The 1951 movie *Detective Story* was nominated for four Academy Awards. Kirk starred along with Lee Grant in her first film. She said that Douglas was "dazzling, both personally and in the part.... He was a big, big star, gorgeous, intense, amazing." In 1956, he played the part of Vincent van Gogh in *Lust for Life*, for which he was again nominated for an Academy Award for Best Actor. Regarding his role, Douglas said, "Playing Vincent van Gogh was a painful experience. Not only did I look like Van Gogh, I was the same age he was when he committed suicide." Douglas won a Golden Globe Award for his acting. This movie was an adaption of Irving and Jean Stone's first historic novel. Irving had met a Van Gogh relative in 1920s Paris. It took him ten years and the help of wife Jean to get it published. Douglas went on the next year to portray Doc Holliday in the famous *Gunfight at the O.K. Corral*.

In 1955, Douglas was one of the first big-name stars to establish his own production organization, the Bryna Company. Bryna was his mother's first name. The company's first film was the antiwar epic, *Paths of Glory*, in which Douglas starred as a French officer during World War I. Stanley Kubrick, the director, said, "I think the movie is a classic, one of the most important pictures, possibly *the* most important picture." The scenario depicts an event where senior officers sacrifice their men to cover up their own blunders. The production of this film illustrated Kirk Douglas's deep respect for justice. Then, in 1960, came the great production *Spartacus*, where Kirk was the co-executive producer as well as the star.

Throughout the sixties, Douglas starred in 20 movies, some of which he also produced. In 1960, he was in a Broadway production of *One Flew Over the Cuckoo's Nest*. Even though Kirk wanted to make it into a movie, he couldn't convince a Hollywood studio to fund it. Interesting enough, Kirk's

World War II Veterans in Hollywood

Douglas as Colonel Mickey Marcus in the big-budget action film *Cast a Giant Shadow* in 1966 (publicity still).

son, Michael Douglas, produced and directed the film in 1975, starring Jack Nicholson. Kirk costarred with young Arnold Schwarzenegger in the Western comedy *The Villain* in 1979.

* * *

Even though he was then over 60, Douglas was in 12 productions during the eighties, including an episode in *Hollywood Greats* where he played himself, along with John Wayne. During the nineties and on into the new century, Douglas was in three television series and nine more movies.

Unfortunately, he had a severe stroke in 1995 at the age of 80. The stroke impaired his ability to speak. In his memoir, he called it "My Stroke of Luck. My stroke was a blessing in disguise. I learned that we take too many things

24. Kirk Douglas

Douglas starring in the comedy/drama *Greedy* as Uncle Joe in 1994 (publicity still).

for granted in this world. I have begun to appreciate the gift of life. The most difficult thing about a stroke is the depression. The antidote to depression is humor and thinking of others."

Even with his disability, he still wanted to make movies, so he had three years of voice therapy and made *Diamonds* in 1999, costarring with his close friend Lauren Bacall. His very last film was the television movie *Empire State Building Murders*, released in 2008. He was 92.

* * *

Douglas and three others were injured in an accident in 1991 when a helicopter they were in collided with a small plane above the Santa Paula Airport in Ventura County, just north of Los Angeles. The two men in the plane were killed. The crash happened when the Bell Jet Ranger helicopter lifted off the airport helipad. According to the airport manager, "The helicopter apparently drifted over the runway. He got too close to the runway." Kirk, who suffered head cuts and a rib fracture, was treated at the local hospital and later was flown to Cedars-Sinai Medical Center in West Hollywood, where he recovered. For Douglas, it was a near-death experience. It caused him to explore the meaning of his life. After a lot of studying, he turned to his religion, Judaism.

World War II Veterans in Hollywood

Kirk Douglas was not only a great actor, but also a talented author. In fact, he embarked on a second career late in life. His first book, *The Ragman's Son*, was published in 1988 by Simon and Schuster. It is his autobiography. He wrote it without the help of a ghostwriter, very unusual for a Hollywood star. Reviewer Susan Stamberg wrote in the *New York Times*: "This was fun! A big movie star writing a big book about his life. *The Ragman's Son* reads like a collection of stories the actor has been telling over dinner for years. They're charming, they're funny and they're gossipy. It has the freshness and pell-mell quality of firsthand telling."

Then he wrote three novels. The first was *Dance with the Devil*, a story of a Hollywood producer who, as a boy, was the only one to survive a Nazi concentration camp. A critic wrote, "It is a highly readable, entertaining drama." (As an aside, your author, Art, has read the book. I couldn't put it down.) His last adult novel was *Last Tango in Brooklyn*, published in 1994. Some critics thought it was his best: "His most satisfying novel so far. It's a love story with a powerful finale that will haunt the reader long after he or she has closed the book."

He wrote two books for children: *The Broken Mirror: A Novella* and *Young Heroes of the Bible*. But neither was well received, and they didn't sell well. Then came three memoirs: *Climbing the Mountain: My Search for Meaning*, *My Stroke of Luck* and *Let's Face It: 90 years of Living, Loving and Learning*, published in 2007. Finally, there were two more: *I Am Spartacus!: Making a Film, Breaking the Blacklist* and *Life Could Be Verse: Reflections on Love, Loss, and What Really Matters*, another autobiography, published on his 98th birthday in 2014. His last was *Kirk and Anne: Letters of Love, Laughter, and a Lifetime in Hollywood*, where he wasn't afraid to express his emotions, especially about his wife, Anne. It came out in 2017.

Kirk Douglas and his wife, Anne, are active philanthropists. He donated $5 million to his alma mater, St. Lawrence University. Among other recipients were the Anne Douglas Childhood Center for Homeless Women and the Anne Douglas Childhood Center at the Sinai Temple. The two donated some $40 million to Harry's Haven, which is an Alzheimer's treatment facility, and another $15 million to build the Kirk Douglas Care Pavilion there. Anne and Kirk have traveled to many countries for the United States State Department to spread the word about democracy and freedom. In 1981, President Jimmy Carter presented Kirk with the Presidential Medal of Freedom and said, "Douglas has done this in a sacrificial way, almost invariably without fanfare and without claiming any personal credit or acclaim for himself." He also received the Jefferson Award for their efforts.

Douglas has received more awards than can be listed. But some of the

24. Kirk Douglas

most significant ones are the American Cinema Award, an honorary Academy Award, the American Film Institute's Lifetime Achievement Award and a star on the Hollywood Walk of Fame.

In 2004, Kirk and Anne renewed their wedding vows to celebrate their 50th anniversary. More than 300 friends and family joined them to party at the famous Greystone Mansion in Beverly Hills. Lauren Bacall, Nancy Reagan and Tony Curtis were a part of the celebration. Kirk sang "I'm in the Mood for Love," plus a new song he had just written for Anne, "Please Stay in Love with Me."

When Kirk's grandson, Cameron, and his wife had a daughter on December 18, 2017, Douglas became a great-grandfather. Kirk had celebrated his 101th birthday on December 9. On December 30, 2018, he and his wife were seen in wheelchairs having an outing near their home. He had just turned 102 and she was 99. Kirk Douglas died on February 5, 2020, at the age of 103.

25

Charles Durning

Charles Durning is best known as a supporting actor. He was seldom the leading man, but even so, he has credits for more than 200 stage plays, movies and television appearances. He was twice nominated for an Academy Award for Best Supporting Actor. During World War II, he served with valor and was a highly decorated soldier. Unfortunately, there is much controversy about his claims, which are contradicted by documents. Complicating the argument is the fact that many World War II records were destroyed in the 1973 fire at the Military Personnel Records Center in Overland, Missouri. His acting career began after the war, when he became one of the greatest character actors in Hollywood. His impressive voice, with a hint of Irish, was in constant demand for narrations and voice overs.

* * *

Durning was drafted into the Army on January 20, 1943. He was assigned to C Battery of the 386th AAA (anti-aircraft) Battalion at Camp Edwards, Massachusetts. After 14 months of training stateside, his outfit was shipped to England on February 12, 1944, in preparation for the D-Day invasion of Normandy. On June 15, 1944, several miles inland from Omaha Beach, Durning and Leo Forster were seriously wounded by a German shrapnel mine. Durning had severe wounds from head to foot. Forster lost his right arm. The S Mine, called a Bouncing Betty, pops up to three feet in the air before exploding and scattering shrapnel over a wide area. The injured pair were received at the 24th Evacuation Hospital at Le Combe, two miles inland from Omaha Beach. After initial treatment, Durning was sent to a hospital in England. After five months recovering in the hospital, he was transferred to the 10th Replacement Control Depot.

With the outbreak of the Battle of the Bulge, the U.S. Army situation became chaotic. The green 106th Infantry Division had been sent to cover the Ardennes sector just five days before the Germans attacked. The Germans captured two of the division's regiments, 6,000 men. This created the chaos in the Army's disbursement of replacements and their record keeping.

25. Charles Durning

Charles Durning as Fr. O'Reilly in the 1986 film *Where the River Runs Black* (publicity still).

There is no record of what outfit Durning was assigned to or where he fought. He was awarded a Silver Star, but there was no citation or explanation of the circumstances. He is listed on the 20th Special Services morning report on July 31, 1945, in Untergroningen, Germany. His discharge report states he was returned to the U.S. on January 24, 1946, and discharged on January 30. He was listed as a rifleman with the 398th Infantry Regiment. He was awarded one star for the Battle of Normandy and the Silver Star for gallantry and a Purple Heart for his wounds.

According to other reports, Durning and 12 others were transferred from the 386th to Unit 2, Replacement Detachment 06E of the 17th Replacement Depot, two weeks before D-Day. The hospital roster and his Purple Heart citation list his unit as Unit 2, 06E. That was a replacement detachment.

In 2008, the French consul presented him with the National Order of the Legion of Honor.

Charles Edward Durning was born on February 28, 1923, in Highland Falls, New York, on the Hudson River, about 30 miles north of New York City. His parents, James Durning and Louise Leonard, had ten offspring, but five sisters died of scarlet fever and smallpox in childhood. His father joined the Army during World War I to gain U.S. citizenship. He saw a lot of combat, lost a leg and suffered from the lasting effects of a mustard-gas attack. He died when Charles was 12 years old. His mother worked as a laundress at the nearby U.S. Military Academy at West Point.

Durning attended Highland Falls elementary and high school (near West Point). A school counselor recommended that he learn office skills, but after seeing the movie *King Kong*, he decided he wanted to be an actor. Charles left school at age 16 in 1939 to work in a munitions factory and in a barbed-wire factory. Then along came the war. After he left the Army, he was continually troubled with post-traumatic stress disorder. He had a variety of different jobs including doorman, dishwasher and cab driver. In addition, he was a professional boxer and taught ballroom dancing at the Fred Astaire Dance Studio in New York City.

Then in 1951 he got a job in a Buffalo, New York, burlesque house where he worked as an usher and dancer. When an actor there became so drunk he couldn't go on stage, Durning was asked to replace him. And this led him to pursue the career he had wanted all along. He returned to New York and used the G.I. Bill to enroll at the American Academy of Dramatic Arts. Told that he had no talent, he left in less than a year. Even so, he had small parts in a number of plays on Broadway until he became a part of the New York Shakespeare Festival in 1961.

Next, he went to Hollywood to try to break into the movies. He played the part of an American GI in the 1962 film *The Password Is Courage*. Then he went back to Broadway, where he was an understudy in five plays; the last was the 1964 *Poor Bitos*, which closed down after 13 performances. This was followed by *Drat! The Cat* in 1965 and three more small roles in plays. Then he went back to Hollywood again for three more movies; the last was *Hi Mom* in 1969.

In 1959, he married Carole Doughty, a fellow instructor he had met while teaching at the Fred Astaire Dance Studio. She came with a daughter, Anita; Durning and his stepdaughter became very close. Charles and Carole had three children: Michele, Jeanine and Douglas. The union lasted for thirteen years and ended in divorce in 1972.

Two years later, he married his high-school sweetheart, Mary Ann Amelio. Both had been married and had children, but they were reunited when Mary's daughter greeted Mr. Durning backstage after his performance in *That Championship Season*. The next night, the couple had their first date in more than 30 years. They separated in 2010 after 36 years together.

By the 1970s, Durning, now in his fifties, was a widely acclaimed actor. During that decade, he appeared in almost 30 movies. His first starring role was in *The Sting*, where he played a corrupt police lieutenant opposite Paul Newman. One of his favorite roles was his depiction of Santa Claus.

25. Charles Durning

He played the part in four different movies made for television. In the 1975 television movie *Dog Day Afternoon*, he was nominated for a Golden Globe Award as Best Supporting Actor—Motion Picture. Back on Broadway, he was in four plays and on television; he appeared five times including in *Captains and the Kings*, for which he was nominated for a Golden Globe and an Emmy.

Durning continued to pursue his acting career right up to his death in 2012. As a matter of fact, two films were released afterwards. His last was *Bleeding Hearts*, released in 2015, in which he played his favorite role: Santa Claus. For the rest of the twentieth century, Charles was in some 50 movies. Outstanding was *The Best Little Whorehouse in Texas*, in which he played the governor, singing and dancing the two-step. This role got him nominated for the Academy Award for Best Supporting Actor. An interesting role was in *Unholy Matrimony*, where he costarred with Patrick Duffy. His stepdaughter, Anita Gregory, had a small role as a secretary. He earned his second Academy Award nomination for playing a Gestapo colonel in the 1983 *To Be or Not to Be*. In *Tootsie*, his character fell hard for a cross-dressing man—Dustin Hoffman—whom he believed was a woman. In a movie made for television he played John "Honey Fitz" Fitzgerald in *The Kennedys of Massachusetts*. A mini-series for television followed, garnering him a Golden Globe.

Even with all this going on in Hollywood, Charles Durning still acted on Broadway. Plays included *Cat on a Hot Tin Roof*, where he won a Tony playing Big Daddy. Another play he appeared in

Durning as Detective Lt. Bobby Mallory in the 1991 crime/action movie *V.I. Warshawski* (publicity still).

was *Inherit the Wind*. He also continued on television 15 times, including in *Evening Shade*, for which he was nominated for a Primetime Emmy Award for Outstanding Supporting Actor in a Comedy Series. For *Homicide: Life on the Street*, he was again nominated for an Emmy. In 1999, he was in *Now and Again*, narrating 20 episodes. He also narrated the documentary *Normandy: The Great Crusade*.

Durning was 77 years old in 2000. Still active in his eighties, he appeared in 13 television shows including the two series, *Rescue Me* and *NCIS*, both of which got him nominations for Emmys. His last was an episode in 2007 in *Monk*. Back on Broadway, he was in Gore Vidal's *The Best Man*. He was in an almost unbelievable 43 movies during the new century. In an Associated Press interview in 2008, he said he had no plans to stop working. "They're going to carry me out, if I go," he said.

* * *

Charles Edward Durning died from natural causes at his home in Manhattan on Christmas Eve, December 24, 2012. He was 89 and surrounded by his three children and his stepdaughter, Anita. She said, "Not only was Charlie a World War II hero, but he was also a hero to his family." She went on, "Charlie loved Christmas and if he could have chosen a time to pass, he would have chosen this day. He loved that holiday and played Santa Claus many times. He brought joy and a smile to everyone's life. He lit up the world by his wonderful sense of humor and his amazing talent." There was a private memorial service, and he was laid to rest at the Arlington National Cemetery.

Durning at the May 25, 2008 National Memorial Day Concert in Washington, D.C. (U.S. Navy).

* * *

25. Charles Durning

During his 50-year acting, singing and dancing career, he received nine Emmys, the Screen Actors' Guild's Life Achievement Award, a Tony, an Academy Award for Best Supporting Actor and a star on the Hollywood Walk of Fame. There were also four Golden Globe nominations and six Emmy nominations.

26

Henry Fonda

Henry Fonda had a 50-year career in the movies, on stage and on television. He was one of the most beloved actors during the Golden Age of Hollywood (1915–1963). He was nominated twice for the Academy Award for Best Actor and won once. In addition, he won a number of other awards, including a Golden Globe, a Grammy and a Tony. During World War II, he served in the Navy for five years, winning a Bronze Star. He had complicated relationships with his family members and a tumultuous marital history.

Henry Jaynes Fonda was born in 1905 in Grand Island, Nebraska. One of his ancestors fled persecution in Italy, came to the U.S. and founded the town of Fonda, New York. Henry's father was a commercial printer and operated the W.B. Fonda Printing Co. in Omaha, Nebraska. Henry liked to write. At the tender age of ten, he won a short story contest and had an article published in a local newspaper. When Fonda was 12 years old, he worked part-time in the printing company, for which his dad paid him $2 a week. His father took Henry to witness the lynching of Will Brown during the race riot of 1919. The experience would affect his performance in a future role. He went to Omaha Central High School, where he ice-skated, swam and ran. He had an after-school job at the Northwestern Bell Telephone Company. By his senior year, he had grown to more than six feet tall. Henry graduated from high school in 1923.

That same year, Fonda enrolled at the University of Minnesota to major in journalism. His time at the university wasn't "a particularly fruitful or eventful time," he later wrote. His dad told him he had to have a job while he was in college, so he got two. He continued his part-time job at the telephone company and was a physical education instructor for $30 a week at a settlement house. But the strain of both going to school and having two jobs proved too much for him. In 1925, he dropped out of college and returned to his home in Omaha.

After trying a few jobs while looking for a job in journalism without success, Henry decided journalism wasn't for him. His mother Helberta's friend, Dorothy Brando (Marlon's mother), offered to let him audition as an actor

26. Henry Fonda

at the Omaha Community Playhouse. Mrs. Brando was an amateur actress and involved in the Playhouse. In Fonda's first acting role at age 20, he played the part of Ricky in the play *You and I*, which ran for a week. It turned out that he liked acting. Next he starred, along with Mrs. Brando, in *Merton of the Movies* in 1926. It played for a week and received good notices. According to Henry, "The idea of being Merton taught me that I could hide behind a mask." In addition, Henry ushered and helped build sets at the Playhouse.

In 1927, Henry Fonda wrote a sketch for George Billings, an impersonator of President Abraham Lincoln. This led to a role for Fonda, who played the part of Lincoln's secretary and traveled for three months on the vaudeville circuit. When he returned to Omaha, he worked as assistant director at the Playhouse.

Henry Fonda in an official U.S. Navy portrait.

Having decided on acting as a career, Henry had the ambition to be on Broadway. He read all the show business magazines available in Omaha and was aware of the summer stock theaters in New England as a steppingstone to Broadway. When an Omaha banker's widow was looking for someone to drive her to the family's summer home on Cape Cod, Henry jumped at the opportunity. He acted in summer stock at the Cape Playhouse in Dennis, Massachusetts, in 1928. Henry joined with the University Players Guild, an intercollegiate stock company based in Falmouth, Massachusetts. There, Henry appeared in a number of plays, first in smaller roles, then in bigger ones. He also did other work there, including setting up lighting and painting sets. While at the Guild, Fonda met Margaret Sullavan, whom he married in 1931. They had starred together in *The Moon's Our Home*. He also met James Stewart there, who became his best friend. After appearing in *The Jest*, Fonda left the Guild in 1932.

World War II Veterans in Hollywood

Margaret Sullavan was a stage and screen actress nominated for an Oscar for her performance in *Three Comrades* in 1938. She was known to be blunt and temperamental.

Meanwhile, Fonda had a small part on Broadway in the 1929 play *The Game of Life and Death*. Next came three more roles in plays. In the 1934 *New Faces*, critics began to notice Henry when he did comic sketches with Imogene Coca. When *New Faces of 1934* opened on Broadway, it was a commercial and critical success.

These were the days of the Great Depression, and actors in plays didn't make much money. Fonda and other actors sometimes didn't have enough money to take the subway. For two years, Henry, Jimmy Stewart and Joshua Logan shared a small apartment in New York. In 1934, Fonda arrived at the top when he starred on the stage in *The Farmer Takes a Wife*, and it led him to his decades-long career in movies.

Hollywood producer Walter Wanger came up with the concept of making a movie based on the stage play *The Farmer Takes a Wife*. He needed a star to play the lead role. Since Henry had created the part on Broadway, Fonda was his choice. His movie debut was in 1935, playing the lead along with Janet Gaynor. Gaynor had won the Academy's first Oscar in 1929. A review of the movie in the *New York Times* stated, "Mr. Fonda, in his film debut, is the bright star of the occasion. As the virtuous farm boy, he plays with an immensely winning simplicity which will quickly make him one of our most attractive film actors." The movie was a big hit. After just scraping by in New York, Fonda made $3,000 a week in Hollywood.

That same year, Henry starred in two more films, *Way Down East* and *I Dream Too Much*. The *New York Times* again took notice: "Henry Fonda is the most likeable of the new crop of romantic juveniles." While shooting a film together, Margaret and Henry had a disagreement, so she jumped up and emptied a pitcher of water on Henry. They had divorced on March 14, 1933. Nevertheless, they stayed on friendly terms and in 1936, he starred with her in *The Moon's Our Home*. Shortly after, Fonda came to California and his buddy James Stewart followed. As before, they shared an apartment.

The year 1936 was an even busier one. Fonda traveled to England to star in the Technicolor movie *Wings of the Morning*. During shooting, Henry met an English socialite, Frances Seymour Brokaw, whom he married that same year. She had been previously married, widowed and had a daughter, Frances, whom Fonda later adopted. Their own daughter, Jane, was born in 1937, with Peter following in 1940.

Through 1943 Fonda starred in a total of 31 movies. For the 1941 movie *The Grapes of Wrath*, he was nominated for an Academy Award as Best Actor

26. Henry Fonda

in a Leading Role. In 1939, he won the Best Acting NBR (National Board of Review) award for *Young Mr. Lincoln*. In 1940, he won two more NBR awards for *The Grapes of Wrath* and *The Return of Jesse James*. According to critics, his best screen performance was in *Young Mr. Lincoln*. In 1937, he returned to Broadway to star in *Blow Ye Winds*. His last film appearance before entering the Navy was in *The Ox-Bow Incident*, released in 1943. The movie was about the lynching of an innocent man. It dredged up Henry's memories of the lynching he had witnessed when he was 10 years old.

Also, in 1942, he starred in the World War II movie *Immortal Sergeant*. Having decided to join in the war effort, he remarked, "Well, I don't want to be here, I wanna be out there. I'm sick and tired of being a lousy spectator." When he enlisted in the Navy on August 24, 1942, he was quoted as saying that he no longer wanted to "be in a fake war in a studio." He was on the edge of being too old at age 37. Nevertheless, he insisted and was finally accepted.

Fonda as Tom Joad in the film adaptation of John Steinbeck's classic novel *The Grapes of Wrath*. This 1940 drama traces the migration of the Joad family to California from the Dust Bowl of Oklahoma and the many hardships they endured (publicity still).

Before joining the Navy, Fonda and his pal Jimmy Stewart helped raise funds for the defense of Britain. Stewart joined the U.S. Army in 1941. Since Fonda had attended a university for two years, he was eligible to apply for a commission when he enlisted. Other movie stars who joined at the time spent their war years selling bonds and encouraging enlistment. Henry joined the Navy to be a sailor, not a movie star. At the time of his enlistment, Fonda was married to Frances, and they had three children. When he volunteered, he was working in the movies and making a lot of money, so his service was a significant financial sacrifice.

As a seaman, Henry Fonda went through basic training and was then sent to Quartermaster School, where he scored near the top of his class. He was promoted to quartermaster 3rd class. The destroyer USS *Satterlee* was being commissioned (newly built and ready for sea), and Fonda was in the initial crew, a "plank holder."

His ship sailed to the Pacific, but after almost a year serving as a quartermaster, Fonda decided he wanted to be an officer, so he made an application. He was 38 by then. Henry was commissioned in the rank of lieutenant junior grade, which was rather unusual. A beginning Navy officer's first rank is ensign. In making the recommendation, his commander wrote that he had "officer-like qualities of leadership."

After receiving his commission, Fonda became an assistant air combat officer as well as an air operations watch officer in the Pacific Theater. He assisted in the planning and execution of Navy air operations for the Mariana Islands and the Western Carolinas as well as for two Iwo Jima campaigns. Fonda rendered valuable assistance in planning and executing air operations that effectively neutralized hostile installations on enemy-held islands and atolls. For his actions during this period, Lieutenant Fonda was awarded a Bronze Star and the Navy's Presidential Unit Citation. His awards were accompanied with a complimentary letter from Secretary of the Navy James Forrestal.

Henry was recommended for promotion in 1945 by Vice Admiral J.H. Hoofer, who stated that Fonda was an outstanding officer who was "intelligent, determined, zealous, loyal and thoroughly cooperative in all and every respect." Fonda was relieved from active duty in November 1945. Even so, he remained in the Naval Reserve until he resigned in 1948.

After leaving active duty, Fonda returned to his home to spend some time with family and friends. Returning to Hollywood in 1946, he starred as Marshal Wyatt Earp in *My Darling Clementine*. He rounded out the forties with six more movies. In 1948, Henry returned to Broadway to star in *Mister Roberts*, a comedy about the U.S. Navy in the South Pacific during the war. He was said to have worn his own Navy hat during the play. He won a Tony award for his depiction of Lieutenant Roberts. The play ran for 1,077 performances on Broadway and went on a national tour.

Meanwhile, things at home weren't going so well. After 13 years of marriage, Fonda told Frances he wanted a divorce because he wanted to marry someone else. Frances had had emotional problems for a number of years. After his announcement, she went into the Austen Riggs Psychiatric Hospital in Stockbridge, Massachusetts. The doctor who treated her described Henry as a "cold, self-absorbed person, a complete narcissist." Frances committed suicide in the hospital on April 14, 1950.

26. Henry Fonda

Fonda had been having a two-year affair with 21-year-old socialite Susan Blanchard, and they were married on December 27, 1950. She was said to be in awe of him. He was 44 at the time. During the marriage, they adopted three-year-old Amy Fishman. The marriage lasted only three years and ended in divorce on May 2, 1956. Fonda told about the breakup, "We were living in Rome when she came down to breakfast and told me. I was devastated and cried, and she said, 'I'm young, I want to dance and tell jokes. I need to cut loose.' I knew exactly what she meant."

A year later he married Afdera Franchetti, who was 25 years old. She was descended from an Italian Jewish family. Afdera's father was Baron Raimondo Franchetti, so she was a baroness. She was just off a previous marriage that had ended in 1957. Fonda was in Italy shooting *War and Peace*, starring with Audrey Hepburn. Audrey was acquainted with Afdera's sister, Simba, who introduced her to Henry.

Afdera told the story: "I was in Rome in 1956. I was walking along Via del Babulino with Audrey Hepburn and we entered a place because we saw two paintings in the window display, two strange paintings of nuns playing tennis. They told me that an American had reserved them, but I paid cash and took them. A few days later at a small party at my house, Fonda, who was filming *War and Peace*, came up to me with Audrey. He was amazed to find his paintings there. With him [Fonda] it was a clandestine relationship in the beginning." After the marriage when they were living in Hollywood, she said, "Fonda was always working. He was a wonderful man, fantastic, perfect."

They were divorced in 1961. (When this was written, Afdera was single and living in London.)

After returning to Hollywood, Fonda's first film was *Mister Roberts*, for which he reprised his stage role. Henry and the director, John Ford, had differing ideas that resulted in on-set clashes. Ford became sick and was unable to continue, so Mervyn Le Roy became the director. Even so, Henry wasn't happy with the resultant film.

Fonda made a total of seven movies during the fifties, including such acclaimed films as *War and Peace* and *12 Angry Men*. Henry also appeared in four plays on Broadway during that time. The sixties were perhaps Fonda's most active time. He appeared in 18 movies and four Broadway plays. Outstanding films were *The Longest Day*, *How the West Was Won*, *Fail Safe* and *Once Upon a Time in the West*. On December 3, 1965, Fonda married Shirlee Mae Adams, an American Airlines flight attendant whom he had met on a trip. She was 33 and he was 60, but even so, the marriage lasted for the rest of his life.

World War II Veterans in Hollywood

Fonda (left) as Lt. Col. Daniel Kiley, with Robert Ryan as Gen. Gray, in the 1965 war movie *Battle of the Bulge*, dramatizing Nazi Germany's final western front counterattack of World War II in December of 1944 (publicity still).

In the nineteen seventies, Fonda was in his seventies. He appeared in an unbelievable number of movies—23—as well as in four plays. His last appearance on Broadway was in *First Monday in October*, playing a justice of the Supreme Court. Also, he was in two television mini-series: *Captains and the Kings* and *Roots: The Next Generation*.

In the eighties, even while his health was declining, Fonda appeared in two television movies, *The Oldest Living Graduate* and *Gideon's Trumpet*. His very last film was the 1981 *On Golden Pond*, where he played an irascible father trying to make peace with his daughter, played by his real daughter, Jane. The film was an outstanding success. Vincent Canby wrote in the *New York Times*, "Mr. Fonda gives one of the great performances of his long, truly distinguished career. Here is film acting of the highest order—as you watch him in *On Golden Pond*, you're seeing the intelligence, force and grace of a talent that has been maturing on screen for almost 50 years." The film won a number of Oscars including Best Actor for Henry Fonda.

He was ill when the Academy Award ceremony took place and was unable to attend. His daughter, Jane, was there to accept the honor. She said, "My

26. Henry Fonda

father is so happy. Me and all the grandchildren are coming over with the award to see him right away."

Henry Jaynes Fonda died from heart failure on August 12, 1982, at age 77. His wife, Shirlee, daughter Jane and son Peter were at his side. His friend, President Ronald Reagan, said that Fonda was "a true professional dedicated to excellence in his craft. He graced the screen with a sincerity and accuracy which made him a legend."

27

Clark Gable

When World War II broke out in 1939, Clark Gable was considered the exemplar of masculinity and the "King of Hollywood." Acting as a glib newspaper reporter in *It Happened One Night*, he received the Academy Award for Best Actor. He was the dashing young naval officer in *Mutiny on the Bounty* and in the movie of the century, *Gone with the Wind*, was the epitome of masculinity with just the right touch of the rascal. Clark Gable was the poster boy for the "Golden Years of Hollywood." In 1942 Gable was truly king of his world. He had fame, fortune, and the girl of his dreams, Carole Lombard. Then disaster struck. Carole was killed in an airplane crash and Clark fell into a deep depression.

William Clark Gable was born on February 1, 1901, in Cadiz, Ohio. Dr. John Campbell came to the home to deliver Clark. His fee was ten dollars. His father, a roughneck, worked on oil rigs as a driller. His mother died when he was only seven months old. When young Clark was five years old, his father married Jennie Dunlap. She raised him as if he were her own. Gable was always devoted to his stepmother. He was remembered as a "quiet boy who carried a lantern at night because he was afraid of the dark." Jennie played the piano and taught Clark how to play it, but he preferred brass instruments. He was the only youth in the Cadiz town orchestra.

In grade school, Clark acted as a Teddy bear in a school play, and he was also in the school band. He was the only kid in the school who had a bicycle. He spent two years at Cadiz High School. In his freshman year, he made a solid C average in most subjects. The second year he did somewhat better, even getting an A in spelling.

Gable had to quit high school in 1917 when he was 16 years old. Clark had wanted to become a doctor, but that was not to be. His father had run into financial troubles and the family moved to Texas, where the senior Gable resumed his work in the oil fields.

Nineteen-year-old Clark, however, didn't go along. He went to Akron, Ohio, in 1920, where he found work in Firestone's rubber factory and took

27. Clark Gable

a night course in medicine at the University of Akron. While there, he went to see a play, *The Bird of Paradise*. This inspired him to become an actor. He went on the road working in stock shows and little theaters. In Portland, Oregon, he hooked up with actress and coach Josephine Dillon, who mentored him, got him his first movie roles and set him on his way to becoming one of the "greatest screen legends," according to the American Film Institute.

Before World War II, Gable had had a very successful career as a movie actor that started in 1924. Clark was coached by Josephine Dillon, and later that year they were married. Dillon had seen great promise in Gable. She

Clark Gable in uniform.

paid to have his teeth fixed and hair styled. She guided him in building up his chronically undernourished body and taught him better body control and posture. She spent considerable time training his naturally high-pitched voice, which he slowly managed to lower, and to gain better resonance and tone. After a long period of rigorous training, she considered him ready for Hollywood.

First, he worked as an extra in silent films. Then he was in Erich von Stroheim's *The Merry Widow*, released in 1925. This was followed by a number of films. Then came *The Johnstown Flood*, where he first met another extra, 17-year-old Carole Lombard. In 1928, he starred in *Command Decision*, another Army film, in which he appeared as a brigadier general supervising aerial attacks on Germany.

Unfortunately, none of this led to much of anything in the movies, so Gable went to New York to try the stage. Initially, he joined the Laskin Brothers Stock Company, where he acted in many different roles. Then he had a

World War II Veterans in Hollywood

major role in the play *Machinal* in 1928, for which he received good media reviews.

Gable was unhappy with his marriage to Dillon. Eventually, they legally separated in 1929 and divorced on April 1, 1930. Back in Los Angeles, he appeared in the play *The Last Mile*. This got him a movie contract with Metro-Goldwyn-Mayer. Clark's first sound film was in a Western, *The Painted Desert*, released in 1931.

During the thirties, Gable was a ladies' man and had quite a few romances. One of his first was with Texas socialite Maria "Ria" Langham. After Clark and Josephine Dillon had divorced in 1930, a few days later he and Ria were supposedly married in Texas. She had been married twice before and had two children, Jana and Alfred. She had become a wealthy widow due to the death of her husband, Alfred Lucas. She was 47, Gable was 30. Ria's young daughter, Jana, had introduced the two. Jana had seen Clark when he was performing in Houston. After her family moved to New York, Jana took her mother to see Gable when he was starring in the play, *Machinal*. Afterwards, they went backstage to meet Clark. When Ria met Gable, she fell madly in love with him, while he saw her as elegant and worldly.

She accompanied him when he went to Hollywood, and they were "remarried" on June 19, 1931. The "real" marriage was coerced by Ria and the studio by using the morality clause in Gable's contract. Their eight-year marriage turned out to be not that happy; during that time, they lived in a mansion in Beverly Hills. According to Jana, "He liked to 'get under her skin' and 'ruffle her feathers' about things." His affair with Joan Crawford became well known, but Ria became even more upset when he began his relationship with Carole Lombard. Ria was granted a divorce on March 8, 1939, and got $300,000, which Gable was able to get in an advance on his *Gone with the Wind* salary (about $5 million in today's dollars). Afterwards, Ria dated George Raft for a while, but finally retired to Houston and died on September 24, 1966.

Another dalliance Clark had was with Loretta Young, with whom he had fathered an illegitimate daughter, Judy. Years later he gave Judy away when she was married. Loretta told everyone that she had adopted Judy. His romances became infamous. The one with Joan Crawford was dubbed "the affair that nearly burned Hollywood down." They even lived together for a time. And he was said to be "a very close friend of Norma Shearer." Gable also had very brief affairs with Paulette Goddard and, much later, a young Grace Kelly. Clark even proposed marriage to Nancy Davis, but she chose Ronald Reagan instead. Being modest, Clark said, "Hell, if I'd jumped on all the dames I'm supposed to have jumped on, I'd have had no time to go fishing."

After the "Roaring 20s" and during Gable's "Roaming 30s," he starred

27. Clark Gable

in a large number of films including *A Free Soul* (with Norma Shearer), *Red Dust*, *Hold Your Man* and *Wife vs. Secretary*, paired with James Stewart. Then came a biggie: *It Happened One Night* won five Academy Awards, including Best Actor for Clark Gable. But perhaps the most famous was *Gone with the Wind*. Playing Rhett Butler, he recited the never forgotten words, "Frankly, my dear, I don't give a damn."

Gable and Myrna Loy starred in the 1938 movie *Test Pilot*. Clark played the pilot who, after he crashed, met Myrna, whom he later married on screen. Perry King told me about meeting Ms. Loy at a Hollywood party in 1976. King says that he told her "*Test Pilot* was one of my favorite movies ever. She said it was her favorite also and that she loved working with Gable. 'They really had the rapport and fun you see on the screen,' she said. What a joy that was, talking with her—I'll never forget it. At 71, she was still just as beautiful as ever, just as alluring."

Just before World War II, Clark Gable married actress Carole Lombard. Gable said, "It is an extra dividend when you like the girl you've fallen in love with." He said that the following years were the best of his life. They had gotten to know each other during the filming of *No Man of Her Own* in 1932.

Clark Gable (center) in the 1935 movie *China Seas* (publicity still).

World War II Veterans in Hollywood

Then, after meeting again at the Mayfair Ball, a party for Hollywood's elite in 1936, they started dating and became a couple. They decided that they would be life partners and wanted to get married. Tabloids and magazines called them an "official couple." But the problem was that Clark was already married to Maria Langham. It took a while, but eventually he was able to get a divorce in 1939.

In the spring of 1939, while Gable was making *Gone with the Wind*, there was a production break and he and Lombard drove to Kingman, Arizona, where they were married on March 29. They bought a large property in Encino, California, not far from Hollywood, where they lived happily. They had horses and a lot of pets on their little "ranch." Al Jolson and other stars lived nearby.

Gable as Rhett Butler, and Vivien Leigh as Scarlett O'Hara in the award winning 1939 historical romance, adapted from the 1936 novel *Gone with the Wind* by Margaret Mitchell (publicity still).

27. Clark Gable

Both became involved in helping in the war effort. Lombard was on a war-bond tour when the DC-3 airliner she was in crashed into the east face of Mount Potosi, Nevada, on January 16, 1942, killing all on board. Carole was with her mother and Otto Winkler, a friend who had been Clark's best man at the wedding.

Gable was stricken with grief. From their first dance together on the night of the Mayfair Ball in 1936, they had never been apart more than six days. President Franklin Roosevelt sent Clark a letter expressing his condolences. The press wrote that Carole Lombard was the first woman casualty of the war. Gable traveled to the location of the crash to recover the bodies and return them to California for services and interment. Afterwards, he returned to their ranch where he mourned, started drinking heavily and lost a lot of weight. According to a friend, he was never the same again. She was the love of his life. He even contemplated suicide.

Finally, Gable pulled himself together and decided that he would get involved in the war effort. He wrote to President Roosevelt, asking him for an active role in the war. Roosevelt wrote back, telling him to keep on with his war-bond promotion efforts. But that was not enough for Clark, so he joined up.

On August 12, 1942, Clark Gable enlisted in the Army. He was 41 years old. The induction was held at the Federal Building in Los Angeles and was heavily covered by the press. First, like all other enlistees, he underwent basic training. Because of his fame, General "Hap" Arnold, commanding general of the Army Air Corps, assigned him to make motion pictures in order to encourage men to become aerial gunners, a skill that was badly needed at the time. (Another famous actor, Jimmy Stewart, was also shooting movies to promote enlistment in the Air Corps.)

In order to follow up on the Arnold assignment, Gable's friend, Andrew McIntyre, a professional cinematographer, joined the service with him. Both were sent to Officers' Candidate School and graduated on October 28, 1942, as second lieutenants. Then they were sent to Flexible Gunnery School at Tyndall Field, Florida, to learn how to be aerial gunners. From there they went to Fort George Wright, Washington, for a course in aerial photography. After training, both were promoted to first lieutenant.

Lieutenants Gable and McIntyre were assigned to the 351st Bombardment Group at Briggs Army Airfield in Texas. They trained with a film team that included a writer, two cameramen and a soundman. The 351st, now a part of the Eighth Air Force, along with Gable's team, arrived at the Royal Air Force base at Polebrook, England, in early 1943, where they spent most of that year.

World War II Veterans in Hollywood

The bombardment group flew bombing missions over Europe. Gable and his crew flew five missions in several different B-17 Flying Fortresses, including one to Germany. Clark, himself, was an "observer" gunner. Even though he was supposed to be an observer, Gable actually manned and fired a .50 caliber machine gun. Their first mission was over Belgium on May 4, 1943. Clark got the opportunity to fire his machine gun at German fighters but suffered frostbite on his hands because he was using the wrong type of gloves. At altitude the temperature can be 40 degrees below zero, and the waist guns on a B-17 are open to outside air. The pilot, William Hatcher, remarked, "The damn fool insists on being a rear gunner on every mission. Know what I think? Gable's trying to get himself killed so he can join up with his wife."

The second mission was over France in July, and the third mission that month was over Norway. The reason for the flight was to bomb war matériel plants. It was the longest mission to date for the Eighth Air Force. Gable was the top turret gunner in the lead aircraft on his last mission on September 23, 1943. A 20 mm shell from a German Luftwaffe fighter came so close to him that it shot off the heel of his boot. Luckily for Clark, the shell failed to explode, thus sparing his life. The mission had been over Germany, and Luftwaffe fighters shot out an engine and damaged the tail. One crewman was killed and two were injured. MGM immediately launched a campaign to get Gable removed from combat operations.

Gable was grounded, promoted to captain and was awarded the Distinguished Flying Cross and the Air Medal. In addition, he received his Aerial Gunner Wings.

During Gable's 1943 stint with the Eighth Air Force, the German Luftwaffe had superiority over Europe, and its top ace, Adolf Galland, had a squadron of yellow-nosed Messerschmitt 109s flying out of Abbeville, France, just across the English Channel from our bomber bases. Eighth Air Force casualties during World War II numbered 47,000, with over 26,000 killed. That was more than the total losses sustained by the U.S. Marine Corps during the war.

Adolf Hitler liked American movies, and Clark Gable was his favorite actor. When he got word that Gable was flying missions to bomb Germany, Hermann Goering offered a reward to anyone who could shoot Gable down, and the führer offered $5,000 to anyone who could capture Clark and bring him to Germany without injury. Gable was fearful that if captured, Hitler would put him in a cage like a gorilla and send him all over Germany for the populace to view.

Gable and his crew returned to the U.S. with more than 50,000 feet of color film. But by then, the Air Corps found they had sufficient gunners, so a

27. Clark Gable

recruiting film wasn't needed. To make use of all the valuable footage Gable and his crew had shot on their dangerous missions, the Army assigned Gable to make a documentary film, an account of aerial combat over occupied Europe and a testament to the Eighth Air Force's brave crews. Clark Gable played himself and also narrated. Also playing themselves were General "Hap" Arnold, Prince Richard Duke of Gloucester, Bob Hope and the members of bomber crews. The 62-minute film, *Combat America*, was released in 1945 and produced by the First Motion Picture Unit, Army Air Forces. William Wyler's documentary *Memphis Belle* reached the movie theaters in 1944 and overshadowed *Combat America*.

At his request, Major Clark Gable was discharged on June 12, 1944. He had wanted to fly more combat missions, but that request was refused. His discharge papers were signed by Captain Ronald Reagan.

After leaving the service, Gable returned to his ranch in Southern California to take a rest and wind down. Soon, however, he went back to acting in movies. The first was *Adventure*, released in 1947. He costarred with Greer Garson, and the promotional spiel was "Gable's back and Garson's got him." It was not a success.

Englishwoman Sylvia Ashley and Clark Gable were married on December 20, 1949. Her birth name was Edith Louisa Sylvia Hawkes. She had been married three times prior to Clark; her first marriage was to English Lord Ashley, whom she had married in 1927 and divorced in 1934. She kept the lord's name and became Lady Sylvia Ashley. Her second marriage was to Douglas Fairbanks Senior. Her third marriage was to Edward Stanley, 6th Baron of Sheffield, in 1944, divorced in 1948. A model, dancer and singer, she and Gable were divorced on April 21, 1952. Her extravagant, aristocratic lifestyle didn't set well with Clark Gable, the mostly homespun and casual American boy.

Gable was unhappy with the MGM studio contract, refused to renew it, and from then on worked as a free agent. He made *Soldier of Fortune* and *The Tall Man*, both released in 1955. Although both made a profit, neither was a runaway hit. That year, Clark married his fifth and last wife, Kay Williams. She had previously been married three times. Kay had a son, Bunker, by her third husband, the sugar baron, Adolph Spreckels. After their marriage, Gable, who had always longed to have a son, became an active stepfather. Bunker went on to become an internationally known innovative surfer. Tragically, he died at age 27 of a suspected drug overdose.

Later in 1955, Clark ventured into producing with partners Jane Russell and her husband, Bob Waterfield, the Los Angeles Rams' Hall of Fame pro football quarterback. They made *The King and Four Queens*, starring Gable.

World War II Veterans in Hollywood

During filming, he began experiencing health problems and he found that both producing and acting in the same movie was too much for him, so he quit producing.

Gable starred in *Band of Angels*, released in 1957, but it was dumped on by critics. The next year came *Teacher's Pet* with costar Doris Day. A number of films followed, the best of which was *It Started in Naples*, which received an Academy Award and two Golden Globes. Gable's very last movie was the 1961 film *The Misfits*. He starred with Marilyn Monroe; it was also her last film. Critics hailed it as Clark's best, with which Clark agreed. His favorite, however, was always *Mutiny on the Bounty*. Both of these movies put Gable in a reel role he fancied for himself in his real life: a macho man taking on nature with various tools devised by man. Off screen he had amused himself with airplanes, cars, boats and guns. He drove his Jaguar XK120 sports car and could often be seen with buddy, Keenan Wynn, riding their motorcycles around the San Fernando Valley in California.

Gable was an active Republican who supported Dwight Eisenhower, a close friend. He also supported Richard Nixon, and Ronald Reagan in 1940. At the urging of Carole Lombard, although he was a Republican, he had supported Franklin D. Roosevelt.

On November 6, 1960, Gable suffered a heart attack at his home and was taken to the Hollywood Presbyterian Hospital in Los Angeles. There, he seemed to have been improving, but then on November 16, as he was sitting up in bed and reading the paper, he suddenly suffered his final heart attack and passed on. He smoked three packs of cigarettes a day plus his pipe. He was only 59 years old. It was just after the making of *The Misfits*. To fit the role he played, Gable had dieted down from 230 pounds to 195. "Working with Marilyn Monroe," he said, "nearly gave me a heart attack, I have never been happier than when the film ended. Everything Marilyn does is different from any other woman, strange and exciting, from the way she talks to the way she uses that magnificent torso."

Four months later, on March 20, 1961, his widow, Kay Gable (Williams) was rushed to that same hospital, where she gave birth to their son, John Clark Gable. Clark had always longed for a son.

The funeral, held at Forest Lawn in Glendale, was attended by more than 200 Hollywood luminaries including Spencer Tracy, Robert Taylor, Jimmy Stewart, Frank Capra, Keenan Wynn, Roy Rogers and Marilyn Monroe. The U.S. Air Force Guard of Honor provided military services. He was interred at Forest Lawn right next to Carole Lombard's grave.

Clark Gable dominated the world of Hollywood like nobody else ever has, before or since. He was called "All man … and then some," by *Life* mag-

27. Clark Gable

azine. *Empire* magazine said he was one of the "sexiest stars in film history." He was voted one of the "greatest movie stars of all time" by *Entertainment Weekly*. *Premiere Magazine* accorded him the same words. Gable was called the "king" of Hollywood and was one of its highest paid stars. Clark Gable's death brought the Golden Age of Hollywood to an end.

In 2019, a special 80th-anniversary showing of *Gone with the Wind*, starring Clark Gable and Vivien Leigh, generated $2.3 million in box office grosses, a record for a classic movie brought back to the big screen. Warner Brothers hosted six screenings over four days.

28

Mel Brooks

Mel Brooks is a film producer and director, actor, comedian and composer. His movies have been hailed as some of the greatest comedies ever made. He is one of the few who have won an Oscar, Emmy, Grammy and a Tony. He served in the Army during World War II and fought in the Battle of the Bulge. At this writing (2019) he is still living, at age 93.

Melvin Kaminsky was born in Brooklyn on June 28, 1926. His parents were Jewish refugees from Eastern Europe. He had three brothers: Irving, Lenny and Bernie. Their father died of kidney disease when Mel was only two. The result was that the four boys were raised by their widowed mother and grew up in tenement housing. Brooks was a small and often sickly boy, bullied and teased by others at Public School 19 in the Williamsburg neighborhood of Brooklyn. He had a raspy voice with a Brooklyn accent. His older brother, Irving, was "kind and good to me. He gave me a tricycle." When Mel was nine, his uncle took him to see a show on Broadway. Afterwards, he told his uncle that he was, "absolutely going into show business."

During school, one of Brooks's friends was Mickey Rich, who was the younger brother of the famous drummer Buddy Rich. When Mel was 14, Mickey introduced him to Buddy. Buddy ended up teaching Brooks how to drum. Mel turned out to be so good at it that he was able to find some part-time employment drumming. He spent the summer of his 14th year in the Catskill Mountains working at the Butler Lodge, drumming and playing the piano. When the comic at the club fell sick, Mel was asked to stand in. He told jokes and did movie-star impressions. Soon he became a "tummler" at the lodge. Tummel is a Yiddish word meaning to make noise. It is Borscht Belt's slang for a comedic mover and shaker.

Mel went to Abraham Lincoln High School for a year, but when the family moved, he changed to the Eastern District High School in Williamsburg, where he graduated in 1944 at age 18. It was then that Melvin Kaminsky started using the stage name Mel Brooks. In the school yearbook, Mel stated that his goal was to become president of the U.S.

28. Mel Brooks

Mel Brooks in a military jeep.

After graduation, Brooks enlisted in the Army. When he scored high on the Army General Classification Test, Private Brooks was sent to an Army Specialized 12-Week Engineering Training Program at the Virginia Military Institute. When the Army shut the program down, Brooks was sent to Fort Sill, Oklahoma, for basic training in May 1944.

After basic infantry training, Brooks was assigned as a combat engineer to the 1104th Engineer Combat Battalion, 78th Infantry Division. The combat engineers were similar to the Navy Seabees; they performed battlefield construction and when necessary dropped their tools and fought as infantry. The 1104th cleared mine fields and built bridges all the way from the Hurtgen Forest, near Aachen, in December 1944, to the Elbe at the war's end in May 1945. During their march they bridged the rivers Roer, Rhine, Weser, and many tributaries. Twice they had to fight strong German resistance as infantry. The Battle of the Bulge began on December 16, 1944. It was the last major German attack that delayed the American offensive drive into Germany until January 25, 1945. Mel's battalion was sent to join in the battle. Corporal Brooks's job was to go ahead of the American front line in order to deactivate enemy land mines, a dangerous task indeed. Afterwards, Mel observed, "War isn't hell. War is loud. Much too noisy. All those shells and bombs going off all around you. You thought about how you were going to stay warm at night, how you were going to get from one hedgerow to another without some German sniper taking you out."

World War II Veterans in Hollywood

When the Germans played propaganda recordings over loudspeakers, Brooks, a Jew, used a bull horn and mimicked songs by Al Jolson, the famous Jewish singer.

When Mel's unit entered Germany, it constructed the first bridge over the Roer River and built similar structures over the Rhine and Weser rivers as well as the Lippe and Aur-Oker canals. It also destroyed pillboxes and cleared roads. At the end of the war in Europe, the 1104th was conducting a reconnaissance of the Harz Mountains. After the German surrender, Mel, who had been noticed as the company clown by senior officers, was given a special services assignment. Since he was a late arrival to the war, he was not eligible for immediate discharge. He was assigned to the 1262nd Service Command Unit. For his new duties he was given an old Mercedes-Benz sedan and as his outfit's "tummler" he roamed the division's occupied area, entertaining the troops.

Brooks was finally discharged on June 27, 1946. He was awarded the Battle of the Bulge Commemorative Medal and, of course, the World War II Victory Medal. Recalling his Army years, Mel said, "I was a Combat Engineer. Isn't that ridiculous? The two things I hate most in the world are combat and engineering."

In the summer of 1947, Brooks began acting in Red Bank, New Jersey, in a theatre troupe. Then he was a comedy writer on Sid Caesar's NBC television series *The Admiral Broadway Revue*, where he earned $50 a week.

Sid Caesar created a variety comedy television series, *Your Show of Shows*, that ran on NBC for three months starting in January 1949. He brought Mel Brooks along with him to do some of the writing. The show was broadcast live for 19 episodes and was an immediate success. It ended when the lead performer, Imogene Coca, left to do her own show.

In 1952 Mel Brooks wrote the show *New Faces of 1952*, which ran on Broadway for most of that year. It was a musical revue featuring songs and comedy skits. It was made into a movie in 1954 with Brooks credited as the writer.

Mel Brooks and actress Florence Baum were married on November 26, 1953. She had appeared in the 1948 movie *Places Please*. They had three children: Stephanie, born in 1956, Nicky in 1957 and Eddie in 1959. They were divorced in 1962. Years later, Mel worked with his son Nicky, who was the story editor on three movies produced, directed and written by his father.

Sid Caesar created *Caesar's Hour* in 1954—more or less a continuation of Sid's previous programs, with many of the same writers and actors. A sketch comedy, it starred not only Caesar but also Nanette Fabray and Carl Reiner, among others. It debuted on ABC television in September 1954 and it ran into

28. Mel Brooks

1957. Brooks and fellow Caesar's writer Carl Reiner had become friends. Together, they wrote and performed comedic skits at parties in New York. After seeing them perform at a party in 1959, a critic wrote, "Brooks was the most original comic improviser I had ever seen."

Brooks and Reiner moved to Hollywood in 1960 to perform in two episodes of their "2000 Year Old Man" act on *The Steve Allen Show*. Their performance was made into a record that sold more than one million copies in 1961. On January 20, 1962, Florence Baum divorced Mel Brooks because Mel was having a torrid love affair with Eartha Kitt.

Brooks's August 5, 1964, marriage to Anne Bancroft was a turning point in both their lives. He was 38, she 33. Anne was previously married and divorced. She had had a successful show business career with her film debut in 1952. Bancroft won an Academy Award for Best Actress for her lead role in the 1962 movie *The Miracle Worker*. A stage play based on the film won her a Tony Award for Best Actress in a Play.

According to Mel, "I'd been dating Jewish girls with short waists." The two met when Brooks saw her rehearsing a musical number for the *Perry Como Show*. Bancroft remembered, "A guy with an aggressive voice from the other side of the theater said, 'Hey, Anne Bancroft, I'm Mel Brooks.'" According to Mel, "She was wearing a white dress and her voice was beautiful. I didn't let her out of my sight from the day I met her." The day after meeting him, Anne told a reporter, "I've met the right man. He never left me from that moment on." They were married at New York's Municipal Building by a judge. A passer-by served as their witness. Afterwards Brooks said, "I'm married to a beautiful and talented woman who can lift your spirits just by looking at you."

Get Smart was a television series created and written by Mel Brooks and Buck Henry. It was a highly successful comedic parody that won seven Emmy Awards including Outstanding Comedy Series. It starred Don Adams, who also directed some segments. It went on the air on September 18, 1965, on NBC and ran for five seasons with 138 episodes.

The Producers was Brooks's first feature film. A musical comedy about Hitler that he produced, composed the music for and wrote, it had initial problems regarding distribution. It was so satirical that it was an underground hit and shown as an art film. The story is about two Broadway producers who put on a play they call *Springtime for Hitler*. It makes fun of Adolf Hitler and Nazi Germany. The film, later called a classic, won Brooks an Oscar for Best Screenplay. It was somewhat successful at the box office, and Mel said, "I'm the only Jew who ever made a buck offa Hitler." He credited Anne Bancroft with being "the guiding force" behind his doing *The Producers*.

Mel and Anne's son Max was born on May 22, 1972. Maximillian Michael Brooks became an actor and author. He appeared in 15 movies or television shows; his first was in his father's *To Be or Not to Be* in 1983. He wrote a number of fiction and non-fiction books and was a member of the writing team at *Saturday Night Live*.

Mel Brooks wrote, directed and acted in the 1974 Warner Brothers film *Blazing Saddles*. A satirical comedy–Western, it was Brooks's first stab at directing. He also appeared in three supporting roles. The movie satirizes racism with the hero being a black sheriff in an all-white town. The music in the film was composed by Mel. It won the Writers Guild of America Award for Best Comedy Written Directly for the Screen. Made with a budget of $2.6 million, it ended up grossing $119.6 million.

Brooks followed up that year by directing *Young Frankenstein*. Written by Brooks and Gene Wilder, the 105-minute movie is a parody of the classic monster film genre. Mel's voice is heard in three different roles. It was well liked by critics. The film was made for less than three million and viewers paid $86.2 million at the box office. It, along with *Blazing Saddles* and *The Producers*, were among the American Film Institute's "100 Funniest Movies."

Mel Brooks created the television series *When Things Were Rotten* in 1975, a parody of the Robin Hood legend. Mel was the executive producer

Brooks as Dr. Richard H. Thorndyne, played opposite Madeline Kahn as Victoria Brisbane in the 1977 movie *High Anxiety* (behind the scenes photo).

28. Mel Brooks

and wrote one episode. The half-hour show ran for 13 episodes on ABC. Although liked by critics, it didn't do well with viewers and was cancelled after one season.

During the rest of the decade, Brooks directed, produced and wrote three movies: *Silent Movie*, *High Anxiety* and *The Muppet Movie*. In 1981, Mel produced, directed and wrote the *History of the World, Part 1*. In addition, he played a number of parts in the film, including those of Moses and King Louis XVI of France. The film cost $10 million to make and grossed $31.7 million. A critic wrote, "Although in bad taste, you let yourself laugh at the obscenity in the humor." Brooks sang a rap song for the soundtrack called "It's Good to Be the King." It became a successful dance hit that year.

Brooks formed his own production company, Brooks Films, and produced *To Be or Not to Be* in 1983. He costarred in it with his wife, Anne Bancroft. He sang the song "Hitler Rap" with the lyric, "Don't be stupid, be a smarty, come and join the Nazi Party." The movie made fun of Adolf Hitler and Nazi Germany. His son Nicky worked at Brooks Films and was the story editor on *The Fly*, *The Fly II* and *Spaceballs*.

Mel Brooks directed, produced and wrote the screenplay for *Robin Hood: Men in Tights*, released in 1993. It is a musical adventure movie, a parody of the Robin Hood story. Mel appears in a minor role and he wrote three of the songs. Made by Brooks Films, it had a budget of $20 million and took in $35.7 million at the box office.

Anne Bancroft convinced Brooks to turn the movie *The Producers* into a Broadway stage presentation in 2001. He produced, wrote the music, lyrics and book. It was a critical and financial success and ran for six years, winning 12 Tony Awards. At its opening, a reporter asked Mel if

Brooks in 1981 (publicity still).

he was nervous about the play's reception since it cost $40 million to produce. Brooks joked, "If it flops, I'll take my other 60 million and fly to Rio." A hit on Broadway, it led to a musical version in 2005, which he also produced and wrote.

Anne Bancroft died on June 6, 2005, while battling uterine cancer. Remembering her, Mel said, "You know, it [their marriage] took because Anne and I both grew up during the marriage, we both grew up, we both knew what was really important and what love meant, and what doing for each other meant." She had remarked, "You know, we're like any other couple. We've had our ups and downs, but every time I hear the key in the door, I know the party is about to begin." During her career, she won not only the Academy Award but also three BAFTA Awards, two Golden Globes, two Tonys and two Emmys.

After partially recovering from Anne's passing, Brooks produced a stage version of *Young Frankenstein*. It was a musical that had had a summer try-out at the Paramount Theatre in Seattle in April 2007 and opened on Broadway at the St. James Theatre on October 31, Halloween night. Promoted as "the New Mel Brooks Musical," *Young Frankenstein*, closed in January 2009 after 484 performances.

Brooks was awarded a star on the Hollywood Walk of Fame on April 23, 2010. The American Film Institute presented him with its Lifetime Achievement Award on June 6, 2013. On April 28, 2015, Mel Brooks appeared in his first and only solo stage show at the Geffen Playhouse in the Westwood neighborhood of Los Angeles. It was a sold-out performance. He told stories from his life, including personal anecdotes and reminiscences about his career in television, movies and musicals.

Mel Brooks went to Washington, D.C., on September 22, 2016, to receive the National Medal of Arts from President Barack Obama, who said that the award is "for a lifetime of making the world laugh." When he received the medal, Brooks pretended to "pants" the president and faked falling down from the weight of the medal before shaking Obama's hand. This brought the house down.

In what may be his last movie, Brooks acted as one of the monsters in *Hotel Transylvania 3: Summer Vacation*, released on July 13, 2018. It's about a monster family that takes a vacation on a luxury cruise ship. It brought in box office sales of $528.6 million for Sony Pictures. *To Tell the Truth* is a television game show with four celebrity panelists. On August 26, 2018, Mel Brooks was one of the panelists.

These days Mel Brooks and his best friend, Carl Reiner, pass the time together reminiscing about their careers and going on about entertainment

28. Mel Brooks

and politics. Reiner remarked in an interview with *Vanity Fair*, "We see each other almost every night. We watch movies and comment on the world. And now we have Trump to work with." For Brooks, his friendship with Reiner continues to make him laugh hysterically. In June 2020, Mel was 94 years old while Carl was 98.

29

Rod Steiger

Rod Steiger had a prolific career as an actor. He had more than 50 credits in movies and television and on the stage. He played in almost anything that came his way, in roles that ranged from leading man to cameo appearances. Steiger was noted for his portrayal of offbeat, often volatile and sinister characters. He won an Academy Award, a Golden Globe and a star on the Hollywood Walk of Fame. Rod was cited as "one of Hollywood's most charismatic and dynamic stars." During World War II, he saw action with the Navy on destroyers in the Pacific Theater.

Rodney Stephen Steiger was born on April 14, 1925, in Westhampton, New York. He was the only child of Frederick Steiger and Lorraine Driver. They were traveling vaudevillians, a song and dance team. They were divorced when Rod was only one year old. As far as Rodney was concerned, his father disappeared, so he never knew him. Rodney and his mother moved to Newark, New Jersey, where he grew up. In elementary school, he experienced his first taste of acting in a play. He attended West Side High School in Newark, where he played softball and was in a number of school plays. Unfortunately, his mother had become an alcoholic, so he didn't have much of a home life.

Steiger dropped out of high school and enlisted in the Navy on May 11, 1942. He had just turned 17. He was sent for boot camp training at the U.S. Naval Training Station in Newport, Rhode Island. Afterward, he was trained to be a torpedo-man on the USS *Benham*, stationed in the Pacific Theater. The ship was a destroyer involved in the Battle of Midway in June and then the Guadalcanal campaign in August 1942. Torpedoes are a main component of a destroyer's fire power.

The destroyer USS *Taussig* was commissioned on May 20, 1944. Steiger was assigned to be on its first crew (a "plank holder"). Upon launching, the ship embarked on a five-week shakedown cruise. After more training, the *Taussig* transited the Panama Canal to join a destroyer squadron, part of the Third Fleet. She was involved in the Luzon campaign, the Iwo Jima operations and the Okinawa operation.

29. Rod Steiger

Late in 1944, the squadron was struck by a horrendous typhoon, known as Halsey's Typhoon, during which three of the destroyers were lost. Admiral "Bull" Halsey was so intent on chasing down the Imperial Japanese Fleet and sinking it that he ignored the danger and sailed the Third Fleet into the teeth of the typhoon. Steiger told about it: "The typhoon was so bad—80-foot waves with 115 mph winds—that when your vessel rolled from side to side, you could see nothing but the superstructure above water. I saw a smaller destroyer than ours that turned over and went down. No one survived. I volunteered to go out on deck in that storm after a depth charge had broken loose. So, I put a rope around myself, and I slithered out and lashed it down. As I turned to go back, I looked up and there was this wave—it was ten feet above me. The wave hit me, carried me along the deck. Then I had to lay there and time my breathing because every time the ship went over on my side, I would go about four feet under. I'd come up for air while the other side was under, take a breath and then finally, when I got my strength back, I crawled inside." Steiger had survived by tying the rope around his waist and flattening his body on the deck as waves engulfed the ship.

The battle of Iwo Jima was unforgettable. The ship's guns were firing on Mount Suribachi, the highest point on the island. According to Steiger, "We were throwing shells in so fast, and the Marines were advancing so quickly, that communication wasn't fast enough to keep up. We were knocking off our own men. That's where that horrible, inhuman phrase comes from, 'They were expendable.'"

After Iwo Jima, the *Taussig* supported a carrier-based bombing of Tokyo. The ship didn't encounter enemy warships, only sampans. The

Rod Steiger portraying Victor Komarosky in the 1965 award winning movie, *Dr. Zhivago*. The film is an historical war story set during the Russian Civil War of 1917–1922 and is based on the 1957 novel by Boris Pasternak for which he received the 1958 Nobel Prize for Literature (publicity still).

fishing fleet was Japan's resource for first alerts. The small boats had women and children on them, but, since they could have radios on board, they had to be destroyed. This memory always haunted Steiger.

The fast carrier squadrons were used not only to strike Tokyo but also to range far to the north to strike air bases out of the reach of the U.S. B-29s. Misawa, at the northeast tip of Honshu, was a kamikaze training base.

The *Taussig* continued to support operations against the Japanese islands until the end of the war. On August 14, 1945, Japan surrendered unconditionally. Steiger was discharged on September 3, 1945. He had a number of ribbons including the Combat Action Ribbon, the Asiatic/Pacific Combat Ribbon and the WWII Victory Medal.

Initially, Rod returned to New Jersey and worked for the Veterans Administration oiling machines and washing floors. While there, he became part of an amateur acting assembly called the Civil Service Little Theater Group. Steiger made his stage debut in 1946 at the Civic Repertory Theatre of Newark in a play called *Curse You, Jack Dalton!* In 1947, he had bit parts in two different television shows: *Amityville Horror* and *American Playhouse*.

Always interested in acting, Rod rented a room in New York City and, using the GI Bill, studied at the Actors Studio and the Dramatic Workshop. In 1950, he secured a small part in the Broadway play, *An Enemy of the People*, that ran into 1952. This was followed by another play, *Night Music*. Steiger made his Hollywood debut in the film *Teresa*, released in 1951. This was followed by 14 more movies. In addition, he was in the television show *Screen Directors Playhouse* and appeared in three more Broadway plays including *Rashomon*, in which he starred with Claire Bloom. A critic noted that Steiger gave "an effortless and persuasive performance."

Playing the title role in *Marty*, in an episode of the Goodyear Television Playhouse, Steiger depicted a lonely butcher in search of love. It was a success and a critic wrote, "He brought striking intensity to his performance, particularly in giving us Marty's pain." Rod got a Sylvania Award for it. He played opposite Marlon Brando in *On the Waterfront* in 1954. Although Steiger had great respect for Brando as an actor, the two didn't get along personally. Rod was nominated for the Academy Award for Best Supporting Actor.

Steiger performed his own singing in the movie version of *Oklahoma!* He portrayed an emotionally disturbed Jud. One critic believed he gave "a complexity to the character that went far beyond the musical version." He costarred with Jack Palance and Ida Lupino in *The Big Knife*, a Hollywood movie released in 1955. Also, that year he was in *The Court-Martial of Billy Mitchell* along with Gary Cooper and Charles Bickford.

In 1952, Steiger had married actress Sally Gracie. The union lasted six years but then ended in divorce. In 1959, he married actress Claire Bloom. They had a daughter, Anna, who was born in 1960 and, when grown, became an opera singer. Steiger said, "Bloom was all I ever wanted in a woman. Maybe our marriage was better than most because we were both established when we met." They bought a home in Malibu, on the coast near Los Angeles, a surf-side haven for Hollywood personalities. In 1969, Bloom divorced Rod and married Broadway producer Hillard Elkins.

Steiger was in three more movies in 1957 including the British thriller *Across the Bridge*, in which he played a con man who hid in Mexico. One critic thought that Rod gave "one of his greatest performances." The hugely successful movie *Al Capone* was released in 1959. Playing Capone, Rod deglamorized his portrayal. He received another nomination of a Lauren Award for Best Male Dramatic Performance.

The decade of the sixties was, perhaps, the high point of Steiger's acting career. He was in 17 movies. He won his only Academy Award for Best Actor in a Leading Role *In the Heat of the Night*. His salary for the movie was

Steiger (left) as Chief of Police Bill Gillespie, with Sidney Poitier as Virgil Tibbs in the 1967 crime/mystery/drama *In the Heat of the Night*. Steiger won the Academy Award for Best Actor (publicity still).

World War II Veterans in Hollywood

$150,000, a considerable sum in 1967. About his Oscar, he said, "I wanted to win it. It's important. It gives you greater latitude in the business and that means bigger and better parts."

Steiger won an Oscar nomination for his part in *The Pawnbroker*, which he said was the favorite of all his films. He won the prize for Best Actor at the Berlin International Film Festival. He was in *Doctor Zhivago*, which had the biggest international box office sales of the sixties, grossing some $200 million. Rod was in a number of television shows such as *Wagon Train* and *Route 66*. Steiger went overseas to act in a role in *World in My Pocket* in 1961. He felt that he had more esteem as an actor in Europe, and he liked the more relaxed shooting schedules there. When Rod returned to New York, he had a part in *Moby Dick—Rehearsed* by Orson Wells. It played in the Ethel Barrymore Theatre for 62 performances at the end of 1962.

Rod was part of a huge cast in the epic World War II film *The Longest Day*, released in 1962. He joined John Wayne, Richard Todd, Robert Mitchum, Richard Burton, Sean Connery and Henry Fonda. Richard Burton was a close friend and, according to Burton, Rod shared intimate details of his life. He talked of his financial troubles and even admitted to having a face lift. In the 1969 science-fiction movie *The Illustrated Man*, he costarred again with Claire Bloom. They were still married at the time.

Steiger was active in the seventies as well. Although he said he was more selective regarding the roles he took, he was in 13 movies. He played Benito Mussolini in the *Last Days of Mussolini* and Napoleon Bonaparte in *Waterloo*, for which he was paid one million dollars. In 1979, he appeared in *The Amityville Horror* film. Interestingly enough, he had had a bit part in *The Amityville Horror* television show in 1951. After the Claire Bloom divorce, in 1973

Steiger as Napoleon in *Waterloo* (1970). The epic, period war film depicts the preliminary events and the June 18, 1815, Battle of Waterloo in Belgium, and is famous for its lavish battle scenes (publicity still).

29. Rod Steiger

he married his secretary, Sherry Nelson, who had been a ballerina. It lasted six years. He was offered the title role in *Patton* but turned it down. He said, "I'm not going to glorify this thing. I wasn't going to glorify war." He also turned down *The Godfather*, later saying, "That was a big mistake." In 1976, he fell into a deep depression. Even so, he went back to Europe again to play in the French movie *Innocents with Dirty Hands*. It was not well received by critics. The *New York Times* noted, "It is little more than a soap opera. The performances are of a piece—uniformly atrocious." In *W.C. Fields and Me*, his part was also poorly received by critics. Steiger played Pontius Pilate in the television mini-series *Jesus of Nazareth*, a British-Italian production that ran for only two months.

During the next decade, he sometimes fell into more bouts of depression and stayed in his apartment alone. In 1976, he had open-heart surgery and again in 1979. Even so, he was in 11 movies and a television show. Perhaps the highlight of Steiger's movie career then was the critically acclaimed 1981 film *The Chosen*. The eighties ended with Rod playing the New York City chief of police in *The January Man*. He was also in the Canadian films *Klondike Fever* and *The Lucky Star*. He received a Genie Award for Best Performance by a Foreign Actor for each of them. Steiger had a small part in the ABC miniseries *Hollywood Wives*, which aired during February 1985. Also, that year, he and singer Paula Ellis were married. They had a son, Michael Steiger.

In the nineties, he was in an almost unbelievable 25 movies and three television shows. He had turned 65 in 1990. Steiger was the doctor *in Shiloh*, an Army general in *Mars Attacks!*, a Supreme Court justice in *The Hurricane*, and a preacher in *End of Days*.

Steiger and Paula Ellis were divorced in 1997 and he married actress Joan Benedict in 2000. It was the last of his five marriages and lasted until his death. He was in six movies during the new century including his last, *Poolhall Junkies*, released a year after he had passed away. He played Marty again in 2000 in a *Playhouse 90* television show.

In 2002, Steiger had surgery to remove a tumor from his gallbladder. There were complications from the surgery, and he died from pneumonia on July 9, 2002. He was buried at Forest Lawn Memorial Park in the Hollywood Hills.

30

Norman Lear

Norman Lear is not as well known to the public as are some other Hollywood personalities. Primarily, he was a television and film producer and writer. As of this writing, he was 97 years old and still going strong. He is best known for the television shows *All in the Family, The Jeffersons, One Day at a Time* and *Mary Hartman, Mary Hartman*. He only acted in one movie, but he was a guest on some 25 television shows and has more than 30 credits as a producer, director and writer. Ten months after Pearl Harbor, he enlisted in the Army, became an Air Force radio operator/gunner, flew 52 combat missions and was awarded the Air Medal with four oak leaf clusters.

Norman Milton Lear was born on July 27, 1922, in New Haven, Connecticut. The family of his father, Herman, was from Russia and his mother, Elizabeth, was born in the Ukraine. The family is Jewish, and even though Norman had his Bar Mitzvah, they didn't attend temple. He had a sister, Claire, who was three years younger than Norman; she died in 2015.

When Norman was nine years old, his father, a traveling salesman, was arrested for selling fake bonds, for which he served a three-year prison term. His absence resulted in hardships for the family, so his mother sent Norman to live with his aunt and uncle in Hartford, Connecticut, and later with his grandparents in New Haven. Lear remembered, "I had to make my own way. There wasn't anybody going to help me."

When his father was released from prison in 1934, the family reunited, and they moved to Brooklyn, New York, where the children attended elementary school. Four years later, Norman's father was seriously injured in an automobile accident. Consequently, they moved back to Hartford, where his dad recovered. While they were in Brooklyn, Lear had had a part-time job at Coney Island trying to persuade customers to use a swimming pool. The pool was, Norman said, "A seedy piece of real estate famous among young male frequenters because of several knotholes in the boy's bathroom where they could see into the girls shower."

Back in Hartford, Lear attended Weaver High School, where he wrote

30. Norman Lear

for the school paper. He made his mark as an eclectic wit and had the opportunity to interview his idol, Harry Ritz, the lead clown of the famous Ritz Brothers vaudeville act. The piece was titled "Leering Lear and the Rollicking Ritz." Norman had begun his climb to the summit of show business at Weaver and graduated in 1940.

Lear enrolled at Emerson College in Boston in September. "I almost didn't make it to college at all. I didn't expect to go because I was a kid during the Depression," Norman said. But his fate changed when he entered the American Legion Oratorical Contest. Competitors had to give a speech about the Constitution. Lear said that he titled his talk "The Constitution and Me." Lear said, "The reason for that title was I was Jewish, and I had learned there were people who hated people because of their religion.... I wondered if the Constitution wasn't a little more precious to me than someone who didn't need its protection."

Norman won the scholarship and entered the college, majoring in theater. He lived in an all-male boarding house nearby. He remembered rehearsing for a production of *Two Orphans* in a drama class. While there, they got the news that Pearl Harbor was bombed on December 7, 1941. Lear dropped out of college and joined the Army in September 1942.

Norman Lear, 2008 (Matt Stoller, Wikimedia Commons).

World War II Veterans in Hollywood

Lear wanted to join the masses of American youth and enlist right after Pearl Harbor. As a Jew, he wanted to prove he was "apple pie" American. His mother tearfully begged him not to join and his father told him to stay in school and become an officer. He registered for the draft on June 30, 1942, and then enlisted in the Army Air Force in September with the ambition to be a pilot. His mother was distraught.

Called up in early November 1942, Norman Lear was billeted in an Atlantic City hotel for basic training. He learned to march on the boardwalk. From Atlantic City, Lear was sent to radio operator's school at Scott Field in Illinois. He vigorously protested (to no avail), because he had enlisted to be a pilot. Completing the radio school, he was sent to gunnery school at Laredo, Texas. Norman Lear completed his training, was certified as an aerial gunner/radio operator and was promoted to sergeant. Then in the mysterious ways of the military, his protests were honored, and he was sent to Buffalo, New York, for pilot training. While at Buffalo and on emotional overload, he telephoned Charlotte Rosen, a girl from Emerson College he barely knew, and proposed marriage. She accepted, and so began a thirteen-year relationship that produced a daughter, Ellen, born in 1947.

Lear was washed out of pilot training for technical reasons and reassigned as a radio operator/gunner to the 772nd Bomb Squadron of the 463rd Bomb Group, which was undergoing training at Avon Park, Florida. He joined Captain Albert Brown's Boeing B-17 crew, nicknamed "Umbriago." Umbriago was comedian Jimmy Durante's sign-off from his radio show in the 1940s. The radio compartment on the B-17 was a small space above the bomb bay and behind the top turret. It had limited visibility above and to the rear, which provided for the flexible mounted .50 caliber machine gun's field of fire. The radio operator's other duty after hearing "bombs away" was to visually check the bomb bay to make sure that all bombs were away.

In November 1944, the 772nd Squadron flew across the Atlantic Ocean via Gander, Newfoundland, to the Azores Islands, the United Kingdom, and then ended up at Foggia, Italy, as the only B-17 group of the 15th Air Force. The 15th was equipped with consolidated B-24s and was most famous for its raids on the oil fields at Ploesti, Romania. The B-24s had initially flown out of Benghazi, Libya, and then on November 2, 1943, moved up to Foggia near the heel of Italy's boot. The 15th Air Force's missions covered all of Southern Europe, and they would sometimes join up with the 8th Air Force for raids into Germany.

Lear flew 52 combat missions, including bloody raids on the Messerschmitt factory at Regensburg and, on March 24, 1945, a raid on tank factories in Berlin. They received a Distinguished Unit Citation for the Berlin raid.

30. Norman Lear

Lear's B-17 outfit operated off of the pierced steel planked (PSP) runway at Celone Airfield, ten kilometers north of Foggia on the spur that juts into the Adriatic Sea. He and five of the Umbriago's crew lived in a six-man dirt floored tent. Lear, with his theater-prop-making experience and family entrepreneurial talents, scrounged up bricks for a floor, lights and radio leads for each bunk, and even P-51 drop tanks for fuel and water. The Umbriago tail gunner, Danny Carroll, memorialized Lear's genius for scrounging in his memoir, *Crew Umbriago*.

At the end of hostilities, Technical Sergeant Norman Lear had completed 52 combat missions, been awarded the Air Medal with four oak leaf clusters and shared a Distinguished Unit Citation for the Berlin raid.

With the war over, instead of returning to the States, Lear volunteered for transport duty. The bombers were converted to transports in order to ferry the thousands of G.I.s in Europe to ports of embarkation. Lear, with his overactive imagination and curiosity, saw an opportunity to see Europe at low altitude and in friendly skies. Eventually he returned home and was discharged in October 1945.

Lear returned to New York, where he got his first job in publicity at $40 a week. After less than a year, some of Lear's off-the-cuff witticisms were printed, and Lear got fired. Charlotte was in a family way, forcing Norman to join the family business with his father. Lear eked out a living for two years being a jack of all trades at Lear, Inc., until the enterprise finally went under.

So in 1949, Lear moved his family to Los Angeles. To make a lot of money, his father advised him to buy the latest model convertible he could afford, drive it out there and sell it in California. Norman remembered, "It took me nine weeks to sell that bloody car and I got fifty dollars more than I had paid for it."

There he partnered with his cousin, Ed Simmons, selling home furnishings door to door. Also, they took and sold family photographs door to door for $17 each. Both wanted to break into show business, so they started writing together. First, they wrote a parody of *The Sheik of Araby* and sold it to Larry Potter's Supper Club for $35. One day Norman got an idea that he thought comedian Danny Thomas could use, so he wrote it up. Thomas used it at Ciro's nightclub and paid Lear $500.

They really made it in 1950, selling a television show that ran for a year on NBC. It was a musical comedy variety production called *The Jack Haley Four Star Review*. Having seen the show, comedian Jerry Lewis was impressed. He hired them for his *Colgate Comedy Hour*, where they wrote comedy sketches until 1953. Then, Norman Lear wrote his first movie, *Scared*

Stiff, a semi-musical comedy. It was one of 17 films made by the Martin and Lewis team and was released in April.

Next came *The Martha Raye Show*, Lear's first try as a producer. It was a comedy and variety hour that was performed live on NBC. Its first episode was in January 1954, the last in May 1956. The show starred Martha Raye and her boyfriend, who was portrayed by retired championship boxer Rocky Graziano. Lear said Martha Raye was a clown. "I think I use the word, 'clown' very seldom and with great reverence. I think comedians are born often enough, but clowns you get only very rarely."

In 1956 Norman and Charlotte divorced. Later that year, Lear married Frances Loeb. She was 33, a year older than Norman, and had been married twice previously. They had two daughters, Kate in 1958 and Maggie the following year.

Lear and his friend Bud Yorkin established Tandem Productions in 1959. Yorkin had been the stage manager for the *Colgate Comedy Hour*. Their concept was to turn out quality television specials and comedy movies. Their first production was a television series, a half-hour Western called *The Deputy*, starring Henry Fonda. Then there was *The Night They Raided Minsky's* in 1967, with *Cold Turkey* following in 1971. They also made a deal with Paramount Pictures to do a number of television pilots. One that Paramount liked was *Band of Gold*.

Next came the big one, *All in the Family*. It premiered in September 1972 and won four consecutive Emmy Awards for Outstanding Comedy Series. Produced by Norman Lear, who directed four episodes, it was groundbreaking in that it examined controversial and socially relevant subjects. Even though a comedy, it centered on race, sexuality and social inequality via comedy. It was the top-rated series on television for five years.

Norman Lear produced the comedy television series *Maude*, which started in the fall of 1972. All the episodes revolved around Maude, an outspoken, middle-class woman who wore her liberal politics on her sleeve. Lear remembered, "Bea Arthur as Maude made me laugh in places nobody will ever touch again, places that I don't know how to find." In one episode, Lear tackled the subject of the right to have an abortion and, a few months later, the Supreme Court made it the law of the land with the Roe vs. Wade decision.

Norman's wife Frances was diagnosed with bipolar disorder in 1973 and became an activist for the women's movement, civil rights and mental health.

Lear broke ground again by producing two television series that featured black families: *Good Times* in 1974 and *The Jeffersons* the next year. His next series was *Mary Hartman, Mary Hartman*, which ran during the 1976–1977 season. A soap opera, it featured a small-town housewife struggling to

30. Norman Lear

Lear, creator of such television series as *All in the Family*, *The Jeffersons* and *Sanford and Son*. New York City, 2016 (Greg 2600, Wikimedia Commons).

cope with the increasingly bizarre and violent events around her. *The New York Times* wrote, "It was postmodern before postmodern became a name."

In 1980, Lear produced *Palmerstown, U.S.A.*, about families with different racial backgrounds. Its 17 episodes ran for one season on CBS. In 1981, Norman Lear founded People for the American Way, a nonprofit organization dedicated to protecting First Amendment rights, strengthening public education plus promoting electoral and immigration reform. Today, it has more than a million members fighting right-wing extremism and defending constitutional values.

Norman started hosting a game show, *Quiz Kids*, on CBS in 1981 and continued for 14 months. Lear and his partner, Jerry Perenchio, bought AVCO Embassy Pictures in 1982 and merged it with another company to form Embassy Communications, dropping AVCO from the name. In 1985 they sold Embassy Communications to Columbia Pictures for $450 million. Lear was inducted into the Television Academy Hall of Fame in 1984.

Norman and Frances divorced in 1985. The settlement was estimated to be as much as $112 million, one of the largest on record. She used some of the funds to start a magazine, *Lear's*, for women over 45. For this, she was named Editor of the Year by *Advertising Age*. But the magazine folded after only six years. She died of breast cancer in 1996.

In 1986 Norman Lear created Act III Communications, which produced a number of films such as *Fried Green Tomatoes* and the television show *The Powers That Be*. Norman Lear and Lyn Davis were married in 1987. She was 40, he was 65. In 1988 they had a son, Benjamin, and then twin daughters in

1994, Madeline and Brianna. For some reason, it turned out that Lyn could no longer conceive, so they had employed a surrogate mother.

During the nineties, Act III produced three television shows, but none were very successful. Act III was sold in 1997. In 2000, he founded the Norman Lear Center at the University of Southern California. Based at the USC Annenberg School of Communications, it is a multi-disciplinary research and public policy center that explores the convergence of entertainment, commerce and society.

The only time Norman was an actor was on a 2005 episode of the *Jack and Bobby* show. Set in the future, each episode of the fictional show is a complete short story. Lear appeared as an elderly substitute father for Bobby.

Norman Lear's autobiography, *Even This I Get to Experience*, was published (and is still available online). A reviewer wrote, "It is flat out, one of the best Hollywood memoirs ever written, an absolute treasure." The Associated Press called it "an entertaining, penetrating celebration of a richly lived life." And the *Wall Street Journal* wrote that in it, Lear was "engaging and unpompous, an amusing storyteller who pokes fun at himself and writes with brutal honesty about his life."

On October 4, 2015, Norman Lear Day was celebrated at Emerson College, where Lear established the Norman Lear Scholarship Fund. College president Lee Pelton said, "He continues to write with power and grace, and engage us all in important conversations about our country and the world in which we live." Lear said, "I never had a day like this, and I can't believe it now. If there's a luckier person than me in this world, I don't know who it is." Jay Leno, an Emerson graduate, sent a videoed tribute.

An hour and a half historical documentary film, *Norman Lear: Just Another Version of You*, was released in 2016 and premiered at the Sundance Film Festival on July 8, 2016. It takes a look at the life, work and political activism of one of the most successful television producers of all time.

When this was written in the spring of 2019, Norman and Lyn live in Los Angeles. Lyn shares Norman's love for political activism. She is involved with Lyn Lear Productions, an organization that produces documentaries aimed at bringing awareness to climate change.

Norman Lear is on the National Advisory Board of the Young Storytellers Foundation and is a trustee emeritus at the Paley Center for Media. He continues as the executive producer of a number of television shows, and he directed the show *Storage Hunters* and the movie *Way Past Cool*. In 2009, he was a guest on the CBS *Sunday Morning Show* as well as on more than 20 other shows.

When President Bill Clinton awarded the National Medal of Arts Award in 1999, he noted, "Norman Lear has held up a mirror to American society and the way we look at it." In December 2017, Norman received the Kennedy Center Lifetime Artistic Achievement Award.

When asked to sum up his influence on American television and society, Lear thought about a night he was flying in an airliner: "I remember looking down and thinking, it's just possible, wherever I see a light, I've helped to make somebody laugh."

Lear's friend Mark Goodson (of Goodson-Todman Productions) said that Lear is one of the most preeminent, innovative and influential producers in our history. And Lear himself says, "I consider myself a writer who loves to show real people in real conflict, with all their fears, doubts, hopes and ambitions, rubbing against their love for one another."

Commenting on current news media in a 2014 article by Curt Schleier, Lear says, "It's a meaner time. The news was a loss leader on three networks, and it didn't have to make money. We were more relaxed. There was room for Eric Sevareid. … We were in love with the country."

31

Efrem Zimbalist, Jr.

Efrem Zimbalist, Jr., joined the Army on April 2, 1941. This was months before December 7, but the war in Europe was raging and he foresaw the U.S. getting involved. After basic and officer training at Fort Dix in New Jersey and Fort Benning in Georgia, he joined the Ninth Infantry Division as a rifle platoon leader in Company L, 60th Infantry Regiment. The division first fought in Algeria and Tunisia and then landed in Sicily. It helped cut off the Cotentin Peninsula during the battle of Normandy. Then, before the Battle of the Bulge, it fought the Battle of Hurtgen Forest, the longest and nastiest fight Americans were ever in. It started on September 19, 1944, and ended on February 10, 1945. It was an attempt to break through the Siegfried Line and into Germany.

The forest was a directionless, snow-covered landscape. The leadership soon learned that troops no more than a few feet apart couldn't see each other. The Germans had booby-trapped a three-mile-wide zone in the forest to slow the American advance. After nearly a month of fighting, the Ninth had pushed only a few miles into the forest. This was where Second Lieutenant Efrem Zimbalist was wounded on his leg. The Battle of Hurtgen Forest ended in a German defensive victory. The whole American offensive was a failure. American casualties were 33,000 killed or wounded while the Germans lost 28,000. The official U.S. Army history put it succinctly: "The real winner appeared to be the vast, undulating blackish-green sea that virtually negated American superiority in air, artillery and armor to reduce warfare to its lowest common denominator." Major General James Gavin said, "For us the Hurtgen was one of the most costly, most unproductive, and most ill-advised battles that our Army has ever fought." It was a battle best forgotten. Zimbalist Jr. received a Purple Heart plus a Combat Infantry Badge and, after recovery, was discharged in 1945.

Efrem Zimbalist, Jr., was born on November 30, 1918, in New York City. His parents were Jewish immigrants who became famous in the U.S. His father, Efrem Zimbalist, Sr., was a concert violinist and composer who headed

31. Efrem Zimbalist, Jr.

the Curtis Institute of Music. His mother, Alma Gluck, was a renowned soprano opera singer. She sang "Carry Me Back to Old Virginny," and it was the first record to sell over a million copies. He had an older sister, Mary, and a half-sister, Marcia Davenport, who was from his mother's first marriage. When Efrem was young, both parents converted to Christianity, as did he.

His parents sent him to board at St. Paul's School in Concord, New Hampshire, where he got his first taste for acting when he took part in the school's plays. From there he attended Yale University, where his conduct and attention to academics left a lot to be desired. He called his behavior "high jinx and low marks." He was expelled, reinstated and expelled again. In 1936, he got a job with NBC radio as a page. In addition, he did some work on-air. Having determined that he wanted a career in acting, Efrem started training at the Neighborhood Playhouse. Efrem started dating Emily Munroe McNair in 1940 and married her almost two years later on December 23, 1941, when he was already in the Army. He had met her when they both costarred in the Broadway production of *Hedda Gabler*. Their daughter, Nancy, was born in 1944.

After leaving the Army in 1945, he made his Broadway debut in *The Rugged Path*, which starred Spencer Tracy. It ran for three months and closed in January 1946. Then he made his television debut, starring in the movie *Mr. and Mrs. North*. Next he acted in five more shows. Afterwards, he produced his first show, with three more to follow, including *The Consul* in 1950. It brought a Menotti opera to Broadway and won the Pulitzer Prize for Music. Efrem made his

Efrem Zimbalist, Jr., veteran actor known for his starring roles in *77 Sunset Strip* and *The FBI*, in a publicity still taken outside his Los Angeles home in 1982.

movie debut in *House of Strangers*, which came out in 1950. But during its production, his wife Emily was diagnosed with cancer and died on January 18. Depressed and in mourning, Zimbalist left show business and worked for his father for four years at the Curtis Institute.

Returning to acting in 1954, he had a small role in the daytime television show *Concerning Miss Marlowe*, which ran into 1955. On February 13, 1956, Efrem married Loranda Stephanie Spalding. She was 15 years younger than Efrem and an East Coast socialite.

Later that year, they had a daughter, Stephanie, who later became a well-known actress. Zimbalist moved to Hollywood in 1956 and was put under contract to Warner Bros. He started playing tennis with Jack Warner, who persuaded him to act in the television show *77 Sunset Strip*. It started in 1958 and ran into 1964; he was in 163 episodes. The stories were about two private detectives who had their office on Sunset Boulevard in Los Angeles. Each episode was introduced by a catchy theme song. The series had a breezy, light-hearted edge. The series was wildly popular; it made Zimbalist famous

Zimbalist with Jane Fonda in a 1962 romance drama film *The Chapman Report*, based on the best-selling novel by Irving Wallace which was inspired by the Kinsey Report (lobby card).

31. Efrem Zimbalist, Jr.

and wealthy. Even though he was nominated for an Emmy, Efrem found it hard to maintain enthusiasm, saying, "The show is utter boredom. It stopped being interesting." Nevertheless, he was awarded a Golden Globe Award.

In the middle of the *77 Sunset Strip* production, he and Loranda divorced in 1962. Efrem was much in demand at Warners and appeared in a number of different shows and movies. Then there was another big one, the television series *The FBI*, which ran from 1965 through 1974. He was in 241 episodes playing Inspector Lewis Erskine. The storylines came from actual FBI cases. The program had the complete cooperation of the FBI. During the first seasons, J. Edgar Hoover personally pre-approved each script.

During *The FBI*, Efrem played the same role in the television movie, *Cosa Nostra, Arch Enemy of the F.B I*. In the 1967 film *Wait Until Dark*, Zimbalist costarred with Audrey Hepburn as her husband. He remarried Loranda in 1972. He costarred with Charlton Heston in *Airport 1975*, an air disaster thriller and a sequel to the very successful original movie, *Airport*. His role was as a pilot who is blinded during a flight.

During the rest of the decade, Zimbalist was in six movies and quite a number of television shows, including *Fantasy Island* and *The Love Boat*. Ten were made-for-TV-movies. In one series, *Remington Steele*, he played a recurring role as a smooth-talking con artist. The show starred Efrem's daughter Stephanie and was on the air from 1982 through 1987.

At the dawn of the new decade, Zimbalist turned 86 years old. Even so, after using his voice in an animated film, his last movie was *The Delivery* in 2008. It is a short film in which he

Zimbalist as Inspector Lewis Erskine on the ABC police series *The FBI* (1965–1974), based on actual cases using fictitious main characters (publicity still from 1969).

Zimbalist (left) with Pierce Brosnan and Stephanie Zimbalist, Efrem's daughter, in a publicity still for *Remington Steele*, a long-running television series (1982–1987).

played a professor helping a young girl to read. He appeared as himself in the television show *The Brothers Warner*, a historical movie written, directed and produced by Cass Warner Sperling, Harry Warner's granddaughter. And in 2007, he appeared as the Player King in a production of *Hamlet* on Broadway. It was his last.

He wrote his autobiography, *My Dinner of Herbs*, published in 2004. But then, disaster struck again when his wife Loranda died from lung cancer on February 5, 2007. Efrem Zimbalist, Jr., died on May 2, 2014, at age 95. His son,

31. Efrem Zimbalist, Jr.

Efrem Zimbalist III, confirmed the death. He said that his father had been outside his Solvang ranch watering his lawn when a handyman found him lying on the grass. "He had been healthy, played golf three times a week and was always in his garden. We are heartbroken to announce the passing into peace of our beloved father today at his ranch," his daughter Stephanie said. Efrem III went on: "He actively enjoyed his life to the last day, showering love on his extended family, playing golf and visiting with close friends."

Epilogue

This book is the second one in my series on members of the Greatest Generation who helped win World War II and went on to stardom. The first, *World War II Veterans in Motorsports*, was published in 2019. It is about 23 of my friends who grew up in the deprivations of the Great Depression, fought in the war, and went on to become prominent in motorsports. A number were highly decorated for their parts in the war. The book contains a number of facts not generally known about these heroes.

There were many movie stars who served during the war but not in combat. The best known is, of course, President Ronald Reagan. During his lifetime, he accumulated 64 credits as an actor in movies or on television. He was in 31 of them before he joined the Army. He made *Air Force* and *This Is the Army* in 1943 after he had joined and was on active duty. Reagan tried to get a waiver for overseas duty but was refused due to his health. What he did do, however, was significant. Assigned to the film unit, he helped make some 300 training films. When the war started, our Army was very small. Before that, new recruits were trained by other fully trained soldiers. But now, there were not enough to do the job, so films were made to help. The concept was studied at the University of Southern California in order to make the films more effective. According to Reagan, "They were an important contribution to the war effort." Captain Reagan himself never left the continental U.S.

There were other famous movie stars who served during World War II, but not in combat. Many spent their time entertaining the troops. Some of them were Desi Arnaz, Red Buttons, Vic Damone, Van Heflin, Burl Ives, Alan Ladd, Tony Randall and Red Skelton. Women played many roles as Armed Forces members, including as pilots, technicians, radio operators, and nurses, but were not allowed in combat. A number of female stars who contributed, but not in uniform, included Martha Raye, Paulette Goddard, Debbie Reynolds, Dinah Shore, and Rosalind Russell.

The United States after World War II was very different than it had been beforehand. For one thing, it became the world's most powerful country in

31. Epilogue

terms of Armed Forces. It also became dominant economically. But all was not peaceful and happy. For one thing, another war followed some five years afterward: The Korean conflict. By treaty, the U.S. had promised to defend South Korea, so when the North attacked the South in May 1950, the U.S. Armed Forces went to war again and eventually fought it to a standstill. To accomplish this, the draft was re-instated. National Guards and reserves were called up. Some of the Hollywood heroes were involved too.

Bibliography

Websites

Ancestry.com
Biography.com
DestroyerHistory.org
Encyclopedia.com
Fold3.com
Genealogybank.com
Latimes.com
Library of Congress
Medium.com
Military.com
Moviestillsdb.com
National Archives (nara.gov)
Notablebiographies.com
Nytimes.com
WikiMediaCommons
Wikipedia.com

Books

Bennett, Tony. *A Good Life*. New York, NY, Simon & Schuster, 1998.
Borgnine, Ernest. *Ernie, the Autobiography*. New York, Citadel, Kensington, 2008.
Curtis, Tony. *Tony Curtis: The Autobiography*. New York, HarperCollins, 1993.
Douglas, Kirk. *Ragman's Son: An Autobiography*. New York, Simon & Schuster, 1988.
Epstein, Dwayne. *Lee Marvin—Point Blank*. Tucson, AZ, Schaffner, 2013.
Fairbanks, Douglas, Jr. *A Hell of a War*. New York, St. Martin's, 1993.
_____. *The Salad Days*. New York, Doubleday, 1988.
Fonda, Henry. *My Life*. New York, E.P. Dutton, 1984.
George-Warren, Holly. *Public Cowboy No. 1: The Life and Times of Gene Autry*. New York, Oxford University Press, 2007.
Guiles, Fred Lawrence. *Tyrone Power: The Last Idol*. New York, Berkley, 1979.
Harris, Warren. *Clark Gable: A Biography*. New York, Random House, 2005.
Hayden, Sterling. *The Wanderer*. New York, Dobbs Ferry, 1963.
Heston, Charlton. *In the Arena: An Autobiography*. New York, 1995.
Hoopes, Roy. *When the Stars Went to War*. New York, Random House, 1994.
Kennedy, John Fitzgerald. *Why England Slept*. Santa Barbara, CA, Praeger, 1981.
Lear, Norman. *Even This I Get to Experience*. New York, Penguin, 2014.
Munn, Michael. *Jimmy Stewart: The Truth Behind the Legend*. New York, Simon & Schuster, 2005.
Murphy, Audie. *To Hell and Back*. New York, Henry Holt, 1949.
Rooney, Mickey. *Life Is Too Short*. New York, Random House, 1991.
Serling, Anne. *As I Knew Him: My Dad, Rod Serling*. New York, Bingham, 2013.
Smith, David. *The Price of Valor*. New York, Simon & Schuster, 2015.
Wise, James E., Jr., and Anne Collier Rehill. *Stars in Blue*. Naval Institute Press, Anapolis, MD, 1997.
_____ and _____. *Stars in the Corps*. Naval Institute Press, Annapolis, MD, 1999.
_____ and Paul Wilderson III. *Stars in Khaki*. Naval Institute Press, Anapolis, MD, 2000.
Zimbalist, Efrem, Jr. *My Dinner of Herbs*. New York, Proscenium, 2003.

Index

Numbers in **_bold italics_** indicate pages with illustrations

ABC (American Broadcasting Company) 104–105, 137, 198, 201, 221
Aber, Christopher 125
Aber, Mark *see* Rooney, Mark
Achnacarry Castle, Scotland 72
Act III Communications 215–216
Adak Island 79
Adams, Adelaide Efantis 57
Adams, Beige 59
Adams, Carolyn 59
Adams, Cathy 59
Adams, Cecily 58
Adams, Christine 59
Adams, Don **_56_**; early life 55, 58–59; Marine service 55–56; as Maxwell Smart 56–59; wounded 56, 199
Adams, Dorothy Bracken 57–58
Adams, Judy Luciano 58
Adams, Shirlee Mae *see* Fonda, Shirlee
Airplane! (movie) 99–100
Airwolf (TV) 106
Aix-en-Provence Hospital 8
Albert, Eddie 3, 19–25, **_19_**, **_23_**, **_24_**; acting career and awards 19–24; early life 20; military life and awards 19–22; philanthropies 23
Albert, Edward, Jr. 22, 24, 25
Albert, Margo 22
Albert, Maria 22
All in the Family (TV) 210, 214
All Quiet on the Western Front (movie) 106
All the President's Men (movie) 86
Allen, Fred 51
Allen, Leslie *see* Curtis, Leslie
Allen, Steve 41
Ameche, Don 128
Amelio, Mary Ann *see* Durning, Mary Ann
American Academy of Dramatic Arts 88, 165, 174
American Cancer Society 140
American Film Institute 145, 187, 200, 202
American Theatre Wing 112, 152
Andy Hardy Films 119, 121
Angeli, Pier 167
Annabella *see* Power, Annabella

Antioch College 159
Anvil Operation 7
Anzio, Battle of 7, 93, 94
Araujo, Laura Rae *see* Brand, Laura
Archer, Pamela Opal Lee *see* Murphy, Pamela
Arlington National Cemetery 11, 156, 176
Armstrong, Louis 112
Arnaz, Desi 224
Arness, Craig 96
Arness, James 3, **_94_**; early life 93–94; military 93–95; radio and acting career 95–98; wounded 95, 99, 100
Arness, Janet Surtees 97
Arness, Jenny 96
Arness, Rolf 96
Arness, Virginia Chapman 96–97
Arnold, Eddie 10
Arnold, Gen. "Hap" 191, 193
Arthur, Bea 214
Ashley, Lady Sylvia *see* Gable, Sylvia
The Asphalt Jungle (movie) 13–14
Astin, John 66
Atsugi Airbase 159
Attu Island 79
Aurness, James King *see* Arness, James
Aurness, Peter Duesler *see* Graves, Peter
Autry, Gene **_39_**; early life 38–39, **_40_**; entertainment career and awards 38–39, 42–43; Los Angeles Angels 38, 42; as military pilot 38, 41–42
Autry, Ina Mae Spivey 39
Autry Museum of the American West 42
Ayres, Lew 106

Babes in Arms (movie) 119
Bacall, Lauren 85, 90, 92, 122, 165, 166, 169, 171
Bailey, Pearl 113
Ball, Lucille 22
Bancroft, Anne *see* Brooks, Anne
Bari, Joe *see* Bennett, Tony
Barter Theatre 103
Battle of the Bulge 44, 88, 110, 172, 196–198
Battle of the Bulge (movie) 184
Baum, Florence *see* Brooks, Florence

229

Index

Baxter, Anne 130–131
Beach Jumpers 72–74
Beauty by Tova 106
Beech, Patricia *see* Bennett, Patricia
Beery, Wallace 64
Beiderbecke, Bix 166
Benedict, Joan *see* Steiger, Joan
USS *Benham* 204
Ben-Hur (movie) 77, 81
Bennedetto, Anthony *see* Bennett, Tony
Bennedetto Art Gallery 114
Bennett, Antonia 115
Bennett, Daegal 114
Bennett, Danny 114–116
Bennett, Joanna 115
Bennett, Patricia Beech 113–114
Bennett, Sandra Grant 115
Bennett, Susan Crow 115–117
Bennett, Tony **111, 113, 116**; as artist 114–115; early life 110, 112; entertainment career and awards 112–117; military service 110–112
Bergen, Edgar 51
Berle, Milton 51
Bernstein, Arthur L. 64
Betty Ford Center 146
Bickford, Charles 206
The Big Red One (movie) 149–150, 156
Billett, Stu 35
The Black Stallion (movie) 125
Blair, Betsy 104
Blake, Amanda **94**
Blanchard, Susan 183
Blazing Saddles (movie) 200
Bliss-Hayden Theatre School 95
Bloom, Claire 206–208
Bogart, Humphrey 122
The Bold and the Beautiful (movie) 123
Bonanza (TV) 149
Bono, Sonny 11
Boone, Pat 84
Boone, Richard 46
Borgnine, Anthony 108
Borgnine, Cris 106, 108–109
Borgnine, Diana 106
Borgnine, Donna Rancourt 106
Borgnine, Ernest **102, 103, 108**; acting career and awards 101, 103–107; early life 101, 103; military action 101–102; military awards 102, 107, 137
Borgnine, Katy Jurado 104–105, 107
Borgnine, Nancee 103, 109
Borgnine, Rhonda Kemins 103–104
Borgnine, Sharon 106, 109
Borgnine, Tova Traesnaes 106–109
Borgnino, Ermes Effron *see* Borgnine, Ernest
Bougainville Battle 33, 86
Boy Scouts, Sea Scouts 97
Boy Scouts Silver Buffalo Award 26

Bracken, Dorothy *see* Adams, Dorothy
Bradbury, Ray 161
Bradlee, Ben 86, 90
Brahm, Bob 32
Brand, Jean Enfield 46
Brand, Katrina 46
Brand, Laura Rae Araujo 46–47
Brand, Mae 48
Brand, Mary 46
Brand, Michelle 46
Brand, Neville **45, 46, 47**; acting career 44–48; early life 44–45; home library fire 48; military life 44–45, 47
Brandeis Institute 97
Brando, Dorothy 178–179
Brando, Marlon 153, 206
Brandt, Grace 20
Breakfast at Tiffanys (movie) 124
Bridges, Jeff 156
The Bridges of Toko Ri (movie) 123
Brokaw, Frances Seymour *see* Fonda, Frances
Brokaw, Tom 3
Bronson, Charles **135, 137, 138, 139**; acting career 134, 136–140; Army service 134–136; early life 134, 136, 152
Bronson, Harriett Tendler 136–138
Bronson, Katrina Holden 138, 140
Bronson, Kim Weeks 140
Bronson, Pierce **222**
Bronson, Suzanne 137
Bronson, Tony 137
Bronson, Zuleika 138
Brooks, Anne Bancroft 199, 201–202
Brooks, Eddie 198
Brooks, Florence Baum 198–199
Brooks, Maximillian 199–200
Brooks, Mel 57, **197, 200, 201**; early life 196; military service and awards 197–198; entertainment career and awards 196, 200–202
Brooks, Nick 198, 201
Brooks, Stephanie 198
Brooks Films 201
Brown, Capt. Albert 212
Brown, Edmund G. "Pat" 35
Brown, Maj. Gen. Lloyd D. 50
Brown, Peter 48
Bryna Company 167
Bryner, Yul 133
Buchinsky, Charles *see* Bronson, Charles
Buck, Bob 132
Bulkeley, Cmdr. John 73–74
Burch, Ruth 95
Burton, Richard 208
Bush, Pres. George H. W. 82
Bush, Pres. George W. 82–83
Butler Institute of American Art 114
Buttons, Red 224
Buydens, Anne *see* Douglas, Anne

230

Index

Caan, James 58
Caesar, Sid 198
Cagney, James 9, 53
Canby, Vincent 184
Caniff, Milt 60
Canova, Judy 114
Capra, Frank 28, 30, 194
Cardinale, Claudia 138
Carmichael, Hoagie 166
Carnegie Hall 114
Carney, Art **49, 52**; acting career 49, 51–54; early life 49–51; *The Honeymooners* 49, 51–53; military service 49–50
Carney, Barbara Isaac 53
Carney, Brian 51, 54
Carney, Eileen 51, 54
Carney, Jack 50, 51
Carney, Jean Myers 51, 53, 54
Carradine, Keith 84
Carroll, Danny 213
Carroll, Madeleine 13, 15, 129
Carter, Pres. Jimmy 170
Carter, John Charles *see* Heston, Charlton
Carson, Johnny 36
Casablanca, Moroco 6, 94
Cat Ballou (movie) 153–154
Cayuga Lake, New York 160–161
Cebu Assault 34
Chamberlin, Janice Darlene *see* Rooney, Janice
Champs-Elysees, Paris 50
Chaplain, Charlie 60, 62, 63
Chapman, Virginia *see* Arness, Virginia
Charpentier, Suzanne *see* Power, Annabella
Chennault, Gen. Claire Lee 62
China-India-Burma (CBI) "The Hump" 38, 60, 61
Christian, Linda *see* Power, Linda
Churchill, Sir Winston 49
Ciro's Nightclub 122, 213
Cisterna Battle 7
Civil Rights Movement 78, 82, 112
Clark, Gen. Mark 73
Clarke, Lydia Marie *see* Heston, Lydia
Clift, Montgomery 104
Clinton, Pres. Bill 116, 216
Coca, Imogene 180, 198
Cochran, Lt. Col. Philip 60, 62
Cohen, George 133
Colmar Pocket 8
Columbia Broadcasting (CBS) 23, 51, 52, 80, 89, 99, 106, 116, 134, 160–161, 215–216
Columbia Pictures 103, 215
Columbia Records 38, 113, 115, 117
Communism 16, 17, 22
Continental Airlines 105
Conway, Tim 105, 108
Coogan, Ann McCormack 65

Coogan, Christoper Fenton 66
Coogan, Dorothea "Dodie" 66
Coogan, Flower Parry 65
Coogan, Jackie 3, 60, **61, 63**; acting life 60–64; family accident 63–64; military life and decorations 60–62
Coogan, Jackie, Jr. 65
Coogan, Joann Dolliver 65
Coogan, John Henry 62–64
Coogan, Leslie Diane 66
Coogan, Lillian 62, 64
Coogan Law 64
Cooke, Jack Kent 35
Cooper, Gary 12, 30, 104, 206
Cooper, Jackie 65
Corregidor 73
Cota, Maj. Gen. Norman D. 19, 50
Count Basie 114
Crawford, Joan 16, 69, 152, 188
Criterion Productions 70
Crosby, Bing 112
Crow, Susan *see* Bennett, Susan
Curtis, Alexandra 146–147
Curtis, Allegra 146–147
Curtis, Andrea Savio 146
Curtis, Benjamin 146–147
Curtis, Christine Kaufmann 145
Curtis, Jamie Lee 145, 147–148
Curtis, Jill Vandenberg 146–148
Curtis, Kelly 145, 147
Curtis, Leslie Allen 146
Curtis, Lisa Deutsch 146
Curtis, Nicholas 146
Curtis, Tony 1, 10, **142, 143, 144**; acting career 141, 143, 146–147; art 146–147; books authored 147; early life 141; Navy life and awards 141–143
Curtis Institute 220

D-Day 95, 172
Damone, Vic 224
Dana, Bill 57, 59
Darnell, Linda **129**, 130
Davis, Bette 104
Davis, Lyn *see* Lear, Lyn
Davis, Nancy *see* Reagan, Nancy
Day, Doris 166, 194
Dean, Jimmy 167
The Death Wish (movie) 139
Death Hunt (movie) 15
De Carlo, Yvonne 106
The Defiant Ones (movie) 145
de Havilland, Olivia 84
Delon, Alain 138
The Delta Force (movie) 149, 156
de Mille, Cecil B. 80
Demsky, Issur Danielovitch *see* Douglas, Kirk
de Noon, Betty Ann *see* Hayden, Betty

Index

Deutsch, Lisa *see* Curtis, Lisa
Dickinson, Angie 155
Dietrich, Marlene 70
Dill, Diana *see* Douglas, Diana
Dillon, Josephine 187–188
The Dirty Dozen (movie) 137–138, 149
Dixon, Col. Hal 41
Dobbins Air Reserve Base, Georgia 32
Dr. Zhivago (movie) 205, 208
Dole, Bob 32
Dolliver, Lillian Rita *see* Coogan, Lillian
Donovan, "Wild Bill" 14
Doolittle, Gen. Jimmy 85
Doughty, Carole *see* Durning, Carole
Douglas, Anne Buydens 167, 170–171
Douglas, Cameron 171
Douglas, Diana Dill 165, 167
Douglas, Eric 167
Douglas, Joel 165
Douglas, Kirk 145, 147, **163**; acting career 165–171; as author 170; early life 163–165; Navy career 165–166; philanthropies 170
Douglas, Michael 165, 168
Douglas, Peter 167
Dove Audio Company 140
Duffy, Patrick 175
Dugan, Capt. Kathi 107, 109
Durante, Jimmy 51, 212
Durkin, Junior 63
Durning, Anita Gregory 174–175
Durning, Carole Doughty 174
Durning, Charles 1, 3, **173, 175, 176**; acting career and awards 174–176; Army life 172–173; early life 173–174
Durning, Douglas 174
Durning, Jeanine 174
Durning, Mary Ann Amelio 174
Durning, Michele 174
Dutch Harbor, Alaska 79

Eastwood, Clint 139, 155
Ebeling, Betty *see* Marvin, Betty
Edwards, Ralph 35
Efantis, Adelaide *see* Adams, Adelaide
Eisenhower, Dwight D. 49, 194
Eisenmann, Ike **24**
Elkins, Hillard 207
Ellington, Duke 114
Ellis, Paula *see* Steiger, Paula
Elmendorf Field Hospital, Anchorage 80
Emanuel Foundation for Hungarian Culture 146
Embassy Communications 215
Emerson College 211, 216
USS *Endicott* 73–74
Endress, Joan *see* Graves, Joan
Enfield, Jean *see* Brand, Jean
USS *Enterprise* 85–86

Escalante Brothers Circus 21
Espiritu Santo Island 87
Essanay Studio 62

Fabray, Nanette 198
Fairbanks, Anna Beth Sully 68
Fairbanks, Daphne 70, 76
Fairbanks, Douglas, Jr. 3, **67, 74**; acting career and awards 68, 71, 74–75; books authored 75; early life 67–69; military life and awards 67, 71–74
Fairbanks, Douglas, Sr. 67, 70, 193
Fairbanks, Mary Lee Hartford 70, 71, 75
Fairbanks, Melissa 70, 76
Fairbanks, Vera Lee Shelton 75
Fairbanks, Victoria 70, 76
The Farmer's Daughter (movie) 95–96
The F.B.I. (TV) 221
Feeley, Pamela *see* Marvin, Pamela
Feldon, Barbara 58, 59
Fletcher, Lt. Jack 21
Flying Tigers 41
Flynn, Errol 12
Flynn, Harry 109
Fonda, Afdera Franchetti 183
Fonda, Frances 180
Fonda, Frances Seymour Brokaw 180–182
Fonda, Henry 3, 28, 138, **179, 181, 184**; acting awards 178, 184; acting career 178–184; early life 178–179; Navy service and awards 181–182; Will Brown lynching 178, 208, 214
Fonda, Jane 153–154, 180, 184–185, **220**
Fonda, Margaret Sullavan 179–180
Fonda, Peter 180, 185
Fonda, Shirlee Mae Adams 183, 185
Ford, John 183
Forest Lawn Memorial Park 109, 194, 209
Forrestal, Secy. James 18
Forster, Leo 172
Franchetti, Afdera *see* Fonda, Afdera
Franchetti, Baron Raimondo 183
Fred Astaire Dance Studio 174
From Here to Eternity (movie) 101, 103
Fuller, Samuel 150

Gable, Clark 1, 41, 67, 69, **187, 189, 190**; early life 186–188; acting career 186–191, 193–195; Navy service 191–193
Gable, John Clark 194
Gable, Kay Williams 193–194
Gable, Maria "Ria" Langham 188, 190
Gable, Sylvia Ashley 193
Gabor, Eva 22, 24
Galland, Adolf 192
Gardner, Ava 120, **128**
Garland, Judy 119, **120**, 122
Garmon, Chester 64
Garson, Greer 193

232

Index

Gavin, Maj. Gen. James 218
Gaynor, Janet 180
Geller Drama School 45
Get Smart (TV) 55–59, 199
Getz, Stan 111
Gibraltar, Strait of 72
Gibson, Chaplain Thomas 133
Giffen, Adm. Ike 72
Gleason, Jackie *52*, 53
Gluck, Alma (Zimbalist) 219
Goddard, Paulette 224
Goering, Hermann 192
Goldwater, Barry 41
Gone with the Wind (movie) 186, 188–190, 195
Goodman, Benny 99
Goodson, Mark 217
Grable, Betty 64
Gracie, Sally *see* Steiger, Sally
Grant, Cary 71, 142–143
Grant, Lee 167
Grant, Sandra *see* Bennett, Sandra
The Grapes of Wrath 180–181
Graves, Amanda 100
Graves, Claudia 100
Graves, Joan Endress 99–100
Graves, Kelly 100
Graves, Peter 93, 95–96, *99*; acting career and awards 99–100; early life 99
Graziano, Rocky 214
The Great Escape (movie) 137
The Great Houdini (movie) 144–145
"The Great Marianas Turkey Shoot" 151
"Great Performances" (TV) 111
Griffith, Edward 13
Grumman's Chinese Theatre 68
Guadalcanal Battle 33, 55–56, 87
Guam 15
Guinness Book of World Records 126

Halsey, Adm. William F. "Bull" 85, 142, 205
Hamilton, John *see* Hayden, Sterling
Hanson, Dorothea Odetta *see* Coogan, Dorothea
Hardy, Andy Films 119, 121
Hartford, Mary Lee *see* Fairbanks, Mary Lee
Hatcher, William 192
Hathaway, Henry 136, 152
Hayden, Andrew 17
Hayden, Betty Ann de Noon 15–16
Hayden, Catherine McConnell 17–18
Hayden, Christian 15
Hayden, Dana 15
Hayden, David 17
Hayden, Gretchen 15
Hayden, Harry 95
Hayden, Matthew 15
Hayden, Sterling 3, *14*, *16*, *17*; acting career 15–18; early life 13; military and decorations 14–15, 96
Hayes, Helen 30
Hecht, Rabbi Mel 147
Heflin, Van 224
Hefner, Hugh 58
Heimberger, Edward Albert *see* Albert, Eddie
Hellgate (movie) 96
Hendrix, Wanda 10
Henry, Buck 57
Hepburn, Audrey 124, 183, 221
Heston, Charlton 45, 77, *78*, *81*, *83*; acting career and awards 77, 80–84; books authored 82; early life and schooling 77–78; military service and awards 78–79, 221
Heston, Chester 77
Heston, Fraser Clarke 78, 80, 84
Heston, Holly Ann 78, 84
Heston, Lydia Clarke 78, 80, 84
Hewitt, Adm. H. Kent 72
Hirohito, Emperor 21, 34
Hitler, Adolf 192, 199, 201
Hockett, Carolyn *see* Rooney, Carolyn
Hoffer, Vice Adm. J. H. 182
Hoffman, Dustin 175
Holden, William 106
Holland, Robert "Dutch" 31
Hollywood Athletic Club 128
Hollywood Canteen 150
Hollywood Forever Cemetery 126, 133
Hollywood Walk of Fame 33, 43, 76, 117, 126, 140, 171, 177, 202, 204
Holy Cross Cemetery 66
The Honeymooners (TV) 49, 51
USS *Honolulu* 87
Hoover, J. Edgar 107, 221
Hope, Bob 64, 113, 193
Hopkins, Bo 108
Horace Heidt Band 51
Horne, Lena 57
Horner, Robert 63
USS *Hornet* 85, 86
House Un-American Activities Committee 16
How the West Was Won 97, 183
Hueneme, California 79
Hurtgen Forest Battle 197, 218
Hussian School of Art 136
Huston, John 14, 17, 67

The Iceman Cometh (movie) 156
Illinois National Guard 44
Ireland, Jill 137–138, 140
Isaac, Barbara *see* Carney, Barbara
Ithaca College 161
Ives, Burl 224
Iwabuchi, Adm. Sanji 159
Iwo Jima Battle 130, 135, 151, 182, 204–205

Index

The Jeffersons (TV) 210, 214
John, Elton 116
John Wayne Cancer Institute 140
Jolson, Al 112, 118, 190, 198
Jones, Charles 63
Jones, Shirley 24
Jurado, Katy *see* Borgnine, Katy

Kahanamoku, Duke 63
Kahn, Madeline **200**
Kaminsky, Melvin *see* Brooks, Mel
Kaufmann, Christine *see* Curtis, Christine
Kelly, Grace 31, 104, 188
Kemins, Rhonda *see* Borgnine, Rhonda
Kennedy, John F. 70
Kennedy, Joseph 70
Kerkorian, Kirk 147
The Kid (movie) 60, 62–63
King, Henry 133
King, Martin Luther 82
King, Perry 1, **2**, 189
Kingman Army Airfield 135
Kiska Island 79
Kitt, Eartha 199
Klugman, Jack 136
Kohner, Paul 139
Kolombangara Island 87
Kraft Television Theatre 160
Krall, Diana 117
Kramer, Carolyn Louise *see* Serling, Carol
Krupa, Gene 88
Kubrick, Stanley 17, **164**, 167
Kurile Islands 79
Kwajalein Atoll 130, 150–151

Ladd, Alan 104, 224
Lady Gaga 111
LaGuardia, Mayor Fiorello 112
Lahr, Bert 51
USS *Lamberton* 101
Lamour, Dorothy 17
Lamphere, Dorothea *see* Coogan, Dorothea
Lancaster, Burt 104
Landsberg Concentration Camp 111
Lane, Marge *see* Rooney, Marge
Langham, Maria "Ria" *see* Gable, Maria
Laredo (TV) 47
Laskin Brothers Stock Company 187
Laughton, Charles 133
Lawrence, Gertrude 70
Lear, Benjamin 215
Lear, Briana 216
Lear, Charlotte Rosen 212–214
Lear, Ellen 212
Lear, Frances Loeb 214–215
Lear, Kate 214
Lear, Lyn Davis 215–216
Lear, Madeline 216

Lear, Maggie 214
Lear, Norman **211**, **215**; Army service and awards 212–213; early life 210–211; entertainment industry and awards 210, 213–217; philanthropies 216
Lear's (magazine) 215
Lee, Robert E. 149
Leigh, Janet **144**, 145
Leigh, Vivian **190**, 195
Leno, Jay 216
Leone, Sergio 139–140
LeRoy, Mervyn 183
Letterman, David 36
Lewis, Jerry 144, 213
Lewis, Judy 188
Leyte Island 34, 158
Life (magazine) 9, 132, 194
Lockwood, Adm. Charles A. 142
Loeb, Frances *see* Lear, Frances
Logan, Joshua 180
Lollobrigida, Gina 132
Lombard, Carole 186–191, 194; plane crash 191
Long, Jimmy 39
The Longest Day (movie) 19, 22–23, 183, 208
Los Angeles Angels 38, 42
Loy, Myrna 1, 189
Lucas, Alfred 188
Lucas, Alfred, Jr. 188
Lucas, Jana 188
Luciano, Judy *see* Adams, Judy
USS *Ludlow* 71
Lupino, Ida 206
Lust for Life (movie and book) 167
Lux Radio Theatre 132
Luzon Campaign 204
Lyn Lear Productions 216

MacArthur, Gen. Douglas 73, 159
Maldin, Karl 165
Malta Mission 72
Manila Battle 159
Mare Island, California 87
Margolin, Stuart **139**
Mariana Islands 151, 182
Mark of Zorro (movie) 129–130
Marshall Islands 130, 150
Martin, Dean 145
Marty (movie) 101, 104
Marvin, Betty Ebeling 152, 154–155
Marvin, Lee **137**, **150**, **153**, **154**; acting career 149, 152–156; early life 149; military and awards 150–152
Marvin, Michelle Triola 154–156
Marvin, Pamela Feeley 155
Marvin, Robert 149
Massey, Raymond 133
Matheson, Richard 161
Matthau, Walter 53, 143

Index

Maude (TV) 214
Maverick Playhouse 152
McCallum, David 138
McCartney, Paul 116
McClure, David "Spec" 10
McConnell, Catherine Devine *see* Hayden, Catherine
McCormack, Ann *see* Coogan, Ann
McGovern, George 82
McGuire, Phyllis 147
McHale's Navy (TV) 101, 104–105, 107
McIntyre, Andrew 191
McKenna, Siobham 52
McLean, Gloria Hatrick *see* Stewart, Gloria
McNair, Emily Munroe *see* Zimbalist, Emily
McNair, Lt. Gen. Lesley J. 50
Meredith, Burgess 129
Merman, Ethel 105
Metro-Goldwyn-Mayer (MGM) 28, 96, 119, 121, 160, 188, 192
Metropolitan Museum of Art 146
Michener, James 123
A Midsummer Night's Dream (movie) 118
Midway Island 79, 86, 204
Mifune, Toshiro 138
Mills Brothers 114
Milne, Martin 46
Milosevic, Milos 124
Minardos, Deborah Ann *see* Power, Deborah
The Misfits (movie) 194
Mission: Impossible (TV) 99–100, 106
USS *Mississippi* 72
USS *Missouri* 142
Mister Roberts (movie) 183
Mitchum, Robert **19**, 208
Monroe, Marilyn 81, 145, 194
Monte Cassino, Italy 7
Motion Picture Academy of Arts and Sciences 68, 70, 80
Mount Suribachi, Iwo Jima 205
Mountbatten, Lord Louis 70–72
Mullin, Adm. Michael G. **108**
Murphy, Audie Leon 3, **6**, **9**, **11**; acting career and awards 9–12; books authored 10; early life 5; military life and deorations 5–9; wounded 8
Murphy, James Shannon 10
Murphy, Pamela Archer 10, 12
Murphy, Terry Michael 10
Museum of Modern Art, New York 147
Mutiny on the Bounty (movie) 186, 194
Myers, Jean *see* Carney, Jean

National Art Club, New York 114
National Portrait Gallery 114
National Rifle Association 82–83
National Velvet (movie) 120–121
NBC 20, 52, 53, 114, 160, 162, 198, 213–214

NBC Radio 128, 219
Nebenzahl, Mildred *see* Wapner, Mildred "Mickey"
Nebraska National Guard 79
Neff, Bill 27
Nelson, Sherry *see* Steiger, Sherry
New York Dramatic Workshop 143
New York Post 129
New York Times 115, 170, 180, 184, 209, 215
New Yorker magazine 28
Newman, Paul 46, 174
Nicholson, Jack 168
Night at the Museum: Secret of the Tomb (movie) 126
Night Gallery (TV) 125, 161–162
Nimitz, Adm. Chester 79, 142
Nixon, Pres. Richard M. 32, 82, 86, 90, 194
Normandy landing 44, 49–50, 95, 172–173, 218
USS *North Hampton* 85–87

Obama, Pres. Barack 202
O'Brien, Edmond 46
O'Connor, Lois Elaine *see* Robards, Lois
Office of Strategic Services (OSS) 14–15
O'Hara, Maureen **75**
Okinawa Battle 130, 135, 204
Olivier, Laurence 81, 145
Omaha Beach 44, 50, 172
On Golden Pond (movie) 184
On the Waterfront (movie) 206
O'Neill, Eugene 87, 88
Operation Anvil/Dragoon 7, 73
Operation Bowery 72
Operation Cobra 50
Operation Petticoat (movie) 143, 145
Operation Torch 72

Paget, Debra 114, 132
Paint Your Wagon (movie) 155
Palance, Jack 46, 206
palimony suit 156
Paramount Pictures 13, 15, 65, 69, 136, 144, 214
Parry, Flower *see* Coogan, Flower
Pasadena Playhouse 96, 129, 136
Pasternak, Boris 205
Paths of Glory (movie) 164, 167
The Pawnbroker (movie) 208
Payne, John 17
Peabody, Richard 47–48
Pelton, Lee 216
Pennsylvania Coal and Coke Company 134
People for the American Way 215
The People's Court (TV) 33–37
Perenchio, Jerry 215
The Perry Como Show (TV) 199
Perske, Betty Joan *see* Bacall, Lauren
The Philadelphia Story (movie) 29
Philippine Sea Battle 151

Index

Pickfair, Mary 68, 133
Pickfair Estate 68
Pittman, Eleanor *see* Robards, Eleanor
P. J. Clarke's Nightclub 105
Planet of the Apes (movie) 157
Play and Players Theatre 136
Playboy Mansion 58
Poitier, Sidney 145, **207**
Power, Annabella 129, 131
Power, Anne 127
Power, Deborah Minardos 132–133
Power, Helen "Patia" Reaume 127
Power, Linda Christian 132
Power, Romina 132–133
Power, Taryn 132–133
Power, Tyrone, Sr. 127–128
Power, Tyrone III **128**, **129**, **131**; acting career and awards 127–133; early life 127; Marine life and awards 130–131
Power, Tyrone IV 133
Presley, Elvis 46
The Producers (movie) 200–201
USS *Proteus* 142
Purdom, Edmund 132

QVC Network 75

The Ragman's Son (book) 170
Raid on Entebbe (movie) 135
Rancourt, Donna *see* Borgnine, Donna
Randall, Tony 224
Randall School of Drama 103
Rase, Betty Jane *see* Rooney, Betty Jane
Rathbone, Basil 130
Rawhide (TV) 47
Raye, Martha 214, 224
The Razor's Edge (movie) 131
RCA 20
Reagan, Nancy 171, 188
Reagan, Pres. Ronald 16, 20, 32, 82, 140, 153, 185, 188, 193–194, 224
Reaume, Helen Emma *see* Power, Helen "Patia"
Red Oak Electric Company 45
Redford, Robert 46
Reed, Donna 30
Reiner, Carl 198–199, 202–203
Reiner, Rob 84
Remington Steele (TV) 221–222
Republic Pictures 15–16, 41
Reynolds, Debbie 108, 224
Richards, Kim **24**
Rickles, Don 58, 108
Ritz Brothers 211
RKO Studios 64, 95
Robards, David 88
Robards, Eleanor Pittman 88–89, 91
Robards, Jake 90

Robards, Jason **86**, **89**, **91**; acting career and awards 88–92; car accident 90, 138; early life 88; military life and awards 85–88
Robards, Jason, Sr. 88–90
Robards, Jason III 88
Robards, Lois O'Connor 90, 92
Robards, Rachel Taylor 89–90
Robards, Sam 90
Robards, Sarah Louise 88
Robards, Shannon 90
Robinson, Edgar G. 50–51, 70, 82
Rochefort, Cmdr. Joseph 79
Rogers, Buddy 133
Rogers, Roy 194
Rogers, Will 38
Roi Namur Island 150
Romano, Frederick 166
Romero, Caesar 133
Rooney, Barbara Ann Thomason 123–123
Rooney, Betty Jane Rase 121–123
Rooney, Carolyn Hockett 124
Rooney, Charlene 125–126
Rooney, Elaine Devry 123
Rooney, Janice Chamberlin 125–126
Rooney, Jonelle 125
Rooney, Kelly Ann 124
Rooney, Kerry Yule 124
Rooney, Kimmy Sue 124
Rooney, Marge Lane 124
Rooney, Mark 125–126
Rooney, Martha Vickers 122–123
Rooney, Michael Joseph 124
Rooney, Mickey **119**, **120**, **122**; acting career and awards 118–126; books authored 125; elder abuse 125; early life 118, 161
Rooney, Mickey, Jr. 121
Rooney, Theodore 123
Rooney, Tim 122
Rooney, William "Jimmy" 123
Roosevelt, Pres. Franklin D. 3, 49, 51, 71, 191, 194
Roosevelt, Mrs. Franklin D. 71
Rosen, Charlotte *see* Lear, Charlotte
Route 66 (TV) 149
Ruby, Thelma 132
Russell, Gail 17
Russell, Jane 193
Russell, Rosalind 224
Ryan, Robert 156, **184**

St. Mathews Episcopal Church 84
Saipan Battle 151–152
Salerno Landing 7, 73
San Cristobal Battle 86
Sanders, George 132
Santa Cruz Island Battle 86
Sanvio Corporation 104
USS *Satterlee* 182

Index

Savio, Andrea *see* Curtis, Andrea
Schary, Dore 95–96
Schleier, Curt 217
Schuster-Martin School of Drama 127
Schwartz, Bernard *see* Curtis, Tony
Schwartz, Julius 141
Schwartz, Robert 141
Schwarzenegger, Arnold 53, 84, 147–148, 168
USS *Sea Pike* 158
Selasie, Haile 132
Selleck, Tom 84
Selznick, David O. 95, 143
Selznick, Joyce 143
Senate Special Committee on Aging 125
Serling, Anne 159–160, 162
Serling, Carolyn Kramer 160–161
Serling, Jodi 160
Serling, Robert 157
Serling, Rod **158, 162**; early life 157; entertainment industry career 160–162; military life and awards 157–159
Seven Days in May (movie) 157
77 Sunset Strip (TV) 220–224
Shaw, Artie 120
Shearer, Norma 119, 188–189
Shelton, Vera Lee *see* Fairbanks, Vera Lee
USS *Sheridan* 21
Sheridan, Gen. Philip 21
Shiloh Horse Rescue 147
Shore, Dinah 224
Short, Walter C. 91
Sicily Campaigns 6, 71–72, 93, 218
Siegfried Line 44
Simmons, Ed 213
Sinatra, Frank 17, 103–104, 114, 120
Six, Bob 105
Skelton, Red 224
Slapsy Maxie's Nightclub 65
Smith, Gov. Al 51
Smithsonian American Art Museum 114
Smuts, Jan Christian 132
Solomon and Sheba (movie) 132
Some Like it Hot (movie) 145–146
Sony Pictures 202
Spalding, Loranda Stephanie *see* Zimbalist, Loranda
Spartacus (movie) 145, 167
Special Services Band 111–112
Sperling, Cass Warner 222
Spivey, Ina Mae *see* Autry, Ina Mae
Spreckels, Adolph 193
Spreckels, Bunker 193
Stalag 17 (movie) 44, 46, 100
Stamberg, Susan 170
Stanwyck, Barbara 166
Stapleton, Maureen **89**
Steenburgen, Mary 92
Steiger, Anna 207

Steiger, Joan Benedict 209
Steiger, Michael 209
Steiger, Paula Ellis 209
Steiger, Rod **205, 207, 208**; acting career and awards 206–209; early life 204; Navy service and awards 206
Steiger, Sally Gracie 206
Steiger, Sherry Nelson 209
The Steve Allen Show (TV) 199
Stevenson, Adlai 71
Stewart, Gloria Hatrick McLean 30, 32
Stewart, James 3, **27, 30, 31**; acting career and awards 26, 28–32; early life and schooling 26–27; military service and awards 26, 29, 30, 32, 41, 67, 80, 144, 179–181, 189, 191, 144
Stewart, J. M. and Company 26, 28
Stewart, Judy 31
Stewart, Kelly 31
Stewart, Michael 31
Stewart, Ronald 31
Stillwell, Lt. Gen. "Vinegar Joe" 61
Stone, Irving and Jean 167
Streisand, Barbra 116
Sugar Babies (stage) 125
Sullavan, Margaret *see* Fonda, Margaret
Sully, Anna Beth *see* Fairbanks, Anna Beth
The Sun Also Rises (movie) 128
Surtees, Janet *see* Arness, Janet
Sweet Smell of Success (movie) 145
Swope, Herbert 70
USS *Sylph* 102

Tagaytay Ridge 158
Talisay Beach Landing 34
Tandem Productions 214
Tarawa Battle 21
Tassafaronga Battle 86–87
Tatum, Art 111
USS *Taussig* 204–206
Taylor, Elizabeth 120–121
Taylor, Rachel *see* Robards, Rachel
Taylor, Robert 129, 194
The Ten Commandments (movie) 80
Tendler, Harriett *see* Bronson, Harriett
Texas National Guard 9
Thomas, Danny 213
Thomason, Barbara *see* Rooney, Barbara Ann
Thomson, David 118
Thunderbolt Division 44
Tipton, Lattie 7
Tito, Josip 14–16
To Be or Not To Be (movie) 175
To Hell and Back (book) 10
To Hell and Back (movie) 9–11
Todd, Richard 208
Tokyo Bay 142
Tora! Tora! Tora! (movie) 47, 91
Tracy, Spencer 1, 119, 194, 219

237

Index

Traesnaes, Tova *see* Borgnine, Tova
Trapeze (movie) 145
Triborough Bridge, New York 112
Triola, Michelle *see* Marvin, Michelle
Trow, Capt. Ken 135
Tulagi Island 56
Turner, Judy *see* Turner, Lana
Turner, Lana 33, 119–120, 122, 131–132
Turner, Scott 10
Tutuila, United States Naval Station 56
20th Century Fox 129–130
The Twilight Zone (TV) 149, 153, 157, 161

"Umbriago" Unit 212–213
Underwood, Carrie **116**
Universal Studios 10, 31, 143, 145
Universal Television 105
The Untouchables (TV) 153
USO 42

The Valachi Papers (movie) 139
Valdovinos, Navy Chief Marco 109
Vandenberg, Jill *see* Curtis, Jill
Van Dyke, Dick 155–156
van Gogh, Vincent 167
Vanity Fair (magazine) 148
Vickers, Martha *see* Rooney, Martha
Vidal, Gore 176
Vincent, Jan Michael 107
Von Stroheim, Erich 187
Voyage (book) 17

Wagner, Robert 46
Wagon Train (TV) 149, 153, 208
Wake Island 85
Wall Street Journal 216
Wallace, Irving 220
Wallis, Hal 166
Walter, Sterling Relyea *see* Hayden, Sterling
Wanderer (book) 17
Wanderer (schooner) 15
Wanger, Walter 180
Wapner, David 35
Wapner, Fred 35
Wapner, Joseph **34**; early life 33; military career and awards 33–35; *People's Court* and other shows 35–37
Wapner, Mildred "Mickey" 35, 37
Wapner, Sarah 35, 37
War and Peace (movie) 183
Warner Brothers 20, 62, 200, 220, 222

USS *Washington* 72
USS *Wasp* 72, 86
Wasserman, Lew 133
Waterfield, Bob 193
Waterloo (movie) 208
Wayne, John 12, 67, 168, 208
Webb, Clifton 131
Webb, Jack 46
Weeks, Kim *see* Bronson, Kim
Weintraub, T5C Louis 122
Wells, Orson 81, 208
Wharton, Brig. Gen. James E. 50
Widmark, Richard 46
The Wild Bunch (movie) 106
The Wild One (movie) 153
Wilder, Gene 200
William White Committee 71
Williams, Kay *see* Gable, Kay
Winehouse, Amy 114
Wingate, Maj. Gen. Orde 60, 62
Winkler, Otto 191
Wolf Packs 102
Woodward, Bob 90
Wyler, William 81, 193
Wyman, Jane 20
Wynn, Keenan 194

Yamamoto, Admiral 79
Yamashita, Gen. Tomoyuhi 159
Yarmy, Donald James *see* Adams, Don
Yarmy, Gloria Burton 55, 59
Yarmy, Richard 55, 58
Yokohama 159
Yorkin, Bud 214
Young, Loretta 95, 129, 188
Young Storytellers Foundation 216
Yule, Joseph, Jr. *see* Rooney, Mickey

Zanuck, Darryl F. 23
Zimbalist, Efrem, Jr. **219**, **220**, **221**, **222**; acting career and awards 219–222; Army service and awards 218; early life 218–219
Zimbalist, Efrem, Sr. 218
Zimbalist, Efrem III 223
Zimbalist, Emily McNair 219–220
Zimbalist, Loranda Spalding 220–222
Zimbalist, Nancy 219
Zimbalist, Stephanie 220–221, **222**, 223
Zitterling, Mai 132

www.ingramcontent.com/pod-product-compliance
Lightning Source LLC
Chambersburg PA
CBHW052059300426
44117CB00013B/2197